Let no man deceive you by a
    for [the Day of the Lo]
    unless there come a revolt first,
    and the man of sin be revealed,
    the son of perdition,

Who opposeth and is lifted up
    above all that is called God
    or that is worshipped,
    so that he sitteth in the temple of God,
    showing himself as if he were God.

...And now you know what withholdeth [him],
    that he may be revealed in his time.
    For the mystery of iniquity already worketh...

And then that wicked one shall be revealed...
    Whose coming is according
    to the working of Satan,
    in all power and signs and lying wonders:

And in all seduction of iniquity
    to them that perish:
    because they receive not the love of the truth,
    that they might be saved.

And for this cause
    God shall send them
    the operation of error,
    to believe lying,
    that they all might be judged
    who believed not the truth
    but have consented to iniquity.

               2 Thessalonians. 2:3-4, 6-11

In Memoriam

Fr. F. John Murphy

Fr. Ron Wolf

Fr. Morrie Crocker

Fr. Tom Economus

They fought the good fight

Sons of Perdition

New Mexico
in the
Secret History
of the
Catholic
Sex Scandals

Jay Nelson

To Paulette —
In honor
of the good times &
the weird.

PS I'll never ~~forgive~~ forget you for stopping me from mooning the Pope.

ISBN: 1-4392-3482-5

Library of Congress Control Number: 2009903049

www.sarabite.info

TABLE OF CONTENTS

PREFACE:
BY WAY OF AN APOLOGY

When do events really begin?

History shows that the roots of current situations often sink much deeper than at first imagined. Since creation at least, no thing has emerged fully formed out of nowhere. Dates matter mainly as signposts of changing times.

Even books, then, have pedigrees, even prehistories. Readers, particularly of such a potentially troublesome historical critique as this, deserve to know where it came from, its origins, and intent. Therefore, in order to illuminate the reasons behind *Sons of Perdition*, I am afraid I must explain a bit about myself, too. This then, is my "apology," not merely in the sense of asking for forgiveness for offense, but also with the theological meaning of being a justification or vindication of my work.

By far, the most memorable date leading to its creation occurred exactly seventeen years ago today. On that day, during a return visit for Good Friday services to the parish I grew up in, I first remembered being sexually molested there as an altar boy by a priest.

That stunning realization has propelled this entire quest. But though I figure in it slightly, it is not my personal story. While events from my childhood provided an initial point for a horror novel I wrote, *The Harrowing*, the tale told here is more terrible in nature as it is true but also gigantic in scope.

Coincidentally with my own awakening, the abuse scandals began in earnest across the nation. It soon became obvious that this mess involved much more than a few unlucky altar boys like me off way in the boondocks. In fact, the full dimensions of the disaster remain undetermined. But any one person's individual tale of woe is no more than a tiny footnote to this immense tragedy that strangles the entire history of Catholicism like a python.

Sexual issues have engaged popes, councils, inquisitions, entire orders, and the very nature of the priesthood itself. This account is not really that of the victims, nor their clerical perpetrators, but mainly concerns the saints and sinners who were forced to deal with them. Most importantly, it's about the system of secrecy that evolved to covertly cope with such problems.

Surprisingly, after Vatican II, that system largely pivoted on a peculiar order of monks, the "Servants of the Paraclete," whose mission was and is to care for troubled priests. The Paracletes, as they are often called, were then headquartered in the northern mountains of my New Mexican homeland.

Up the road from their monastery, an uncle of mine owned a cabin where my siblings and I summered on weekends throughout the 1960s. As the second son in a large Catholic family, I seemed destined for the Church from birth. So it was, that in one of the small nearby communities, some of the very first Masses I ever served as an altar boy were for the monks' wards, men who might well have been sex abusers. Later during college while earning a history degree on medieval Europe but still quite clueless, I occasionally attended church at another facility of theirs south of Albuquerque.

In between, I suffered through two years at the local Catholic high school and several near misses with the notorious Art Perrault despite warnings from older boys. There I also became acquainted with other prominent local figures, including the future archbishop, Robert Sanchez.

Unfortunately, my luck had already run out in parochial school. There, a parish priest, Thomas P. Wilkinson, had repeatedly molested me, though I repressed all awareness of the attacks for decades. As did so many back in the early '70s, I left the Church in college, experimenting with various alternatives. But as inevitably and often as the turning tide, unsatisfied religious longings drew me back before intractable questions drove me out.

Trying to work out these inner conflicts, I even played at being a "Friar Tuck" kind of monk in a medieval recreation society for some years. I probably learned more about how religion actually works than I might have had with either a doctorate or a stint as a missionary to heathen lands. Sacred things, even those made just for fun, I soon found, take on lives of their own.

Such antics, however, only aggravated my private turmoil, so I eventually decided to take the calling seriously. In August 1991, almost seven months before my memories surfaced, I was ordained as a priest in the Catholic Apostolic Church of Antioch, an Independent Catholic Church; that is, one of many small Catholic churches derived from but free of Rome.

Like many such autonomous denominations, the Church of Antioch claims apostolic succession, boasting of the sacraments without traditional Roman restrictions. Antiochan clergy can be male, female, straight or gay, married, divorced, in a relationship or not. Ignored by the titanic Ark of Peter, such tiny churches are like lifeboats offering those who cannot in good conscience serve in the Roman priesthood a real opportunity to minister.

Then patriarch of the Church of Antioch, Archbishop Richard Gundrey, was generously welcoming of me despite my many difficulties. I am most grateful for his wisdom and patience as well as the safe place to worship that he provided. But though I tried, a pastor I was never meant to be.

Eruption of abuse issues made any religious calling at all extremely difficult for me. Just wearing a clerical collar could be intensely triggering, so I soon abandoned any hope of building a congregation. Instead, I mostly engaged in behind the scenes supportive work for the Church until I officially retired a year ago, having earned a rank equivalent to monsignor.

My resignation was to spare them any repercussion resulting from my activities, including this book. To keep my vision uncompromised, for better or ill, I even chose to self-publish, designing and editing as well as writing. Thus, neither the Church of Antioch nor anyone else is responsible, approving, or even necessarily cognizant of my conclusions here in any way. Everything in this volume is mine: opinions and mistakes included.

Though never actually a Roman priest, I do appreciate the clerical Catholic view. Having administered the holy sacraments, I have partaken of the awful responsibility that all priests bear and borne the profound loneliness in which most live, too. To this day, I have a deep and abiding respect for the men and women of the cloth who truly live up to their high calling. They are better people than I. It is therefore not the clergy itself that I blame, but a moribund hieratic system terminally overdue for reform.

In any case, back then, my true vocation suddenly took a most unexpected twist: helping other victims and survivors of clergy abuse. I spoke out locally and soon found myself embroiled in protests along with others. Although I didn't win the "Catholic lottery," I, too, sued the Church. Due to lack of evidence at the time, I settled merely for legal and medical costs. This proved sufficient and by then I had no wish to be beholden to the Archdiocese. I should also mention that the noted attorney, Bruce Pasternack, who played such a critical role here, did not represent me. There is therefore no financial influence on my assessment of his efforts on behalf of victims.

Meanwhile, I had eagerly volunteered to produce *The Missing Link*, the quarterly journal for the leading national victim's support and advocacy group at the time, the Linkup. Compiling each issue from reports submitted from all around the world allowed me to watch as the crisis grew and spread like a plague for over a decade. This proved invaluable, as most information about clergy abuse cases remains even now sequestered in local regions.

In the process, I amassed an ungodly mass of news clippings (many since donated to Bishop Accountability), along with an extensive library, including numerous exposés and hefty nineteenth-century academic histories. At the same time, at local meetings, national conventions, demonstrations, through correspondence and over the phone, I networked with hundreds of victims and heard many touching stories of abuse and recovery.

After a decade of this, I left the Linkup, totally burnt out, and it folded not long after. I then wrote a psychological horror novel and even a dark comedic screenplay, but so many troubling mysteries remained. Not even requesting and being most graciously granted a formal excommunication from the Roman Church by Archbishop Michael Sheehan helped much.

But, as in my own life, the origins of this crisis in the life of the Church lay also long wrapped unsuspected in the shadows. Yet, the two are linked in ways that seem almost foreordained. God, fate, or chance put me in a unique position to recover a far larger story than just my own. Whether I liked it or not, I found myself smack dab in the right place at the right time.

Having toyed with writing a memoir involving the crisis in New Mexico, I began to probe into its history. Once started, I was driven to dig ever deeper, because none of the links I uncovered was more astonishing or critical than that of the hidden hand of the Inquisition. The trail then inexorably led to Vatican II and the complex, remarkable role of the current pope, revealed here for the first time anywhere in print. Only then did I begin to appreciate just what a unique perspective and opportunity I had been given.

Putting it together with what I already knew seemed simple. But information kept providentially popping up all the time, most especially when "Father Pious," as he prefers to be called, contacted me. This gentleman claims that he'd been a novice with the Servants for some time in the mid to late 1960s. Though he has not provided any documentary evidence, his local knowledge plus assertion of certain obscure facts about the Paracletes which later research verified have convinced me that he was indeed present then.

Another source, a nurse who once worked for them also, had already helped out, but Pious seemed to have an even deeper insider's view. His contributions, with his most disturbing allegations, all carefully noted, have provided some final pieces of the puzzle for which he has my sincere thanks.

My gratitude is even greater, however, to the many victims and survivors of clergy abuse whose true-life stories have both appalled and inspired me over the years. I could not have written this without them; nor would I have needed to. There are far too many to be named, but public recognition should be given at least to those survivors selflessly providing resources online. I am indebted to Kay Ebeling of the City of Angels blog as well as Terry McKiernan and the dedicated staff of the Bishop Accountability website. S.N.A.P., the Survivors Network for those Abused by Priests, the major victims organization these days, must also be recognized for its efforts.

The learned input of experts with whom I've had the pleasure of occasionally sparring, especially Father Tom Doyle and A.W. Richard Sipe, needs to be respectfully acknowledged. So too, should be the works of the great American historian, Henry Charles Lea, from which I freely plundered.

As for what it all truly means, the central issues were clearly stated by Christ himself in the Gospel of Matthew, laying the foundation for all of the Church's later policies concerning sex and scandals. His well-worn remarks are still worth quoting. Like most of the challenges that Jesus set for his disciples, the test might seem simple but is really almost superhuman:

At that hour the disciples came to Jesus, saying: Who, thinkest thou, is the greater in the kingdom of heaven?

And Jesus, calling unto him a little child, set him in the midst of them.

And said: amen I say to you, unless you be converted, and become as little children, you shall not enter into the kingdom of heaven.

Whosoever therefore shall humble himself as this little child, he is the greater in the kingdom of heaven.

And he that shall receive one such little child in my name, receiveth me.

But he that shall scandalize one of these little ones that believe in me, it were better for him that a millstone should be hanged about his neck, and that he should be drowned in the depth of the sea.

Woe to the world because of scandals. For it must needs be that scandals come: but nevertheless woe to that man by whom the scandal cometh.[1]

From these few words, both the clerical secret system and the abuse crisis stem. Jesus thus not only set up outraging the innocent as the worst sin, he also foretold its inevitable occurrence and terrible consequences.

My hope in writing has been simple: to help break this awful cycle by exposing how it works. In the process, certain unpleasant truths about the Roman Church that I have discovered have been expressed, maybe occasionally with too much passion. I am sincerely sorry for this. I have cherished Catholic culture and spirituality since I first learned to pray at my mother's side. But that heritage turned out to be much different than I was taught. Its dark and ugly side must also be lit, blemishes and all, no matter how shocking because the stakes are too high for any more naïve sentimentality.

Despite its high spiritual toll on me, however, this research has had one unexpectedly positive result. The soul-numbing magnitude of this calamity is just too unimaginably huge for me to sustain any more personal rancor.

The gnashing demands of sex and religion have devoured many unguessed millions of souls throughout history, as if by the very jaws of Hell. Only in the brief window provided by the sex scandals have we been allowed a sobering glimpse into this theological inferno that is two thousand years in the making. It is a disquieting and depressing vision indeed.

To all unto whom *Sons of Perdition* becomes a stumbling block, I apologize for the scandal it gives — but not for any disturbing facts it contains. The secret system even now being resurrected by the Vatican like Frankenstein's monster needs be exposed in all its arrogant folly.

The first step is to recognize the realities involved as they truly are, stripped of any comforting euphemisms that can make it all too easy to minimize or soften the unpleasant, fleshy, and urgent issues at stake.

Sexual relationships between priests and women are not genteel "affairs" as if a bout between equals, all just part of the dating game. Instead, they usually involve violations of solemn vows and betrayal of sacred trust. Altar boys are said to be "abused" when they have been orally and anally raped by their pastors, schoolgirls "molested" when they have been groomed, seduced, and finally trapped by smooth talking predators as sly as serpents.

Crimes or not, these are all grave sins that strike the very heart of faith.

Yet, Christ promised that "you shall know the truth: and the truth will set you free."[2] To the myriads of suffering, bewildered victims of clergy sexual abuse, this remains an abiding assurance of hope as well as an eternal threat to their deceivers. For he also commanded, "Therefore fear them not. For nothing is covered that shall not be revealed: nor hid, that shall not be known. That which I tell you in the dark, speak ye in the light: that which you hear in the ear, preach ye upon the housetops."[3]

God help me; here I have humbly tried to do that to the best of my poor abilities. Make of it what you will, but this really is how it all happened.

Jay Nelson
Albuquerque, New Mexico
April 17, 2009

AN ECCLESIASTICAL CHART
OF NEW MEXICO

UTAH   COLORADO   KS.

OKLA.

Navajos

TEXAS

Taos

Los
Alamos

Hopi ←

Jemez
Springs

Las
Vegas

JEMEZ

Santa Fe

Gallup

PECOS

ZUNI

ARCHDIOCESE
OF SANTA FE

ACOMA

Albuquerque

DIOCESE
OF GALLUP

PECOS
RIVER

ARIZONA

Socorro

Navajos

Roswell

Apaches

NEW
MEXICO

RIO
GRANDE

DIOCESE OF
LAS CRUCES

† *Las Cruces*

† *El Paso*

MEXICO   TEXAS

† Bishoprics
Towns
◆ PUEBLOS
◇ RUINS

ARCHBISHOPS OF SANTA FE

1. JOHN BAPTIST LAMY, *1875-85*
2. JOHN BAPTIST SALPOINTE, *1885-94*
3. PLACID LOUIS CHAPELLE, *1894-7*
4. PETER BOURGADE, *1899-1908*
5. JOHN BAPTIST PITAVAL, *1909-18*

6. ALBERT THOMAS DAEGER, OFM, *1912-32*
7. RUDOLPH ALOYSIUS GERKEN, *1933-43*
8. EDWIN VINCENT BYRNE, *1943-63*
9. JAMES PETER DAVIS, *1964-74*
10. ROBERT FORTUNE SANCHEZ, *1974-93*

11. MICHAEL JARBOE SHEEHAN, *1993-*

CHAPTER I:
A CHURCH EXPOSED

A catholic crisis

By the opening years of the third millennium after Christ, it has become appallingly obvious that the Roman Catholic Church has some enormous problems with sex. For several decades now, there has been a seemingly endless litany of disturbing revelations about priests, bishops, brothers, and nuns sexually seducing and even raping children, women, and men — not to mention each other.

First begun in the United States and Canada in the early 1980s, during the 1990s the scandals spread like an unholy pandemic to Ireland, across Europe, Australia, and then to the rest of the world. Taken altogether, they comprise a truly "catholic" or universal catastrophe. The once-stainless reputation of Catholic clergy as angelically chaste is now tarnished and tattered, perhaps beyond repair.

Here in the first days of the twenty-first century, predatory priests have become standard fodder for late-night comedians; headlines regularly carry tidings of the latest multi-million dollar legal settlements along with parish closings, while prelates in public nervously watch out for angry victims. Church attendance has plummeted along with offerings; laments of poverty and excuses of misunderstanding ring out from bishops' palaces, while seminaries and convents empty. The demoralization down in the pews is palpably manifest as the shameful disclosures grind on and on.

These sordid sex scandals undoubtedly form the greatest challenge facing the Roman Church at least since the Protestant Reformation half a millennium ago. Almost as horrific as the crimes themselves have been the shocking disclosures that time and again, in country after county, the Church reacted by covering up the sins of its clergy, transferring offenders, stonewalling authorities, and blaming victims.

As supreme head of the Roman Church, the pope should naturally bear the greatest public burden for this crisis. Yet, the pontiff goes about his daily business in time-honored fashion, seemingly unconcerned. No sweeping reforms have been ordered. No internal investigations or soul-searching are underway. Any discussion whatsoever of abandoning clerical celibacy or ordaining women as possible remedies is still completely forbidden.

At best, the pope has ordered Church-wide perpetual prayer to cleanse it of pedophile clergy.[1] But in terms of practical action, it would appear that the Vatican cares little about these issues and does even less.

Perhaps that is because this particular pope, His Holiness Benedict XVI, Joseph Ratzinger, bears a unique personal responsibility for this entire crisis. Unsuspected before now, Ratzinger has had a far greater influence on the course of this crisis than is widely believed. Astonishingly enough, these calamities are book-ended, both coming and going, by the figure of this man.

Over forty years ago, a speech written by him as a young theologian helped set the conditions for the scandals to break out in the first place. Two decades later, he labored secretly as a powerful cardinal to undo those fateful words. His patient efforts may have already succeeded. There is good reason to believe the whole sorry mess is already fading away like a bad dream. Unfortunately, along with it, may go any prospects of real and lasting reform.

These remarkable events all occurred even before Ratzinger ever ascended the papal throne. This incredible story only happened due to his impact at different times on the most powerful department in the Vatican. Now called the Sacred Congregation for the Doctrine of the Faith, before that, the Holy Office, for centuries previously, this agency enjoyed the sinister title of the Roman Inquisition.

Indeed, it's like that old Monty Python punch line: no one expected the Spanish Inquisition. As the abuse crisis unfolded, nobody even imagined that the Inquisition, Spanish or otherwise, had ever been concerned with clergy sexual abuse along with heresy and witchcraft. And for good reason: that interest had become a closely guarded secret.

But as will be shown, the policies of the Inquisition – or rather, "inquisitions," for there were several incarnations – are central to the secret history of the clergy abuse scandals. And though rooted far in the past, their continuance today in a secretive and ruthless form pose deep questions about the separation of Church and State in the future.

Many ideas have been floated for why the scandals occurred when and where they did. Commentators have focused on vague social forces, celibacy, Vatican II, gays, the 60s, but all such assertions are insufficient in themselves. History demands greater precision and clearer connections. Yet, many of the necessary facts have already been publicly accessible for years in forgotten tomes and neglected archives. They just have never been put together before.

Other clues needed lurk behind ancient walls of secrecy built by the Vatican for over a thousand years. Like a forbidding castle, they jealously guard the hidden sex lives of priests and monks, and are next to impossible for outsiders to penetrate. Unwilling victims have, but few have had the training or desire to piece it all together. Most simply want to forget.

To understand how this entire mess came about and will end requires a very broad view. Uncovering the actual historical causes behind the scandals needs a sweeping examination of the entire history of sex in the Church and its relations to the papacy, and most particularly, the Inquisition.

But critically examining the scandals globally everywhere in depth as they appeared, however, is not yet practical. Sadly, it is no exaggeration to say that sex crimes by Roman Catholic clergy have been reported in every country where they have established a substantial presence. These wildfires are far too fresh and widespread. Too many embers still smolder.

The overall situation can perhaps be better understood by looking in depth at how the scandals manifested in one single area. Of all the various regions that could be investigated for numbers or intensity, one place particularly sticks out like the proverbial sore thumb: the western American state of New Mexico, and the ecclesiastical realm within it known as the Archdiocese of Santa Fe.

This ancient, poor land has a critical importance in this story far belying size, wealth, or population. Not just because scandals happened quite early and are hopefully over, nor because they quickly toppled the very highest ecclesiastical office in the land. Here the crisis hit like the so-called "perfect storm." New Mexico was a laboratory where many elements of the modern cover-up that would reappear later elsewhere were honed and tested. But all those effects resulted from to the centrality of "Land of Enchantment," as the state is typically called in tourist brochures, to the global crisis.

What happened in New Mexico is one of the key parts of this entire epic tale. Extraordinary historical circumstances made this forgotten place serve – in the notable phrase – as a "dumping ground for ecclesiastical waste."[2] It became the source of many of the scandals elsewhere as well. Fateful decisions secretly made here sent some of the worst clerical sexual predators into unsuspecting parishes across the land, and possibly, the world.

This chronicle thus extends far beyond the American Southwest, just as it involves much more than popes and inquisitors. Official suppression by the doctrinal police at the behest of the Holy See was but the most savage weapon in the eternal struggle to avoid scandal through secrecy.

This "secret system" as various authors have rightly named it, constitutes a consistent set of strategic policies for the concealment of clerical sin. It has been directed and maintained from the highest levels of the Roman Catholic hierarchy on down for centuries upon end. The resulting cover-up of clergy sex crimes has been far larger and longer than most people, including many experts and churchmen, have ever imagined. Few even dream that it continues today, as unchecked as it remains unknown.

Up until the Second Vatican Council, the system was as successful as it was hermetically sealed. Once it broke, a profound shock from the revelations of priest sex abuse echoed around the world. This distress raises profound questions about the entire system of the Church. At the very least, the stench alone will take years to fade away.

The stigma of scandal

The history of sex and the Church is filled with ironies. Perhaps the greatest paradox, however, is that the scandals were essentially caused by the Catholic Church's eternal dread of them. By ruthlessly suppressing scandal for two thousand years, the pressure of those unacceptable truths is what in our day has created this massive eruption of shame.

The driving aversion to public humiliation goes back to the very earliest days of Christianity. Embarrassing questions were raised even while Jesus was alive about his parentage, relationships, and practices. But all that was nothing compared to the "scandal of the cross." The Roman state inflicted on Jesus the most degrading and painful form of capital punishment it could devise, one reserved mainly for runaway slaves and foreign rebels. The Crucifixion traumatized his first followers, most of whom would face their own ends in violent disgrace as well.

For centuries, Christianity remained a laughingstock. Few educated citizens of the Empire would take any religion that worshipped an executed criminal seriously. The earliest image of the Crucifixion, in fact, a bit of Roman graffiti from the third century, showed a Christian worshipping a crucified man with the head of an ass.[3] Though largely left alone, Christ's followers would be periodically rounded up and executed as atheists and anarchists in waves of persecutions for the mob's amusement.

So, the young faith soon became hypersensitive to shame. For better or worse, it has stayed that way ever since. Scandal, defined as actions or attitudes that lead another to sin, *must* be avoided at all costs.

As a reviled, outlawed criminal organization, the Church developed its most basic institutions both in secret and in opposition to the surrounding pagan society. No matter how accepted the institution later became as an essential part of the social fabric, its leaders could not fail to remember the disgrace imposed upon its founder. The grotesque instrument of Jesus' execution was in fact made the religion's chief emblem.

Nor have the bishops ever forgotten the fact that the faith could depend on no power beyond its walls save God. "Outside of the Church there is no salvation," became its watchword. Thus, the Catholic Church has ever jealously maintained its dignity and root independence. Moreover, it keeps its own counsel. As an institution, it is neither inclined to seek permission from civil rulers nor to answer to them for anything because basically, it still does not trust them. The deep traumas engendered by the Age of Martyrs have not been forgotten.

But within three centuries, the Church had triumphed over the Empire. Crucifixion was immediately banned and pagan temples were one by one transformed into churches. In the West, however, the Roman Empire did not last. Less than a century after conversion, Rome crumbled under the weight of barbarian invasions and internal rot, though the Eastern portion of the now-Christianized Empire endured for another thousand years.

Christians found themselves with the few institutions still standing in Western Europe. These became the basis of a new civilization, Christendom. Though religious leaders stood apart from the rickety pillar of barbarian kingship, they both propped each other up. In exchange for its military protection, the state was blessed with sacred legitimacy and clerks who could read and write the tax rolls. So, the faith formed the vital heart of the medieval West, becoming thoroughly intertwined with the secular order. Yet, the Church ever remained a "perfect society" set apart with its own goals, laws, and instrumentalities.

Believing itself established by God and thus fundamentally superior in every way to the secular order, Christianity has thus historically sought to dominate and use the instruments of mundane government for its own purposes. Whenever free to safely do so, the Church would simply ignore the state and proceed according to its own whims.

Even today, it still connives to prevent any interference by civil rulers, be they popular democrats or atheist dictators. As shall be shown in this modern crisis, it has utilized every legal tactic in the book and then some to avoid revealing the sins of its priests and bishops. Its lawyers have also sought to use the separation of Church and State to its advantage. They have argued that its internal affairs are none of the state's business. So far, at least, they have managed to stymie every attempt to legally attack it as some kind of corrupt, racketeering Mafia.

Not just ignorant anti-Catholic bigots have referred to the Church as a crime syndicate, either. Indeed, Frank Keating, the first head of the National Review Board the bishops established to investigate the Church's record in the US, had to resign after publicly comparing the Roman Catholic Church to organized crime. Refusing to later apologize for his "deadly accurate" remarks, the former governor, FBI agent, and federal prosecutor said, "To act like La Cosa Nostra and hide and suppress, I think, is very unhealthy... To resist grand jury subpoenas, to suppress the names of offending clerics, to deny, to obfuscate, to explain away; that is the model of a criminal organization, not my church."[4]

Nor he was alone in his views. His replacement, former judge Ann Burke, had almost as harsh words about their deception and public relations tactics in a letter to the bishops just a year later.[5]

Keating probably should have apologized to the Mafia for his remark, however, for they have never been singled out as willfully concealing and abetting pedophiles. While that may seem callous, the Roman Catholic Church has been rightfully criticized, even by some of its most ardent supporters, as having woefully mismanaged its pastoral obligations.

Victims and their families have been lied to by bishops, parishioners have been kept in the dark about the predators in their midst, and perpetrators have been empowered to continue to molest time and again in fresh locations. These are not radical opinions, but simple facts, demonstrated repeatedly in countless cases.

Scandal of scandals

Clergy sexual abuse is a crime committed under the color and authority of religion. That spiritual component is what distinguishes it from incest or molestation by other authority figures like coaches or teachers.

What makes sexual abuse by priests particularly heinous is that the spiritual power and authority claimed by an ordained Roman Catholic priest is literally God-like. It is far greater than any mere preacher or minister of the Gospel, however revered. The hands that touch improperly are holy, consecrated to bless the bread and wine in order to bring Christ to Earth.

So, when avowed "men of God" commit sexual assaults, the damage to the victim incorporates all the pain and confusion associated with sexual abuse of any kind, plus a particularly damning sense of sin. But whether or not a cleric uses religious sensibilities to actively manipulate his victim, any violation at all of his own chastity becomes both a defilement of his own sacred office and an abuse of its divine authority.

In the Catholic system, the priesthood is not just a job; it is a state of being. It cannot be separated from the rest of the man's existence. "Thou art a priest forever," as the ordination rite once proudly proclaimed. This exclusive, eternal character was determined quite early on. Even while still outlawed, the Church struggled over whether clergy who had succumbed to pressure and offered incense to the pagan gods during the persecution could ever effectively minister at Christian altars again. It decided finally that indeed they could, only to be faced with the same questions again due to the corruption in the Middle Ages.

The theological principle finally enshrined by the Council of Trent is *"ex opere operato,"* "by the work performed" – that is, by the sacramental act itself properly executed with the right materials, intention, and so forth. It is completely uninfluenced by any personal sanctity, or lack thereof, of the clergyman performing it. The right to minister the sacraments may be forbidden by higher authorities, but the actual ability cannot be taken away under any circumstances: "a priest's ordination never becomes invalid, even if he loses the clerical state."[6]

Nor is this power ever diminished at all by sin, even the worst kind of spiritually deadly or "mortal" sin. Administering any sacrament while in a state of mortal sin, as the gravest type is called, is itself a mortal sin. But according to established doctrine, the spiritual efficacy of that sacrament is not weakened in the slightest. Yet, the fear of scandal reigns supreme here as well. As it would be scandalous for a priest in a state of sin to cancel or delay Mass just so he can go confess, so he is allowed to perform the service with just mumbling a quick private Act of Contrition and intending to confess as soon as is practical.[7]

And so it is, that a priest could sodomize an altar boy in the sacristy, tidy up, and then go out to calmly say Mass as if nothing had happened.

According to testimonies, this unfortunately is exactly what has occurred on not a few occasions. Moreover, since it would also be scandalous if the priest were noticed doing penance, so as long as his sins have been undetected by his flock, so any payment due must also be hidden. "If the punishment cannot be secret, there must be no punishment, and no admission of priestly weakness."[8]

Thus, the pious horror of leading others into sin by shocking them can actually enable clerical criminals rather than stop them.

In any case, the numbers alone – doubtless far more than the official estimate of nearly 11,000 child sexual abuse victims of over 4,000 Catholic priests just in the United States over the last 50 years – show a disturbing pattern of depravity.[9] But the real distress lay not in numbers, ages, or conditions of victims.

The true horror was simply that Catholic priests could even commit such sins at all. When most of the crimes in the news were committed, trust in the heroic sanctity of men of the cloth had probably never been higher. In postwar America, for instance, priests were portrayed in movies as being as manly as any soldier and just as heroic in their sacrifice.

Seminarians were taught that priests could justly be "called not only Angels, but even gods" because of their divine powers.[10] The laity accepted them at their word as set apart like living saints, showering them with privileges, economic as well as social: Father driving a brand-new car every year was not an uncommon sight in the 1950s and 60s. Nothing, therefore, had even remotely prepared Catholic parents for the possibility of these revered, consecrated, and pampered men raping their children.

The Catholic Church had completely convinced the people that their leaders' elite station somehow miraculously transformed their human natures. Events have since sadly proven that many were not. The real mystery, then, may be not why scandals erupted, but what had kept them from breaking out before.

How much had the Inquisition to do with this suppression? The archives of the Spanish version show its continued involvement in sex cases until its final extinction in the nineteenth century. As full access to the Roman records is most unlikely and current cases are secret, the full extent of the cover-up may never be completely clear. As will be demonstrated, the evidence, however, sufficiently shows that the Holy Office, in all times and places, constituted the main pillar of the secret system.

CHAPTER II:
FROM CHASTITY TO CELIBACY

From Jesus to "zero tolerance"

By the time the Inquisition was handed its mandate to suppress clergy abuse, the Roman Church was in trouble such as it had never experienced before. For centuries before Luther's revolt, the moral reputation of clergy had steadily declined. Discipline faltered as repeated assaults of the Black Death reaped the most saintly while rival claimants to the papacy busily cursed each other. Corruption became as open as it was rife. Prelates could easily purchase dispensations to keep female housekeepers, for instance, and then later buy bishoprics on credit for their resulting illegitimate sons.[1]

It had taken over a thousand years for the situation to become so dismal. The root cause was simple, however: mandatory clerical celibacy. Church apologists who so strenuously argue that celibacy has nothing to do with clergy abuse overlook the fact that it serves as the exclusive basis for the claim of the Roman clergy's separate status and privileges. Ironically, only the power of the clergy over a believer based on their presumed chastity makes sexual abuse of him or her possible.

Simple logic indicates the inherently dangerous conflict of combining such awesome authority with the equal demand for absolute chastity. As confirmed continually by history, outlawing sex is futile. Like all such prohibitions, celibacy required of those unwilling or incapable merely perverts this most potent natural urge into more criminal forms, resulting in adultery, prostitution, rape, child abuse, or even worse.

The supreme irony is that it did not have to be that way. Much as the Roman Church dislikes admitting it, as happened during Vatican II, there is nothing inherent in the priesthood that requires celibacy. In many Eastern branches of the universal Church, though priests cannot get married and bishops must be celibate, already married men can be ordained now just as they could a thousand years ago. And indeed, there is sound Biblical precedent, for all the priests of Yahweh were married. It was not optional either, but their solemn religious duty to breed.

Whether Jesus was married or not is not known – the accepted Gospels say nothing about it one way or the other. The fact that he was a Jewish teacher, a rabbi, is often used to argue that he must have been, and it is often speculated that Mary Magdalene was his wife. This is not just a product of modern times either – the *Gospel of Philip*, for instance, which did not make it into the Bible, called her "his companion." And it mentions that Jesus would often kiss her. Exactly where is not specified due to a gap in the text. Most scholars assume it was on the mouth. But wherever the smooch was planted, it certainly offended the rest of the disciples, who complained that he loved her more than them.[2]

Perhaps Jesus' wife and children, if they existed and whoever they were, were not mentioned in the Scriptures simply to protect them. After all, even his revered brother James who succeeded him as head of the movement was himself thrown off of the Temple. If "James the Just" could be martyred despite a universal reputation for sanctity, no one was safe.[3]

In fact, the legions long continued to hunt down Jesus' relatives – after the fall of Jerusalem, the new emperor Vespasian issued an order to wipe out anyone who claimed to be a descendant of David. The last known relative of Jesus was said to be a cousin, Symeon, an extremely old farmer who led the Jerusalem Church. Trajan crucified him at the turn of the first century.[4]

Regardless, the official position of the Roman Church remains firm that Jesus, though a normal male in every other way never married nor even had sex. He stayed eternally chaste and virginal his entire life. Christ also only chose male disciples as apostles, they claim, and thus it is that priests who represent him must also be sexless males. Pope John Paul II raised this to near dogma: "I declare that the Church has no authority whatsoever to confer priestly ordination on women and that this judgment is to be definitively held by all the Church's faithful."[5]

Yet Peter, whom the Roman Church claims as founder and font of authority as the first pope, was most definitely married – the Gospels are silent about his wife and children but do mention his mother-in-law.[6] He would not be the only wedded pope, either.

Paul complained of being alone, and said that bishops should have only a single wife and be able to manage their children.[7] Apostolic celibacy was not the norm but recommended for the practical reason that as the world would surely end soon, the work to be done was great, and a family would only be a burden.

Women were important, powerful, and active in the early church. There was the group of women including the Magdalene that supported Jesus in his ministry; later on, others financially underwrote missions, hosted home churches, or preached themselves. Some served as deaconesses, priests, and quite likely even as bishops.[8]

They were soon pushed aside, however, due to a number of forces, including competition from extreme Gnostic cults, the worsening social situation overall, and probably most important of all, the cumulative effects of centuries of sexual trauma and powerlessness under Roman slavery. These all led to a powerfully ascetic, world-hating, and misogynist revulsion of all things erotic or feminine.

Females became feared for their creative powers, sensuality, and not least for the real possibility of accidental ritual contamination from sexual fluids, particularly menstrual blood. It was for this reason women were gradually ousted from the deaconate. Blood associated with birthing became considered so polluting that mothers up until the 1960s had to undergo a special "churching" ceremony after giving birth before being allowed to attend public services.[9]

Important writers like saints Jerome and Augustine praised celibacy to the heavens. Jerome, for instance, in his Latin version of the Bible that would rule the West until the Reformation, translated a term for "young woman" as "virgin," thus promoting the cult of the asexual, ever-virginal Mother of God. He even falsified the dialog concerning sex and marriage in his rendition of the Book of Tobit to glorify sex for offspring, not pleasure.[10]

This might have been a reflection of certain personal issues, however. It seems that Jerome had to leave Rome forever after apparently being caught in a woman's dress, though he claimed was set up. An evil monk switched the gown in the dark that Jerome was to put on for midnight prayers. Whatever really happened, the embarrassed saint spent the remainder of his days in the desert, clad in hair shirts and beating his chest with a rock instead.[11]

His friend and contemporary, Augustine, bishop of a city in Africa, was equally, if not more, anti-sex. His authoritative influence has severely stressed countless Christian marriages through the ages. Augustine dourly proclaimed that any lovemaking for pleasure, even in marriage, was in itself sinful. His fingering the sin of Adam and Eve as specifically erotic in nature branded sexuality as inherently evil. The only legitimate purpose of sex was therefore procreation in marriage, and that only if done with as little delight in the act as possible. Because of the pleasure involved, the sin of the parents infected the offspring of their passion as if it were HIV.

Only Jesus, who did not originate out of bestial lust, was thus the only human totally free from original sin.[12] It would take a very long time for his mother to be equally honored with the doctrine of the Immaculate Conception, that she, too, was graciously conceived without sin.

Just as the notion of the virgin birth sprang from paganism, so too did celibacy. Priests of Cybele castrated themselves and dressed like women to serve their goddess, as did those of numerous other cults. Ritual abstention from intercourse before sacrifice was required among the Greeks and Romans.[13] Even Jewish priests were forbidden to sleep with their wives the night before beginning their temple duties, and a back up kept ready in case of nocturnal emissions.

But apart from certain fanatics with their castrating "nutcrackers," these were all temporary restrictions. One of those nuts, however, was possibly the greatest Christian thinker of the age, the Egyptian philosopher Origen, who took the Gospel injunction to make himself a "eunuch for the kingdom of heaven" all too literally. His self-mutilation was a "headstrong act" that disgraced him when it was revealed many years later.[14]

In any case, by the time the time the Roman Empire fell in the West, the newly dominant Christian church had turned resolutely against the world and its delights, especially sex. Early Church councils soon began to regulate the lives of the clergy, including their love lives.

Before Christianity was even legalized, a local council held at Elvira in Spain in the first decade of the fourth century was the first to declare, "that all concerned with the ministry of the altar should maintain entire abstinence from their wives under pain of forfeiting their positions." It decreed that only sisters or daughters, and solely when bound by vows of virginity, should be permitted to live with ecclesiastics as companions.[15]

If the clergy did not abstain from sex completely, they were to be removed from office, and if guilty of sexual immorality, could not receive Communion even at death, nor could anyone who had sexually abused boys. Moreover, screening candidates for holy orders was already the rule, even at that early date. Those who had sex in their youth or came from outside the province and were hence unknown were also proscribed.[16] Although of very limited authority and not repeated by general councils for a considerable time, these were the first signs of some problems that still haunt the Church.

When Pope Gregory the Great died in 604, celibacy was not yet the rule, but strict chastity was. He proclaimed a policy of "zero tolerance." A single lapse was all it took to make a cleric unfit to minister at the altar and condemn him to irrevocable degradation from his holy office. Within three centuries, monastic copyists had twisted that rule. In an influential collection of laws altered to increase papal power, the *False Decretals of Isidore*, a paragraph was added to Gregory's letter explaining the necessity for forgiveness after repentance of clerical lechery "of which, among many, so few are guiltless."[17]

The Roman Church would not even consider Gregory's extreme hard line against clergy sex again for another fourteen hundred years. The first prelate to seriously propose it again was the founder of an order known as the Servants of the Paraclete, who plays a major role in the story. For whatever reason, a fateful decision was made to attempt to rehabilitate the offenders instead. The situation continued another forty years, and in time, the scandals blossomed.

At the dawn of the third millennium, another Gregory, this one surnamed Aymond, a bishop in charge of the US Conference of Catholic Bishops, would try to convince the Vatican to give it another shot. The proposed regulations in June of 2002 met little success due to opposition from the Holy See.[18] As virtually every effort to keep priests pure during that long period had been undermined, sabotaged, or ignored by clergy, perhaps Rome's pessimism was not unwarranted.

Medieval immorality

After Pope Gregory, the state of affairs grew steadily worse. By the ninth century, in the depths of the Dark Ages, one of the lowest periods of clerical morality of all, there were regulations such as that of St. Theodore Studita, forbidding even female animals in monasteries for fear of bestiality.[19] So many nunneries had become brothels that a local council in France ordered that convents should not have any dark corners where sex could take place unobserved. Charlemagne's chancellor himself remarked that the licentiousness of nuns often led to the worse crime of infanticide.[20]

The most extreme point of papal misogyny in the Middle Ages was shown in certain curious customs during electoral conclaves. These involved a most unusual throne. One such supposedly still exists in a back room in the Vatican Museum.

> *It is a strange object. There is, for a start, something curious about its proportions. The seat is very high and has cut into it a keyhole shape, the stem open to the front. On closer examination it could be an elderly, rather grand*

commode, once used by popes, but now an embarrassing reminder of their humanity. However, the chair back is at a curious reclining angle, far too relaxed, it would seem, for any practical bodily movement. And the legs, too, are unusual... leaving the centre, under the keyhole, open and uncluttered.

Variously known as the sedia stercoraria – *which translates as the "dung chair" – or rather more understandably, as the "pierced chair," this then was the object used to test the sex of newly installed popes... Any candidate chosen by his peers to occupy the papal throne was required, before his election could be verified, to sit on this elaborate seat while a young cardinal took advantage of the design to touch his testicles.*[21]

Supposedly, if all was found as expected, the story goes, the examining cardinal was to call out, "He has two balls, and they are well hung."

Medieval eyewitness accounts give no doubt that at one time, this very chair or others like it were indeed an important part of the papal coronation ritual. The only explanation ever given for this embarrassing ceremony has to do with a long-rumored feminine papacy.

Ancient and legends persist about "Pope Joan," as she is called. Vigorously denied to this day by the Church, her story was nonetheless recorded in some 500 medieval chronicles.[22]

Their tale is most peculiar. Said to have been a German woman of English parents who, posing as a man, entered the Church, "Joan" became a great teacher and a bishop. She was ultimately elected pope as John VIII in 855. She supposedly reigned for two years, secretly taking a lover. Her secret was shockingly revealed when she gave birth to a child in the street during a papal procession, whereupon she and her lover were either stoned or hung upon the spot. The popes, it is said, have superstitiously avoided taking that same route ever since.[23]

Monuments were built in her honor, but later destroyed or altered, especially after the Reformation, when her tale was used to further embarrass Rome. The Tarot card known as "The Popess" may well be one of the few existing references to her.[24]

Whatever the truth, less than a half-century after her legendary reign, powerful aristocratic women did indeed dominate Rome, albeit from behind the scenes. In fact, the great eighteenth-century English historian Edward Gibbon thought that Joan's story was but a "coded reference" to the most influential of these: a team of "two sister prostitutes" – actually a noble-born mother and her daughter – named Theodora and Marozia. Theodora first achieved infamy by giving the fifteen-year-old Marozia to her candidate, Pope Sergius III, as a reward for his election, and then arranged the succession of two following pontiffs, followed by her own lover, Pope John X.

But Marozia became every bit the equal of her mother in both numbers of lovers and political cunning. She placed her bastard son by Sergius on the papal throne. This "Christian Caligula," Pope John XII, was the son of a pope but the son, grandson, and nephew of papal mistresses who made and unmade so many.[25]

Remembered as possibly the worst pontiff ever, even more wicked than Alexander VI, the Borgia pope five centuries later, John was only eighteen when his ascension was arranged in 955. He crowned Otto as German Emperor but then turned against him. Accused of incest, violating female pilgrims, and converting the Lateran palace into a brothel, among other things, it is likely, however, that he was not that much more wicked than some of his immediate predecessors.[26]

Dethroned by Otto but reinstated by the noble ladies, John's triumph was short-lived. Even as the emperor and his new pope, Leo VIII, marched back on Rome, John was supposedly brutally killed by a jealous husband while in bed with the man's wife in the papal palace.[27]

Only another member of his family could really rival him. Almost a century later, another descendant of Marozia, Benedict IX, was placed on the papal throne by the bribery of his father at age ten, twelve, or fifteen (sources differ). Force to flee by an uprising in 1045, he returned and actually sold the papal office. Deposed by the Emperor Henry III the next year, he later returned yet again as an antipope, or false claimant.[28]

Having had numerous affairs with both married women and virgins, Benedict finally sold the papacy yet again and retired happily to his estates and harem.[29] But his evil reputation was such that a legend grew up that after his death, his spirit appeared to a holy man in the shape of a bear with the ears and tail of an ass, which Benedict would have to wear during his torments in Hell until Doomsday.[30]

Yet, both popes ironically made the papacy appear much more regal. John XII, born Octavius, established the tradition of popes changing their names upon their election, while Benedict IX was the first to bear a coat of arms like a secular king. And it was another bad pope, Boniface VIII, who added a second crown to the papal tiara, to indicate his royal status.[31] Cloaking wickedness beneath the opulent trappings of power is not an option just for secular rulers, it seems.

Many other pontiffs made the Church their family business, too. Two other medieval popes begat future pontiffs, another was the son of a bishop. Priests fathered a further seven, and one was the offspring of a subdeacon. At least three popes were widowers before they were ordained.[32]

In fact, one later long-standing papal tradition became that of the "cardinal nephew" from which is derived the term "nepotism." Usually a young nephew or other relative of the pope (though often rumored to be his own bastard), he held a position of trust and considerable, often excessive, influence. It became such an important position that councils and church law attempted to regulate the practice. Abuses led to Pope Innocent XII banning the position in 1692, yet most pontiffs in the eighteenth century continued to appoint them anyway. It was finally eliminated when the loss of the Papal States and political influence made the post unnecessary.

All this of course occurred much, much later. Back in the ninth century, things could not have been much worse as the papacy sank into a swamp of corruption. With new invasions by Vikings and other barbarians and the collapse of Charlemagne's fleeting empire, civilization in Western Europe was on the ropes. Allegiances shifted as governments failed. Local nobles began providing protection to farmers in exchange for them being bound to the land they rented. The feudal system took shape as society's last chance. Abbots and bishops became important lords and thoroughly invested in secular politics. The effect on clerical morality was not good.

Bishops such as Segenfrid of Le Mans, not only took wives but also stripped their own churches for the benefit of their sons. To say that many bishops lived like secular lords only worse would not be amiss. One such was "Archembald, Archbishop of Sens, who, taking a fancy to the Abbey of St. Peter, drove out the monks and established a harem of concubines in the refectory, and installed his hawks and hounds in the cloister."[33] At the same time, wives of married priests among the Anglo-Saxons were taking the revenues and finery of parish churches for their own.[34] By the late eleventh century the situation had become dire. It was the darkest part of what historians used to call the Dark Ages.

CHAPTER III:
SEX AND THE SINGLE PRIEST

Monks and misogyny

As the Church accommodated itself to the harsh new feudal realities, the priesthood was in real danger of becoming a hereditary office. Church lands, property, and spirituality gradually slipped away as bishops and abbots became as worldly as any other lords. As landholders, they had the same obligations to support their own lords militarily also.

Some prelates actively took up arms. Bishop Odo of Bayeux fought beside his brother William during the English conquest. Possibly, he and other warrior priests may have used maces rather than swords so as not to shed blood. But some, however, including Bishop Adhemar, a leader of the First Crusade, are depicted as wielding the typical weapons of a knight: spear, sword, and shield.

The Church became so feudalized that part of the ordination ceremony of priests up until modern times still incorporated the knightly commendation ceremony or "act of homage." During this rite, the new vassal (a priest in this case) would kneel and put his hands within those of his lord (his bishop) to swear his loyalty and personal obedience. The lord bishop would accept and make promises of his own in return.

If the posture sounds familiar, it should. It is still practiced constantly in churches around the world. This position, kneeling with hands clasped in front, in time became the standard stance of prayer. Previously, people prayed standing erect with hands open and spread apart, as if offering explanations or expecting a gift. This was "orans," the classic pose of prayer.

Kneeling, however, is a position from which it is much more tactically difficult to attack, especially with head bowed. A human version of the universal mammalian gesture of social submission, the posture displays the abject inferiority and total dependence of the petitioner before the more powerful superior. The adoption of such an extreme form shows how desperate the times were.

This kneeling posture is called "supplicium" in Latin, the stance of entreaty and awaiting punishment; that is, beheading. Hence, genuflections or at least bows to acknowledge superiority are still performed before royalty, including princes of the Church.

Perhaps it is therefore not coincidental that God started being regarded more as a conquering king rather than a loving father when bishops became lords. As they are still, for the hierarchs to this day retain many of their god-like medieval powers over their subordinates.

In any case, because of all this political intermingling, their secular over-lords began to demand the right to appoint bishops, priests, and abbots like any other vassals on their lands. The Roman Church drew perilously close to losing its treasured independence altogether.

Finally, however, a violent ascetic reaction against such secular influences began in earnest. St. Peter Damian, "the last monk," who died in 1072, was the firebrand who ignited the reform movement. A noble-born but neglected baby, the compassionate wife of a priest saved his life. He would repay this kindness by devoting most of his life to wiping out her class.[1]

Famed for his asceticism and intellect, Damian became first a prior and eventually the highest cardinal in Rome. His voluminous writings promoted a revolutionary Church that was in effect a theocratic empire, demanding absolute allegiance from the clergy, and separated from the people by self-inflicted austerities whose performance entitled the clergy to their reverence and obedience.[2]

His most famous work was an essay addressed to Pope Leo IX called *The Book of Gomorah*. It was a shocking exposé of the excesses endemic in monasteries, a bitter diatribe against the laxity of monkish morals, and sodomy in particular, "the saddest of all the sad monuments bequeathed to us by that age of desolation."[3] Here is a sample of his ranting:

> *Vice against nature creeps in like a cancer and even touches the order of consecrated men. Sometimes it rages like a bloodthirsty beast in the midst of the sheepfold of Christ with such bold freedom that it would have been much healthier for many to have been oppressed under the yoke of a secular army than to be freely delivered over to the iron rule of diabolical tyranny under the cover of religion, particularly when this is accomplished by scandal to others.*[4]

He condemned not only clerical homosexuality but also marriage, stigmatizing the wives of priests as harlots and their husbands as unbridled adulterers, and also promoted anti-Semitism for good measure. His missions, however, sometimes met with physical resistance. Several times he barely escaped with his life from enraged clerics. In Milan, the solution he imposed sparked almost twenty years of rioting and civil strife.[5]

Though given the highest honors, Damian resigned as cardinal and returned to his cell to die. The praise continued after his death, too. Not only named as a saint, Pope Leo XII gave him the title of "Doctor of Reform" in 1823 – more likely for his efforts in promoting the papacy than for his opposition to clerical sex.[6]

Despite his rhetoric, Damian was more complex than a simple fire-breathing misogynist, however. He acknowledged the power imbalance in any relationship between priest and layperson, or between different clerical ranks, for that matter. He described clerical sex as a kind of "spiritual incest" and stated that bishops who did not discipline errant clergy were just as guilty as the offenders.

He was well aware that power just made the opportunities to abuse greater. "For we indeed punish the acts of impurity performed by priests in the minor ranks, but with bishops, we pay our reverence with silent tolerance, which is totally absurd," he wrote. He even described how bishops who had sex with their own clergy abused the seal of Confession. The bishops would confess to their inferiors or hear their confessions to keep them from revealing the sin.[7]

He suggested that any monk who seduced boys or adolescents be confined to a monastery where he could be watched, given harsh and degrading public penance, and even deposed from Holy Orders.[8] Even though he was the flag-bearer for papal primacy, Damian felt that even the pope could and should be chastised, or worse, if necessary, by the laity. And he was not above calling upon powerful women such as the Duchess Adelaide of Turin to initiate reform if the bishops refused.[9]

He died already revered shortly before the election of another cardinal-monk, Hildebrand, a clerical revolutionary. As Pope St. Gregory VII, he would implement the reforms Damian only dreamed of. Gregory, with his celebrated defiance of the German Emperor, laid the foundation for the Church's dominance over the State that characterized the High Middle Ages.

The new pope demanded priestly celibacy chiefly to prevent the rise of "an hereditary ecclesiastical aristocracy."[10] Absolute chastity was imposed on the clergy to make them dependent upon the Church rather than their families, allowing the Church to maintain its ascendancy over the laity. This may still be one of the bedrock reasons for clerical celibacy. Even today, it seems to have far less to do with morality than property and power.

The Vatican, for instance, will nowadays allow married Anglican or Orthodox priests to be ordained as Romans without putting away their wives. To allow Latin-rite priests to marry, however, not only involves disciplinary changes, but also expensive alterations to insurance and healthcare policies, pay scales, and pensions. Though cheaper and simpler to just open the priesthood to celibate women, this seems even more improbable.

In any case, Gregory's own life was also marred by scandalous innuendo. His enemies spread rumors concerning the Countess Mathilda of Tuscany, a wealthy and beautiful aristocrat who had conspicuously abandoned her husband for the papal court. Gregory was said to be smitten, but ultimately put her aside so he could fruitlessly pursue her own niece, Theodorine, who would have naught to do with him.[11] In any case, the great pontiff died in bitter obscurity and exile, defeated by the armies of the emperor. Only later would his true importance be seen.

Gregory had not hesitated to call upon the nobles to assist in his reforms. William the Conqueror attended the Synod of Lillebonne in 1080 in order to do so by quashing clerical resistance. One of its canons first mentions a practice that became a great disgrace to the Church. It declares that no priest shall be forced to give anything to the bishop beyond the lawful dues and particularly that no money shall be exacted because of their women.

This is the first reference known of a tax called "cullagium," the payment of which allowed ecclesiastics to enjoy their mistresses without fear. Despite repeated and harsh attempts to suppress the custom, it flourished until the Reformation.[12] One reason was that it could provide a great deal of revenue for constantly cash-strapped royalty. Henry I, for instance, reversed William's stand against cullagium just a half century later. He established an extended system that garnered a vast amount of money, in return for which the clerics got royal licenses to keep their women in peace.[13]

Meanwhile in Spain, the admonitions of Elvira had been long neglected. Celibacy had been largely ignored during the desperate early years of the fight with the Muslim invaders. Archbishop Diego of Compostella, under pressure from the pope, tried for years to reform just a single monastery. The abbot, who had many progeny and had wasted the revenues of his convent on riotous living, was admonished no less than seven times. Finally, at trial, he was proved by witnesses to have had no less than seventy concubines. His power was such that although deposed, he was still given a benefice to allow him to survive.[14]

As papal power slowly grew, pontiffs acted with greater ambition and cruelty, not against the clergy, but their women. At a council in Rome in 1051 to restore discipline, Pope St. Leo IX ordered that all the priests' women in the city were to be enslaved and given as property to the Lateran, while bishops elsewhere were to do the same for their own churches.[15]

Other popes, most notably Urban II, who launched the First Crusade, did much the same. Urban, in fact, tried to bribe the nobility to aid in this noble effort by offering them the wives of priests to be their own slaves, although he later backed down and merely forbad such marriages, ordered them dissolved and the couples subjected to penance.[16]

There were few other moments of such relative liberality. Pope Alexander II, for instance, maintained the ancient rule that no married man could take monastic vows unless his wife consented freely and joined a convent at the same time. Less than half a century later, however, the sacrament of marriage was completely trumped by the call of the Church, and consent would no longer be necessary.[17]

Sometimes, the effort by a zealous bishop to enforce celibacy led to actual violence. When Archbishop Geoffrey of Rouen returned from the council in 1119, he held a local synod of his clergy in the cathedral. Among the canons he promulgated was one forbidding "commerce with females of any description," the penalty for which would be excommunication.

The priests grumbled. The archbishop had the loudest complainer arrested and cast into prison. The clergy were appalled by this act against one of their own in the sacred precincts. In a rage, the archbishop then called for his guards and a riot began. The clergy fought off the archbishop's retainers and soon the local cooks and bakers joined in. They savagely beat all the priests they could lay hands upon, including several old and completely innocent men.

They and the offending clergy fled the city and "carried the sorrowful tidings to their parishioners and concubines." The citizens of the town showed pity on "the servants of God who had suffered such unheard-of insults." Yet they could do nothing. When Geoffrey's wrath finally subsided, he calmly purified the cathedral with holy water.[18]

In 1123, Pope Calixtus II called the First Lateran Council, which declared that all ties to the Church were supreme. When a man was ordained, he was set apart from the laity, and all previous bonds were to be dissolved.[19] This marks the final separation of the clergy from the people. Henceforth, no form of clerical sexual relationship would be lawful – unless a special dispensation was obtained.

Not much later at the Second Lateran Council, Innocent II extended the ban. He pronounced that any union contracted despite the rule of the Church was not a marriage. The intent was to brand the mates of priests and their children with an unbearable stigma. By putting them in a most unsupportable position both economically and legally, the Church would thus remove all legitimate sexual options from Western clergy.[20]

The Greeks, of course, were unaffected by this rule. The Eastern Church had never required priests to be celibate. Measures had to be taken to prevent men in Southern Italy where the Byzantine presence was strong from being ordained in the Orthodox Church just so they could marry.[21] Yet every time the popes sought to mend their schism with Constantinople, they had to admit that celibacy was a local rule. This happened first indirectly in the great Fourth Lateran Council in 1215 where the canons mandated even more severe penalties for "those clerics who have not renounced the marriage bond, following the custom of their region, shall be punished even more severely if they fall into sin."[22]

This was repeated in the Council of Florence several hundred years later, and finally, during the Second Vatican Council, a full seven and half centuries down the road. As shall be seen, it was that final, most damning admission that may have helped spur the great exodus of men from the Roman priesthood in the latter part of the twentieth century.

The papal sin tax

Hypocrisy was the inevitable result of outlawing priestly matrimony. No sooner was celibacy was made the rule than the morals of the clergy became an offense to all Christendom. So it was that Cardinal Pierleone could gather enough votes to make a plausible claim to the papacy, becoming the antipope Anacletus II in 1130. This was notwithstanding having had children by his sister Topea and traveling openly with a concubine while a papal legate.

The dissolution of the papal court became so notorious that cardinals even joked about it openly. When Pope Innocent IV left Lyons in 1251 after being there for eight years, Cardinal Hugo made a little speech. "Friends," he said, "since our arrival here, we have done much for your city. When we came, we found here three or four brothels. We leave behind us but one. We must own, however, that it extends without interruption from the eastern to the western gate." Such remarks were not well received by the noble ladies to whom they were addressed.[23]

Prostitution, surprisingly enough, was never outlawed by the Church in the Middle Ages. Basing himself on the authority of Augustine, St. Thomas Aquinas tolerated it as a lesser evil preferable to rape and incest. This explains the prevalence of red-light districts permitted by the civil authorities in some European cities. Houses could legitimately be rented out for this purpose, if in the right locale and "the owner secretly detests the sin."

Moreover, prostitutes enjoyed a privilege not shared with any other class of the faithful save the Holy Father himself – they were exempt from the requirement of yearly confession. Whether this was because recounting all her sins would take too long, the inadvisability of the confessor knowing the names of her clientele, or simple professional courtesy, is not clear. But she was not to confess and be absolved until she quit her profession, at which time the confessor could interrogate her as freely and deeply as he liked.[24]

In the Western Church, outlawing sex was as ineffective as condemning greed. Human nature always found a way. If he was wealthy and resolute, a churchman might be able to buy a dispensation from the papal court. Overcoming the dangers and expenses of a trip to Rome or Avignon, he could obtain permission allowing him to keep his mistress, or if banned from office thereby, even purchase a decree commanding his superior to reinstate him.[25]

No matter how harsh the proclamations issuing from on high or the efforts of zealous reformers to enforce them, letters of absolution could be purchased from the papal chancery to neutralize them. Prelates could even buy permission to grant dispensations to the priests under them.[26]

With the formal transfer of the papacy to Avignon in France in the early fourteenth century and the Great Schism that followed where up to three contenders at a time would each claim to be pope, the need for money became insatiable. It quickly became organized. Pope John XXII framed the infamous *Taxes of the Penitentiary*; a list of current prices for absolutions – in effect, a "papal sin tax." That it was a regular traffic is proved by the fact that among the many forms for scribes to use, there are none for refusing a request, any request.[27] Its importance may be shown in that as early as the end of the thirteenth century, applying to the Holy See for permission to borrow money was often the first thing a new bishop would do, because every function of the Curia was for sale.[28]

The practice of selling dispensations for various purposes continued even after Luther. Many Jewish-born Spaniards desperately sought protection from the papacy against the Spanish Inquisition by such means, usually futilely. The Curia would gladly take their money, but the Spaniards even kept an agent in Rome to counter such moves. In many cases, as a tool of the king, the Spanish Inquisition would simply ignore such documents anyway.

Yet, the papacy, even while insisting on the strictest chastity of its underlings, continually undermined itself throughout the Middle Ages and Renaissance with its avarice. The popes became their own worst enemy. The Roman Church squandered its moral authority, even as it raked in cash through dispensations, indulgences, and jubilees.

The pope had even imposed his own income tax on the clergy early on. Innocent III introduced this to help the crusades in 1199. It started at a fortieth, or 2.5%, but it could be levied at different rates, growing with income. Raised to a tenth in 1228, it soon became a regular and general tax and a substantial source of papal income.[29] But even that was not enough. The greed of officials and the inherent hypocrisy of the system frustrated reformers repeatedly and made the Church a butt of jokes long before Luther's rebellion.

After the Schism, the personal lives of the popes during the Renaissance contributed greatly to this. The corruption of the Borgia pope, Alexander VI, with his mistresses and infamous children, Lucrezia and Cesare, was particularly notorious. Even Julius II, the great warrior pope and art patron, had three daughters.

Long after Luther, the popes still flaunted the rules they made. Paul III was called "Cardinal Petticoat" because his sister had been a mistress of Alexander. He had his own concubine and several children. Pope Julius III had a sexual relationship with a fifteen-year-old boy he made a cardinal. Pius IV, himself the father of three, finally called the Council of Trent in reaction to the Lutheran revolt later in the sixteenth century.

Rumors have surrounded post-Reformation popes, too, including Innocent X. In recent times, Pius XII's long relationship with his confidant, Sister Josefine Pascalina, a powerful German nun, "the only woman to ever lived with a pope in the papal quarters," caused much gossip. Even Paul VI was said to have had a gay relationship as a young priest. The Vatican gave unexpected weight to the stories by stridently denying them at an official "Day of Consolation" to soothe the outraged pontiff on April 4, 1976.[30]

Predictably, the Council of Trent accomplished little that was new or daring, despite high hopes. Recommendations drawn up by a special commission that labored on reform for years in preparation included the suggestion that monastic orders were so corrupt that they should all be gradually dissolved, and all nunneries placed under the rule of the local bishops in the meantime. The report was so damning that Luther himself happily published it. The embarrassed chairman and chief inquisitor, Cardinal Carrafa, quietly condemned his own report by placing it on the very *Index of Forbidden Books* which he had introduced after he became Pope Paul IV.[31]

The Protestants all uniformly denounced celibacy due to clerical immorality, but nobody did more to bury it than Luther himself. He encouraged all religious to abandon their convents and marry each other. The ex-monk practiced what he preached, too, by wedding an escaped nun, Katharina von Bora, who bore him six children.

Luther's reading of Genesis had convinced him that sexuality, created by God, was thus in itself good. The divine command to "go forth and multiply" trumped all the Church's rules. Celibacy was in fact a sin while raising a family became holy work, a sort of new penitential lifestyle.[32] The ancient equation of sex with sin and suffering was broken at last, at least for Protestants, although the suffering part probably still remained.

In reaction, Trent exalted celibacy, like it did other doctrines denied by the rebels. Absolute chastity was raised virtually to the level of dogma, with apostolic origins claimed for it against all history. Aside from making many good Christians of the previous thousand years instant heretics, it froze asceticism solidly into place. Even though punishments were the same as had been repeatedly threatened, henceforth, celibate doctrine itself could not be questioned.[33] At least, that is, until Vatican II when all these issues would be revisited.

Meanwhile however, with the sin tax finally abolished, some lusty clerics would resort to seduction, prostitution, homosexuality, or rape instead. Many would sate their desires by taking criminal advantage of the most sacred of circumstances, during the sacrament of Confession. The misuse of this most solemn rite to procure sex would in time be the lure to attract the Inquisition's ominous attention.

CHAPTER IV:
SOLICITATION AND THE CONFESSIONAL

Rites of forgiveness

The most frequently abused sacrament of the Church is Confession, or Penance, or as it's now called, Reconciliation. Understandably, for in private "auricular" confession – that is, whispered in the ear – a priest and a layperson share the most intimate spiritual encounter possible.

By whatever name, Confession is actually a sacred tribunal, where the priest, taking the place of Christ the final judge, hears a recounting of a sinner's misdeeds and forgives them, ordering a token repayment by prayer, fasting, or good works. In Catholicism, the rite is considered an essential means of returning to and maintaining a state of grace.

Since the twelfth century, most every Catholic has been duty-bound to resort to it at least once a year.[1] Before modern times, the faithful were given little choice as to who would hear their deepest faults either, but had to resort to their parish priest. This allowed ample scope for sexually predatory clergy to approach anyone they desired in the community.

But like the rest of the sacraments, that of Penance did not spring fully formed straight from the mind of Jesus. It has greatly changed through the centuries. But the Council of Trent finally set its dogmatic underpinnings in the sacramental system in stone in the sixteenth century. Alterations since have mainly been merely a result of theologians working out various implications of the dogma. Not even Vatican II, which tweaked its outward form, challenged those basic definitions in any way.

Though the Christian faith quickly settled on Baptism as a once-only purifying initiation, for a long time there was uncertainty whether such a blanket cleansing could be granted more than once. Because of this doubt, baptism for many early believers was something to be put off for as long as possible, especially for those involved in the tumult of public life. Even Constantine waited until his deathbed to wash the blood from his soul.

Infant baptism was only allowed if the danger of death was imminent. Though the practice started early, not until the chaos that followed the collapse of the Empire in the West did baptizing babies become universal. Irish missionaries spread the practice across the continent to the conquering barbarians along with private confession.

Most offenses during the first centuries were expected to be dealt with purely by the sinner's own personal repentance. But Peter and the apostles themselves, by their cowardice at Jesus' crucifixion, had proven that anyone could mess up before the entire group in a big way and require correction.

So something had been needed from very the start to re-incorporate those who had committed grave public errors back into the community. Open admission of their mistakes before the congregation followed by equally public punishment was the answer.

Since Christianity was still an illegal underground movement, only those sins that actually endangered the existence of the local group required communal purging. Confession was thus reserved mainly for serious social offenses like adultery, murder, and idolatry.[3] The latter sin in particular committed by clergy unwilling to be martyred led to great controversies, even outright schisms, when they later sought to regain their former posts.

At first, Penance was a singular grace, granted just once, like Baptism. Administered publicly before the community, its judgments were imposed by the "overseer" of the community – the bishop – often in consultation with the "elders" – the class of men that became the priests. At the time, they could only apply spiritual remedies, not physical or financial punishment.

Yet, penances were usually harsh and prolonged, including austerities such as fasting, wearing sackcloth, and sprinkling ashes on the head. Penitents were excluded from the assembly for up to seven years, then admitted to the congregation but not allowed to receive the Eucharist for another seven. While sitting outside lamenting their sins, they would often implore the faithful as they entered to pray for them. When their penance had been served, the bishop would signify their re-admission to full communion by a formal imposition of hands.[4]

St. Jerome said, "Penance is the second plank after shipwreck." He meant that it was the way to save a floundering soul after it had lost its grip on the first plank of salvation, Baptism.[2] Though it all seems incredibly harsh by modern standards, the system eased those who had made serious errors into gradual re-acceptance by the community. But if they could, often penitents would delay confessing until their deathbeds due to the harshness and length of penalties.

Once the religion was legalized, however, the new political situation changed everything. The influx of all kinds of new members – including government officials – destroyed the cozy closed structure of the early house churches. Public buildings were now being used and strangers could more easily attend. This all soon made communal confession inadvisable, even dangerous. Open acknowledgement of faults and crimes could now have dire, unpredictable effects outside the immediate church community.

Other changes were brought about by the growth of the faith. Penances did not soften but were extended to cover an ever-widening range of offenses. Codes and courts gradually came into being as the Church developed its own system of jurisprudence case by case. "Episcopal police" were obliged to keep track of compliance.

Those seeking forgiveness did not always take these extreme demands meekly, either. At the end of a period of persecution, great numbers of former clerics seeking re-admission would often object to being rigorously punished for their idolatry. After Diocletian's terror, the resentment was so great that the disgraced members of the clergy rose in rebellion, which ended not only in bloodshed, but the banishment of both the pope and his successor.[5]

Meanwhile, those holy men who had acquired a reputation for sage counsel attracted penitents, and in time, were appointed or specialized as confessors. As Christianity spread and congregations grew, the ever-increasing need caused the power to forgive to gradually extend from the bishops down to the presbyters. These trusted elders presided over the local sacred meals and increasingly ran individual congregations. They would become the priesthood.

The evolution of Confession

The same Irish monks during the Dark Ages who promoted infant baptism finished turning a public cleansing into a private consultation and ritual purgation. Confession was still a rare occurrence, a singular event that might require a long journey to the nearest confessor. He would sit for days with the sinner, systematically delving into all his or her misdeeds, and would often be rewarded with a feast when it was done.

Confession was now confidentially whispered into the confessor's ear rather than spoken aloud before a group. The Irish and later Anglo Saxon missionaries carried these practices onto the continent. They composed books called "penitentials" with long lists of sins and the penalties they merited. These were still quite severe and varied greatly, but substitutions of money or other things could significantly shorten them.[6]

Like most of the Church's dogma, the theory behind the practice was not worked out in detail until the Middle Ages. Debated by a great many theologians, St. Thomas Aquinas most fully developed its rules and premises. One of the last subjects that he tackled before his death, his description of how Penance worked became definitive.

Most details are irrelevant here, but several key concepts should be noted. First, Confession is only necessary for mortal sin, those grave offenses against God, which are called "mortal" because if left unforgiven, they result in the eternal death of Hell. Lesser sins need not be admitted at all and can be forgiven by many other means.[7] Secondly, the confession must be made to a priest, although even in the Middle Ages this was not so clear. Others often heard them: deacons, for instance, or even laymen when priests were unavailable at the time of death, and abbesses might hear those of their nuns.[8]

The sacrament itself consists of several parts. Remorse is first necessary on the part of the sinner. "Perfect remorse" or "contrition," the regret for offending God out of pure love, is itself sufficient to gain forgiveness even without ritual, but theologians agree that "attrition" or regret due to fear of God's punishments is quite enough for the sacrament to work. For most people, the rite was essential, as many schoolmen held that true contrition was virtually impossible. The catch was that since anyone genuinely sorry for sin would gladly take the opportunity for sacramental forgiveness anyway, there was just no getting around Confession.

The second part of the sacrament is the actual confession itself. The penitent accuses him or herself of sins, which must include all mortal sins committed since the last time, any forgotten then, and all complicating circumstances. If any mortal sin is deliberately withheld, then the confession is invalid and must be completely repeated the next time along with an admission of concealment.

The third part is the "satisfaction" or the penance that the confessor imposes, followed by absolution. Interestingly, the concrete performance of the given penance is not necessary for forgiveness, just the willingness to do so.[9]

The ordeal has greatly softened down through the ages from years of strict fasting in ancient times to a few muttered prayers today for the same offense. This laxity also is inevitable; for the wise rule is that the confessor must not impose any burden that the penitent will not accept.[10]

But though the sinner escapes Hell thereby, some punishment is still due for the absolved mortal sins, as well as all those unconfessed minor sins. After all, Jesus forgave the apostles for their betrayal of him. But they still all eventually paid with their own lives anyway, save for John the guiltless, the only one to attend him at Calvary.

This remaining need for purification is called "temporal" punishment, to be paid for in full in an afterlife jail called Purgatory. That is, unless the person now reconciled to God acquires "indulgences," credits that cancel such postmortem suffering through the performance of specially approved devotions. These can include monetary donations, which led to the greedy abuses that Martin Luther blasted.

Confession can cover offenses against the Church, too – in fact, these must be forgiven first, so that once the sinner is reconciled to the Church, he or she and can be then accepted by God.[11] These censures are inflicted on people for defiance of the Church. They consist chiefly of individual excommunication or suspension from church activities, although entire countries can be forbidden the sacraments, too.

Censures may be "reserved," that is, not just any priest can forgive them. Usually, only the prelate who imposed them or his superior can forgive reserved censures. Along with certain grave sins such as heresy in all its forms, such censures may be dealt with only by the pope or his authorized representative.[12] In the case of approaching death, however, the humane rule remains that any sin or censure can be forgiven by any priest, even one without proper credentials.[13]

With all these conditions, Confession is obviously not a simple ritual like the other sacraments. It is "iffy;" depending much more on intent, judgment, and circumstance. While it, too, can be reduced to a simple rote recital, since it remains in essence a trial on which depends one's eternal fate, most believers approach it with utter seriousness and dread.

Priests, too, are trained to treat it as a tribunal wherein they are the sole judges sitting in the place of Christ. Manuals school them in what kinds of questions to ask, how to search consciences without suggesting bad ideas to the sinner, and render a proper judgment.

Though reconciliation with God is ever the goal, the power given to the confessor over the soul of the one confessing is absolute. So the Church is emphatic about the so-called "seal of Confession," that nothing said there can be revealed under any circumstances, not even, it is claimed, to save the life of the pope.[14] Of course, in reality, things are not quite so clear-cut – heresy, for instance, is not really completely covered. But in any event, the potential for blackmail by a wicked priest always remains, and the intense, soul-baring intimacy of the encounter provides both temptation and opportunity for all kinds of mischief.

Abuse of the sacrament started just as soon as it became secretive. In 398, the first Council of Toledo forbad relations between virgins dedicated to God – the forerunners of nuns – and their confessors. Later, a forged decree ordered the confiscation of the guilty woman's possessions and confinement in a convent. The seducing priest was warned of deposition and penance lasting twelve years – but only if the crime had become known to the congregation. Scandal had already become more important than sin and so the secret system was born.[15]

The misuse of Confession to seek sex was technically called "*solicitatio ad turpiæ*" in Latin, "solicitation for filth." It did not become a major problem until the High Middle Ages, however. That happened when mandatory celibacy of the priests and equally compulsory yearly confession by the laity were both required. Once the Fourth Lateran Council ordered the latter in 1215 as part of every Catholic's duty, it provided a perfect combination of motive, means, and opportunity for lusty priests. The trouble was made worse because for centuries people were not allowed to choose confessors. They were required to utilize only the services of their parish priest. In fact, without his permission, no other priest was allowed to forgive the sinner.[16]

Canonists soon realized the inherent danger in this and said that parish priests known to be addicted to vice forfeited their jurisdiction over female penitents. Predatory confessors, of course, would neglect to mention this to their congregations. But the Church generally recognized that the responsibility lay exclusively with the priest.

Pope Calixtus II, for instance, compared the situation to a traveler being attacked by a bear. The woman was not to be treated as a partner in crime, "but as an unfortunate who finds destruction where she is seeking salvation" and the blame was to be placed solely on the priest. Nonetheless, while customs like cullagium and the sin tax flourished unchecked, rapacious confessors enjoyed almost virtual immunity.[17]

When at last confronted with the successful Protestant rebellion in the sixteenth century, Rome tried hard to clean up its act. But the Council of Trent merely fortified traditional positions on clerical celibacy, offering few new solutions beyond prescribing seminary training for all priests. Popes scrambled to find tools to enforce priestly discipline.

Malpractice and the confessional

The papacy eagerly seized upon an actual mechanical device: a literal shield to block the most brazen assaults on women by priests. It was the confessional booth, recently invented specifically for just that end. Mentioned first in 1547 in Spain, St. Charles Borromeo had one installed in the cathedral in Milan around 1565. Within a half-century, the *Roman Ritual* ordered their use in all churches around the globe. It was still being demanded as late as 1781. The command was reluctantly obeyed due to opposition of priests who objected to the isolation.[18]

Nor was the arrangement without certain drawbacks. Paradoxically, once fully developed, the booths permitted a brand new sin. Opportunities suddenly existed for laymen to impersonate priests in order to hear the confessions of women for any number of wicked reasons. Cases were not uncommon, but the Inquisition could get involved only if the layman pretended to give absolution.[19]

Before the confessional, the sacrament could be administered anywhere, although precautions for nuns were required since the ninth century. The encounters were usually held in private chambers with the door open or in a secluded corner of a church, often right before the altar, where whispers could not be overheard.

Either way, someone should still be able to observe the parties. Confessors were ordered not to hear women's admissions otherwise, or at night. They were even told to avert their gaze. Yet, with the penitent necessarily quite close by, seated beside him or even kneeling at his feet, temptation had many opportunities to play.[20]

Originally, the confessional was simply a wide seat with a solid partition in the middle to prevent any physical contact of confessors with penitents during the sacramental engagement. A kneeler at some point replaced the penitent's chair. The confessional soon evolved into a set of darkened soundproof booths linked by a closeable window backed by a grille and often gauze. Through this opening, the list of sinful deeds and desires would be whispered and the absolution delivered.[21] Anonymity as well as privacy and security were the intentions.

Lines of sinners could be quite long just before Easter, so many churches placed stalls on either side of the confessor's booth to speed the process. The silence of the eerie darkness within would be barely broken by the hushed murmur of the fellow reprobate opposite to the priest as one waited. It would be followed by a startling, sudden burst of light as the unseen judge opened the window. All these theatrical effects greatly enhanced the rite's mystery, as any pre-Vatican-II parochial school veteran could testify.

In the wake of the council, all this was temporarily undone. Though the fathers had not modified the sacramental theory at all, changes to the outer form happened just as they did to other liturgies, such as the Mass. Prayers were modernized and everything said in the everyday local language. For a while, penitent and confessor would often face each other directly in a private room. It was as if the confessional had never been invented.

But this reversion to the old ways did not last long. Soon, arrangements had to be made so that the encounter was safely visible again. Confession reverted to its previous setting much more rapidly once the scandals began, even though the booths had proved sadly insufficient to prevent clergy sexual abuse. In some ways, the confessional even facilitated it, by making verbal seduction easier. Many victims, even young children there for the first time, were set up by lies whispered in that sacred space.

Few churches had gotten rid of the booths but in any case, the sacrament is much less exercised these days. Every Lent, the Vatican bemoans the lack of penitents and reminds them of their duty. It also objects to the giving of general, group confessions where there is no recitation of individual sin.

Intended for situations such as soldiers going into combat, mass absolutions are still sometimes offered to get people to approach the sacrament at all. However, though the Vatican claims there has been resurgence in recent years, it seems that modern Catholics have generally decided that individual repentance is more important than absolution by a priest.[22]

Siege perilous

Perhaps the faithful unconsciously sense what a dangerous encounter the confessional can be. The Sacrament of Reconciliation is actually meant to be a rigorous examination of their very souls, a "first judgment" as it were, and a foretaste of the final one.

Since the priest as judge must know all the facts and circumstances if he is to render a proper verdict, penitents are taught that they must confess everything and answer all questions. The confessor is instructed to inquire carefully into details as necessary to determine the actual guilt involved.

However, he should not inquire into the identity of any accomplices, except in cases where in concealment "there would rise grave evil which the penitent is bound to prevent." This would include cases where the confessor himself is a religious superior, in order to punish wrongdoers. But it is best if such information is passed outside Confession so the seal of secrecy does not cover the information.[23]

Concealment of accomplices, however, is not done out of any consideration for the embarrassed sinner. If necessary, confessors are empowered to demand names under the threat of withholding forgiveness. But although any such information involving say, robbery, could be used for evil purposes, knowledge of sexual weakness and compromises was particularly dangerous. As late as 1849, Pope Pius IX decreed excommunication for anyone who taught that it was lawful to actually refuse absolution in such cases. Even so, since dire circumstances are conceivable where such threats may be necessary in this post-9/11 world, the temptation also still exists.[24]

Ironically, the complete privacy of the confessional made verbal attacks on chastity that much easier. Old technical manuals for priests are full of warnings about not giving out sexual information in the process that could lead an innocent into sin, but this was a very persistent problem. In the late 1800s, a former priest, and client and friend of Lincoln, Charles Chiniquy, wrote an incensed exposé of innocent maidens shocked, sinfully informed and even aroused, and not infrequently seduced by the probing inquiries of confessors into their sex lives.

He bitterly complained from personal experience of the effect on the confessor:

> *Those unmarried men are forced, from morning to night, to be in the midst of beautiful girls, and tempting, charming women, who have to tell them things which would melt the hardest steel. How can you expect that they will cease to be men, and become stronger than angels?*

> *Not only are the priests of Rome deprived… of* [matrimony,] *the only remedy that God has given them to withstand* [temptation]*, but in the confessional they have the greatest facility which can possibly be imagined for satisfying all the bad propensities of fallen human nature.*[25]

Another customary, virtually inevitable element in any seduction by a priest would be the subsequent forgiveness of his companion. The mere promise to do so could powerfully increase the temptation. By magically removing all burdens of guilt afterwards, he also made it much less likely that she would feel moved by her conscience to denounce him. For according to theology, absolution utterly destroyed the sin that it no longer counted either in this world or the next. It never need be admitted or mentioned again. And although canonists often denounced the frequent practice of priests forgiving their partners, such absolutions were still acknowledged to be valid.

Some theologians even argued that the seductive confessor should grant absolution, not only to soothe his paramour's scruples, but also to avert her defamation.[26] For as always, the shame of the victim was the most effective means of enforcing silence.

Whether a seductive priest's scheme was successful or not, the woman would often be deterred by the infamy that would fall on her if she dared complain. There were rarely any witnesses: it would typically be her word against his and the weight of society was against her. She might also be made to believe that the seal of the confessional covered it though it actually did not, and thus to speak out would incur a mortal sin.[27]

Yet as convenient as all this could be for a lusty confessor, it was also risky. Any abuse of a sacrament touches on heresy. Anything to do with heresy inevitably aroused the Inquisition.

CHAPTER V:
THE EDICT OF FAITH

The prototype of terror

The full power and dread of the Inquisition must be understood to really appreciate how effective it was suppressing scandals of all kinds. Its success prompted much imitation. Repressive regimes of every flavor imposed on suffering humanity ever since the Middle Ages owe considerable inspiration to the Holy Office.

Most recently, its awful legacy has been shown in the haunting pictures of Abu Ghraib and Guantanamo. Even today, the word itself still conjures up a horrible ruthlessness. As the editor of a museum catalog of torture instruments wrote: "*The* Inquisition is no longer; but Inquisition is, and will be forever."[1]

The Inquisition literally wrote the book on torture, psychological assaults, and dehumanizing humiliation. It perfected the use of midnight arrests, secret proceedings, anonymous accusations, indefinite detentions, spies and informers, and the confiscation of property. It was not, however, a single, monolithic entity. Inquisitions appeared in different forms in various times and places. But wherever and whenever its dark shadow fell, the name rightfully struck dread into all.

In its several incarnations, the Inquisition terrorized large sections of Christendom for a score of generations. Kings and bishops fell equally under its scrutiny with errant knights and wandering preachers. Mighty lords, even powerful religious orders answerable only to the pope like the Knights Templar, could be summoned at any time and crushed mercilessly for suspicions of which they would not be told. Nor could they resist in any way. The abuses of such awful power became the basis of the "black legend."

Perhaps this was inevitable in a religion that placed such emphasis on the horrific torture and execution suffered by its founder. Untold numbers also suffered and died as martyrs by means only limited by the imaginations of their tormentors. Many missionaries had died horribly while converting the invading barbarians later as well.

Was the Inquisition, then, some sort of revenge for the ages of persecution? Or had the crucifix everywhere displaying the agony of Christ led to some perverse need to re-enact it repeatedly?

Regardless of psychological underpinnings, inquisitions served as the most ruthless watchdog of the faith. The infamous Inquisition of Spain was primarily a tool of their Most Catholic Majesties, though the neighboring Portuguese version had an even worse reputation. Yet, it was the earlier medieval and the papal varieties in particular that demonstrated the most extreme achievements of clerical power.

Only one branch of the Inquisition survives today, but in some ways it is more powerful than all previous ones. As previously mentioned, the Roman Inquisition, renamed several times, survives as the Sacred Congregation for the Doctrine of the Faith (or CFD). It remains the most influential department in the Vatican, currently presided over by Archbishop William Levada, who handled the scandals in San Francisco. He succeeded then-Cardinal Joseph Ratzinger after he became pope. Though lacking its former brutal means of enforcement, its supreme power now rests on jurisdiction over the entire Church. Only the pope himself has more influence.

That such an institution, which depended on terror and violence, was needed to prop up a religion of love and peace is deeply incongruous. But it took a long time to come about, and the root cause was, paradoxically, the very success of the Church.

Corruption began first in Dark Age monasteries. They got rich from saying prayers for the nobles, who surely needed them in their constant wars and bloody intrigues. Paradoxically, monastic standards of piety and ascetic purity inevitably declined with the cash influx that such self-denial attracted, leading to repeating cycles of reform and relapse. Many would-be reformers sought to transcend this, appealing over the intermediacy of the Church directly to the Gospel and its emphasis on the poor. Some even organized their enthusiastic followers into orders.

A fortunate few, like Francis of Assisi and his contemporary Dominic, won the blessings of the Church. These founders of what would become the greatest mendicant, or begging, orders managed to impress the most powerful pope of the age, Innocent III, who approved them. While some of Francis' followers went on to become heretics themselves in their radical embrace of poverty, others were co-opted to serve as persecutors. The Dominicans, however, started as preachers against heresy and so naturally fell into the inquisitor's role.

Some would-be reformers, like Peter Waldo of Lyons, were less lucky or perhaps more opinionated, having read the Bible for themselves, and were accordingly condemned. Meanwhile, old Gnostic heresies like Manicheanism resurfaced in new forms as Catharism and the Albigensians.

These were even more world denying than medieval Catholicism, which was no mean feat. They saw the Church as ignorant servants of a false creator god. The worldly Catholic clergy contrasted poorly with the extreme asceticism of their consecrated holy men, the so-called *perfecti*. Theologically and morally, the Cathars became the greatest competitors Catholicism would ever face in the ages before Luther.

Fighting faith with fire

The medieval Inquisition was formally created on April 20, 1233, at the behest of Pope Gregory IX. That day he issued two papal bulls that created the groundwork for international strike teams of trusted clerics to sniff out, expose, and eliminate heresy. These doctrinal police would be able to go anywhere, knock on any door, and get answers. It was the culmination of a long and ever more violent process of confronting heresy.

Under his predecessor, the commanding Pope Innocent III, the papacy had recently attained dominance of sorts over the German emperors and other secular powers. These had often, in the pope's view, flirted with heresy by doing completely unacceptable things like choosing their own bishops.

Meanwhile, many lords had dangerously tolerated or even promoted actual heresies. Once freed to deal more directly, Innocent had responded by calling a great council in 1215, the Fourth Lateran. Its purpose: to declare a holy war against the south of France.

Throughout history, the fight with heresy molded the doctrines of the Church, starting soon after Jesus left the scene. For his attempt to buy the power of invoking the Holy Spirit from Peter, Simon Magus had the dubious honor of being named the "father of heresy." The sin of "simony" became the overall term for monetarily trafficking in blessings, sacraments – and church offices, too.

Simony was the cardinal sin of the Middle Ages, more of a problem than heresy, in fact, because it inspired heresy. It was the unavoidable result of divine grace being treated as a commodity. Prayer became monetized and marketable by the monasteries. Indulgences were bought and sold like afterlife insurance investments. Greed lit up the most fateful failure of the Church to live up to its basic ideals. In response, medieval heresy – up to and including Luther – derived almost as much of its appeal as a protest against such gross commercialization of religion as against clerical sexual immorality.

"Heresy" came from the Greek word for choice, or taking. Heretics willfully chose a viewpoint at odds in some fashion with the majority view of the Church. Defining who was a heretic and who was "orthodox" or "right worshipping" involved appeals to Scripture and tradition, and of course, politics. But it was far more than just an intellectual disagreement.

By the Middle Ages, heresy had become a real matter of life or death, for such dissent simply could not be allowed. It denied the cosmic order, which was none too stable to begin with. Though Church and State propped each other up, the marriage was shaky. However, because of their intertwining to survive from the late Roman period on, being at odds with one was to deny the other also. And whoever resisted the power of the Church resisted God.

Ultimately, the pope claimed *"plenitudo potestas,"* that is, "plenitude of power" – that he was the supreme embodiment and source of all ruling authority on earth. Once Pope Boniface VIII declared in 1302 that it was "necessary for salvation that every human creature be subjected to the Roman pontiff," disobedience of any papal command became heresy. Inquisitors thus had the power and duty to declare holy war against heretics in his name and reward hunters with the same indulgences due crusaders who fought the infidel.[2]

Heresy, a sin, thereafter was also a crime of political treason, and treason, heresy. Yet, even so, the Church still realized the role the poor example of priests played in inspiring such a betrayal. Pope Innocent III's opening address at the great Lateran Council had even admitted that corruption of the people derived from that of the clergy. Even so, the schoolmen declared there was no excuse for such a grave offense. Aquinas calmly wrote that heresy was a sin that merited not only excommunication but also death.[3]

Most alarming to the hierarchy was the growth of Catharism in the very heartland of Christian Europe, like a knife pointed at the papacy. The Christian leadership saw the movement as an organized assault from without, blaming wandering minstrels and returning crusaders. They may indeed have a hand in spreading it along with the Bogomils, Gnostic Manichean missionaries from Bulgaria.[4]

The Cathars were particularly successful in southern France and northern Italy, where many crusaders had come from. There, in the elegant courts of Provence, the troubadours invented fanciful tales of chivalry, the Holy Grail, and the very concept of romantic love. These gentle pursuits were powerless to save the sophisticated courtiers from the brutal wrath of Rome.

Engaged in a struggle for the soul of Europe, the Church first sent in trusted teams of mendicant preachers. When one was murdered, Innocent launched his most awful weapon to cauterize the infection. He called down a crusade against a region of Christendom itself.

The Council decreed that any lord who neglected to "cleanse his territory of this heretical filth" would be excommunicated. If he did not do so within a year, the pope would "declare his vassals absolved from their fealty to him and make the land available for occupation by Catholics so that these may, after they have expelled the heretics, possess it unopposed."[5] Anxious princes and peasants rushed to take the cross to prove their orthodoxy. The salvation promised to warriors for Christ would be theirs. Simple greed was also a potent factor.

A coalition of avaricious lords from the north of France led the long and vicious Albigensian Crusade. Having a persistent problem of distinguishing true Catholics from heretics, they quickly resorted to wholesale slaughter. Provence and southern France have never completely recovered.

Machinery of fear

In the aftermath, the problem of actually identifying heretics remained for the investigators of the new tribunals. Heresy was a thought-crime, but unless it was actually taught, detection was difficult for it typically masqueraded as holiness. Many heretics also felt it was perfectly acceptable to lie as necessary to blend in. They had no problem taking the sacraments or making outward shows of orthodox faith, even taking oaths.

Often heretics had been coached in how to seemingly agree with the authorities without actually betraying their consciences or their true beliefs. They would need it to withstand questioning by intellectuals trained in all the subtleties of scholastic debate in the universities. Bernard of Gui, a leading persecutor in Toulouse, even gave a sample dialog in his manual to show how to handle heretics who twisted meanings to seemingly agree with their interrogator.

Heretics craftily spoke in code. Such deceivers had to be forced to expose themselves and their fellow conspirators. So the inquisitors did not hesitate to use deceit themselves, along with torture, secret accusations, and spies both inside and outside of prison.[6]

Once an area was targeted, a "crisis control team" of inquisitors would be sent in. Armed with guards, authorized by pope and prince, they would always travel in pairs. This allowed them to watch over and absolve each other of any blood spilling or other unpleasantness required in their work. This was necessary as the ancient traditions of the Church forbade clerics from performing or even witnessing torture. So Pope Alexander IV graciously allowed inquisitors powers of mutual forgiveness and dispensation in 1256. But secular authorities were always required to provide men for the actual dirty work with pulleys, racks, water-boards, irons, and stakes.[7]

Inquisitors were given immense powers. They could go after virtually anyone, absolve anyone of any sin, and sell the goods they confiscated. They got full indulgences for their pains, too, so they not only enriched themselves in this life but also were assured of a well-earned paradise in the next.

The Inquisition became quite sophisticated in its theatrical displays of power and terror. The inquisitors would ominously parade into a town in their simple habits accompanied by the local lord's men, a chief minion called a "familiar" and his stooges, along with a secretary provided by the bishop to officially record the proceedings.

The entire town would be edgy already due the vigorous preaching of the local clergy, who would be there along with all the faithful under pain of excommunication. There the inquisition would be declared in a "general sermon" in front of the chief church or cathedral. This detailed the crimes, procedures, and penalties. All sinners were invited to come forward and confess. They were given a period of grace in which to secretly do so in order to be granted clemency.

In Spain especially, this official declaration, the "Edict of Faith," would be proclaimed with great ceremony. The clergy processed into church with a black-covered cross. Offenses were announced and a solemn curse leveled on their perpetrators. The Roman Inquisition later adopted similar practices.[8] But, once the tribunal had become thoroughly incorporated into the life of the Church, a papal decree simply outlining the crimes that must be reported would be read in all churches on Holy Thursday instead.

Any guilty parties who had seen an inquisition in action might well be tempted to use the period of grace to either confess or flee. For it was not just a capital crime to be an outright heretic, or to give them aid and comfort, it was also illegal to be in any way favorable or even merely impressed by their seeming sanctity. "Listeners," "receivers," and "defenders" were quite as suspect as hardcore sect members. And any hesitation, resistance, or questioning of the Inquisition might be seen as evidence of a dangerously bad attitude requiring further investigation.

To be forgiven, suspects were required to inform on others in the community. So was everyone else, especially the clergy, who were under even more suspicion to the point that they were forbidden to forgive a sinner of heresy in Confession. Heresy was reserved exclusively to the pope's men to deal with and nobody else could interfere.

Confessors were instructed to interrogate their penitents about it, however, write down what they had learned and try to persuade the sinner to reveal all to the authorities. But if the sinner balked, the priests were to refuse absolution and take themselves to "experts" for consultation – without mentioning names. However, many theologians held that if the penitent did not abandon his errors or reveal his associates, there could be no "seal of Confession." Confessors could thus reveal all to the inquisitors. Faith need not be kept with the faithless.[9]

A panel of judges would be set up, including local experts or representatives of the religious establishment along with the inquisitors. They would quickly begin debriefing the clergy and penitents in secret. Procedures were based on those of episcopal courts and ultimately Roman law. Bishops, whose own corruption and failure to combat heresy effectively had led to the Inquisition, still had a role. They could be present during questioning and torture, and were expected to build the prisons as well as provide the notary.

The inquisitorial process

Unfortunates fingered by their neighbors would be hauled off in the middle of the night by the familiar and his crew. The very fact that the accused had not already confessed was itself suspicious. But the wretches would never be told of what they were accused them or who did so. Instead, they would be asked if they knew why they had been arrested. Even then, Catholic guilt was expected to work wonders.

Suspects had few chances of escaping unharmed. Claiming innocence was not usually one of them. Their best hope was to quickly and accurately name their unknown accuser as a personal enemy. Such accusations would be thrown out as tainted, one of the rare safeguards in the system. Otherwise, if the accused confessed to the right thing, a minor first offense, and cooperated fully by naming others, he or she might obtain leniency. In fact, the Inquisition occasionally treated select reformed heretics conspicuously well to attract others to come in.

But just being accused was often enough to ruin a person even if found innocent. The accused person's goods were seized and auctioned to pay for his own imprisonment and trial. If guilty, fines might also be levied. For the Inquisition pretty much paid for itself, as well as enjoying many favors, gifts, and privileges, though of course, the mendicant friars, sworn to poverty, were supposed to be above bribery.

Under "vehement suspicion" of heresy, victims could be held indefinitely at the whim of the inquisitor, even decades. They could be let out at any time and reeled in again later for the same offense. There were no limits on the number of times they could be arrested. Indeed, most of legal protections for citizens that Americans enjoyed before 9/11 were born out of a reaction against the methods of the inquisitors.

Options for torture were as fertile as the inquisitors' fevered imaginations. They generally used water-boarding, the application of fire, stretching by the rack or pulleys, breaking on the wheel or crushing the feet.[10] Questioning would be methodical but devious, and woe to any unfortunate soul whose answers did not completely satisfy the interrogator.

Showing the instruments to the prisoner was the first stage of torture. The second stage was stripping and binding the victim. All the while, he or she would be entreated to confess and promised mercy. Only then, in the "third degree," would they be actually applied.

Torture would proceed with increasing severity until the inquisitor was contented or the accused perished, though care was taken to prevent the latter. If the questioner detected any evasion or duplicity, however, he was required to be merciless for the sake of his victim's soul. Torment was supposedly limited to one occasion, but inquisitors got around this by scheduling continuances, repeated as often as desired.[11]

Worst that could befall anyone was to relapse into error again after being once forgiven. Deemed irredeemably corrupt, there could be no mercy for them and were usually sent to the stake no matter what they pleaded. The most they could hope for by any further recantation would be the mercy of strangulation before burning.

However, only a small number of victims were actually burnt at the stake. Many lesser punishments involved imprisonment or fasting for years, publicly wearing placards or symbols such as huge wooden dice for gamblers. Other innovations had effects that were more lasting.

For instance, penitential garments of shame, called in Spain *sanbenitos*, were tabards with yellow crosses front and back. They were worn both in prison and in public over their street clothes. In Spanish churches – though never in Italian ones – the tabards would be displayed along with the names of their wearers after their sentences were completed. However, such shameful exhibits were often vandalized by the disgraced families of the condemned.[12] These tunics were distant ancestors of the infamous yellow star of David that Jews would be forced to wear in the ghettos and Nazi death camps.

Punishments public and private

Trials were held in secret. But a closing spectacle even grander than the introductory general sermon would mark the inquisition's grim climax. The Church refused blame for the death penalty any more than the stain of torture; instead, it "relaxed" the victims into the tender mercies of the secular authorities who would then conduct the actual immolation.

But that the Catholic Church was entirely responsible, there can be no doubt. Indulgences were granted those who attended a burning. And an extraordinary indulgence was offered to those who actually contributed wood for the pyres. Priests, oddly enough, had to apply for a special dispensation in order to earn one.[13]

The papal and Spanish *"auto da fé"* or "Act of Faith" became an important festive social occasion to demonstrate the full might of Catholic power, though it also gave the condemned a chance to show their mettle. Pomp and ceremony emphasized the sublime importance of the event. Long lines of gorgeously arrayed clergy with flying banners, streaming incense, and chanting choirs, led the condemned chained in tumbrels through the excited crowds to the waiting bonfires piled high with tinder.

The worst heretics, used as a salutary lesson to others, were not strangled before burning. Giordano Bruno, noted for his outrageous belief in heliocentric theory and life on other worlds, for instance, was burned alive for his crimes in 1600 in a whistling iron mask that also pierced his tongue and palette so he couldn't scream.[14] Afterwards, the smoldering ashes of such infamous heretics would be dumped in the nearest river to keep any remaining bones from becoming relics to sympathizers.

Only clerics condemned for major heresies were usually exposed. They might even be publicly degraded in an impressive ceremony. First they would be stripped of their vestments and shaved to erase their tonsure before the crowd, even having their hands symbolically scraped clean of the holy chrism of their ordination. Dressed in the black *sanbenitos* and mock miters of the condemned, they would then be ritually burnt with the rest.[15]

Houses of heretics were routinely destroyed, their families impoverished and ashamed. Suspects were denied the sacraments and the right to a Christian burial. Years after their death, their bones could be dug up and burnt. Even would-be saints were not immune. Armanno Pongilupo, for instance, was an Italian Cathar who was caught, recanted, led a pious life thereafter, and died safely in the arms of the Church. Assured thereby of his orthodoxy, he was hailed as a Catholic saint soon after. Before long, Pongilupo was given a grand altar over his tomb and said to have caused many miracles.

This greatly displeased the local inquisitors. They fought it for nearly half a century through five inquests. Finally, Pope Boniface appointed a commission that in 1301 decided the blessed Armanno had indeed been a secret Cathar all along. His body was dug up, relics burned, the altar thrown down, and the inquisitor became the new bishop.[16]

The politics of sorcery

As in this case, the Inquisition was all too often shown as political and greedy. Several other episodes that profoundly shocked all Christendom would soon illustrate just how brutally effective the Inquisition could be when used for political ends.

Boniface's declaration of papal supremacy was the most extreme claim to ecclesiastical power ever uttered from the throne of Peter. Though inquisitors took it seriously, the French king defied it. Philip IV, already arguing with the pope over taxes, embarked on a lengthy personal vendetta. His men even attacked the papal residence and briefly captured the pontiff. Boniface survived the ordeal only to soon die from sheer mortification.

Philip then arranged the election of a compliant Frenchman. The papacy was soon moved from Rome to the French city of Avignon. In this period, often called the "Babylonian captivity" of the Church, and the Great Schism that followed, corruption grew enormously as popes scrambled for money – especially after a botched attempt to return to Italy led ultimately to two feuding rivals before a council finally brought the Church back together.

Philip smeared the late Boniface with accusations of heresy, magic, and homosexuality. His official enquiry included charges that Boniface enjoyed familiar relations with demons, constantly calling them to his aid and worshipping them. Others, including Walter Langton, bishop of Coventry and Lichfield, faced similar charges also possibly for political reasons several years before.[17] In 1308, Guichard, Bishop of Troyes, was charged with attempted black magic against the royal family after losing the favor of the queen. He was quietly released and given the title to a new bishopric five years later.[18]

Once he had installed his man as pope, Philip turned his attention to another powerful party to whom he also owed money – the Knights Templar. Their downfall was orchestrated with a coordinated nationwide bust on Friday, October 13, 1304, which is actually why Friday the thirteenth is still considered unlucky by the superstitious.

The inquisitors used their most savage techniques to get the answers the king wanted. Many knights, including their leaders, confessed under torture. Later the Grand Master, Jacques de Molay, and other senior members recanted their confessions and were therefore roasted alive.

Among charges of heresy, blasphemy, and idolatry were also those of sexual depravity. Though dismissed like most similar tales told of the Cathars and other sects, there may be some truth to these rumors of illicit sex. The Templars were armed monks: both a monastic order and an army. Male homosexuality may occur in either kind of group. Even their famous seal showing two knights riding a single horse could be seen suggestively.

The sexual charges fell into two groups. The Knights were accused of "illicit kissing" on the base of the spine, the navel and three times on the mouth during receptions of new members. Others claimed to have been solicited for sex, threatened or beaten if they refused to participate in sodomy, and told "a brother should not deny himself to a brother."[19]

True or not, there was little doubt, even at the time, that greed and jealousy primarily led to Philip's crushing the order, though their treasures escaped. The persecution of the Templars was unique in it was ordered by the state, not the Inquisition itself. And though the property would ultimately go largely to their rivals, the Hospitallers, the French crown got it first.

The greed of those who profited from the pyres, especially in Spain, gradually extended the reach of the Holy Office. Inquisition was tried for social improvement. The experiments gave mixed results in terms of punishing adultery, bigamy, gambling, or intoxication. When it finally turned its attention to witchcraft, however, the Inquisition found new sources of helpless victims and revenues beyond its wildest dreams.

Astrology and "natural magic," depending on inherent mystic properties of objects, were theologically somewhat dubious but had long been tolerated. Invocation of spirits of any kind, even angels, was always forbidden. But at first, all magic was thought to be a superstitious delusion. The enlightened doctors of the schools had believed that witches' sabbats and powers were entirely illusory. In 1257, the pope even instructed inquisitors not to be diverted by diviners and sorcerers unless heresy was obviously involved.[20]

By the time the Templars were thrown down half a century later, the situation had changed so that even the highest officials, secular or ecclesiastic, could be accused of sorcery. Another century and a half later, some theologians decided that any resort to magic whatsoever necessarily involved worshipping the Devil, thus blasphemy. All supposed practitioners of the occult, no matter how seemingly benign, thereby became fair game.

In 1484, this new theory was formally laid out in the infamous inquisitor's manual, *Malleus Maleficarum*. The sinister *"Hammer of the Witches"* opens with the ominous assertion that "the belief that there are such beings as witches is so essential a part of the Catholic faith that obstinately to maintain the opposite opinion manifestly savours of heresy."[21]

Once the dreadful power of witchcraft was accepted as real, its dangers to Christians then had to be opposed at any cost. Confessions under torture soon naturally confirmed the inquisitor's worst imaginings. The resulting "witchcraft craze" was a classic case of creating one's own enemy. Possibly a million or more innocents, mainly women, suffered and died as a result.

In a strange twist, however, there were few outbreaks of panic in Spain or its dominions. Surprisingly, the inquisitors, who seemed unable to decide definitively whether these fantastic stories were delusional or diabolical, reined in the craze. Anything smacking of divination remained completely outlawed: a lay brother got into trouble just for calculating the positions of the planets as late as 1796. But though they kept their doubts about witchcraft, sorcery in Spain was actively prosecuted long after the rest of enlightened Europe had stopped such trials.[24]

A lasting curse

Though the medieval Inquisition helped wipe out the remaining Cathars, it was a hollow victory in many respects. Other heretics, such as the Waldensians, fled to the mountains and survived. Centuries later, neither war, council, nor Inquisition could suppress the Hussites of Bohemia either, despite the betrayal and burning of their leaders. Both groups would make common cause with the Protestants in due course.

Martin Luther's success entirely depended on his successful avoidance of the Holy Office. Shortly after his open defiance of both cardinal and emperor on April 18, 1521 at the Diet of Worms, his noble patron snatched him away, saving his life and the movement.

This unexpected princely protection kept him out the clutches of the Inquisition and free to write. Luther was then able to continue mobilizing public support through a new instrument of communication that Rome could not control, the printing press. In short order, the Protestant Reformation was on. And so the renegade monk spearheaded the long-dreaded heretical rebellion that the Catholic Church had set up the Inquisition specifically to prevent.

Ironically, that same invention had not long before spread the *Hammer of the Witches* all across Europe. In the mad times to follow, the Protestants would do their own share of witch burning inspired by its directions.

The medieval Inquisition never officially ended. It slowly withered over time due to the lack of victims, though it was considerably refreshed by the witchcraft craze. The revived papal and Spanish forms were more settled, bureaucratic versions, with headquarters, prisons, agents, and areas of jurisdiction. Permanent tribunals were established in many cities – the one in Venice, for instance, was famous for capturing Bruno and Casanova, too, although the latter managed to escape.

The inquisitors of Italy were noted as dedicated thought police. They sought to quarantine the Lutheran infection by closely monitoring booksellers and printers, even examining travelers' books as theological customs agents. The Spanish Inquisition, however, rarely ran into Protestants, foreign or domestic. It was much more preoccupied with subversion from supposedly converted Muslims and Jews.

The ultimate failure of the Inquisition to eliminate heresy also showed the fatal weakness hidden at its very heart. For the entire edifice of the Church depends on just how much the faithful are willing to bear. The pope's real power depends not so much on God nearly as much as it relies on the consent of the laity to tolerate the demands laid on them by the clergy.

But in all its incarnations, the Holy Office left a very dark and bitter legacy. It twisted the Catholic Church into an intellectual dictatorship, a religious police state where the appearance of conformity was all-important. And the price has been steep.

With such enforced intellectual rigidity comes a stifling of creativity in all fields. Freedom of thought and expression is lost. Everything from theology to art is falsified by the supreme imperative to conform. Secrecy rules.

Galileo, for example, learned well the lessons left by Bruno. He wisely denied the evidence of his senses and thus escaped the stake – but certain sciences have languished in Italy ever since.

Even worse, the universal terror that was the Inquisition forced everything officially unacceptable into the fetid underground Hell it had created. Both sexual affairs of priests as well as outlawed theology fell into this unholy stew, free to mingle and mutate. Its bloody violence radicalized its victims, too. Like the Templars themselves, some heretics may have willfully incorporated torture and degradation into their own secret cult practices to order to learn to endure capture.

So it is, that the Inquisition is therefore probably more directly responsible for secret rings of criminal clerical perpetrators and black magicians, in and out of the Church, than any other single factor.

If anything could strangle the Spirit, the Inquisition could and did. The tribunals fed papal arrogance with pretensions of power that led directly to the Reformation. And after the schism, the Roman Inquisition made sure that there would never be any reunification save on its own terms of unconditional surrender – then, now, or in the future.

Without question, the Inquisition permanently blackened the reputation of the Roman Catholic Church. Yet, though relieved of their bloodiest tools, the doctrinal police remain quite powerful and vigilant today. And they are as apparently involved in suppressing clergy sex scandals these days as once they were before.

Chapter VI:
Harsh Measures

Seduction as heresy

The foregoing chapter illustrated what terrible punishments a priest who dabbled in illicit ideas might face. Those who dallied with love in post-Reformation times shared much the same risk, at least theoretically.

Originally, of course, mere animal lust was the last thing the terrible Inquisition would be interested in. But perversion of the sacraments by false teaching had always been fair game. However, only in the wake of the Reformation was jurisdiction over all sex crimes by religious officially transferred to the inquisitors. It happened first in golden age Spain.

Up until then, episcopal courts took responsibility for the crimes of priests. Though they became harsher after the Reformation also, some seemed mainly concerned with making money. In Toledo, for instance, Alonso de Valdelamar was charged in 1535 with a list of crimes ranging from theft and blasphemy to cheating on indulgences, charging for confessions, frequenting public brothels, as well as solicitation. The court had evidence that he had refused absolution to a girl unless she had sex with him, that he had seduced a married penitent, and one lady testified he had repeatedly assaulted her within church. For all that, he was given a month's penance, fines amounting to eleven ducats and four reales plus costs, and sent on his merry way.[1]

So, the Spanish Inquisition seemed a handy instrument to try against this burgeoning problem. It was a powerful, well-organized, and effective heresy-hunting machine run by a monarchy ever seeking to increase its power and influence. In February 1559, even as the Council of Trent droned on, reforming Pope Paul IV, a driving force for inquisition everywhere, authorized the inquisitors of Spain to start prosecutions of clergy sexual solicitation in the province of Granada.[2]

Apparently satisfied with the results, his successor, Pius IV, broadened its warrant two years later over all Spanish dominions. His bull of April 14, 1561, empowered the inquisitors investigate all confessors who solicited women. They were to inflict punishment even to the extent of degrading them from the clergy and relaxing them to the royal authorities for burning. This included all priests, even those in monastic orders.

The edict was read in churches on a feast day before the entire population. All who knew of such crimes, directly or otherwise, were required to denounce them to the Inquisition under pain of excommunication. Naturally, it must have caused a huge sensation.[3]

One apocryphal story, not taken seriously by all historians, recalls the shock. Supposedly when the Edict of Faith including solicitation was first read in Seville in 1562, not even forty inquisitors and secretaries were able to record all the denunciations given within the thirty days allowed. Four extensions were supposedly necessary to take them all in.[4]

Meanwhile, the long moribund Inquisition in Rome was also revived and given jurisdiction over clerical depravity in the Papal States. Put under the command of six cardinals, its sway ultimately extended across all Catholic Christendom. Their minions could go anywhere and arrest even high churchmen, and could call on secular powers for help. Following popes also quietly expanded the range of sex crimes covered. More cardinal inquisitors were put on staff to cope with the increased workload. Finally in 1588, the Roman Inquisition was made the most powerful department in the Vatican by Sixtus V, as it remains even today.[5]

On August 30, 1622, Pope Gregory XV issued a bull confirming all previous acts and extended them across the universal Church. He also enlarged the definition of solicitation to counter various legal evasions that had been thrown up. Bishops in regions where neither inquisition was active were empowered to act as special judges over all members of the clergy, including all exempt religious orders. They were given the same powers as inquisitors to inflict even the most extreme punishments.[6]

Penalties were varied and impressive. Suspension from their posts, deprivation of church income and dignities, and for members of orders, loss of voting and speaking rights were the start. Priests caught having sex also faced the possibility of exile, enslavement in the galleys, life imprisonment without parole, and in the worst cases, expulsion from the priesthood and "relaxation" – burning.[7]

Though leniency steadily increased through time, the supreme punishment, however, had never been imposed in any sex case, even the most notorious, as Pope Benedict XIV himself admitted. Even sentencing to the galleys was actually extremely rare.

Spain was less severe in these cases than Rome. The actual penalties seem to be chiefly deprivation of the right to hear confessions if one laywoman had been solicited one time. If there was more than a single occasion, suspension of priestly functions and being sent to a monastery or to serve in a hospital was warranted. Only if the woman was a nun, the wife of an important man, there was a big scandal or many victims involved, would degradation or the galleys suffice.[8]

In Spain, also, torture could only be used if serious heresy was suspected. In Rome, suspicion was automatic. There, the testimony of one woman of good character was enough, if supported by evidence; two, if not.[9]

In both later versions, the Inquisition kept its own terrible processes, jails, a passion for all-enveloping secrecy, and a hard-bitten reputation for ruthlessness. The mere evocation of its despised name was enough to resolve many difficulties. And it had a rationale ready for intervening in clergy sex cases at will.

If a priest, for example, seduced a woman by saying that sex with him was no sin or if he absolved her afterwards, as was typical, such blasphemies automatically made him liable for the Inquisition's remedies. Just seducing her during Confession, in fact, indicated a most improper attitude towards the sacrament.

Clergy were the sole targets – surprisingly, victims were not even to be questioned as to their consent. If volunteered, the Roman Inquisition immediately struck such testimony from the record, though the Spanish considered it fair game.[10]

The ability of some priests to move around – especially those in religious orders who maintained far-flung networks of houses – caused great problems in tracing perpetrators. Then as now, bishops could often reassign a rapacious priest or otherwise squelch scandals before his activities became notorious. Then as now also, denunciations might not come in for years, even decades, after the incidents, complicating matters greatly.

At one point in Spain, where two separate denunciations were required, a special registry of all accused solicitors was attempted. It must have proved too difficult to keep current as the idea was soon abandoned. Instead, letters would be sent round secretly to all the other tribunals concerned once a denunciation was made asking if they had any information.[11]

However, a woman who denounced her confessor would never be told of his other victims, or even what happened to her own complaint. And as offenders were usually punished in secret, not even those whose speaking up had been responsible usually ever had any idea that they had not been simply ignored. No wonder modern Catholics, when told by their bishops that the problem would be taken care of, had to accept it on faith alone.

Letter of the law

There were certain ways out for accused priests. Legal technicalities were important. The inquisitors cared little for the morality involved but greatly about the sacramental details. Records show that the decisive factor was precisely where the incriminating acts occurred. If they took place outside the rigid confines of the sacred act, it lay outside their jurisdiction.

In 1577, the Supreme Council of the Spanish Inquisition ruled that if solicitation did not occur during Confession itself, it could not be prosecuted. At the time, most confessions were still performed in deserted corners of churches. Thus, bold assignations with "incredible indecencies" could be and often were held that only gave an outward appearance of the sacrament. This ruling seriously weakened the legislation.[12]

Other questions, such as that of priests acting as pimps in the confessional, or using it to urge one woman to help procure others, also divided opinions. Probabilism and casuistry were quickly evolving as Jesuitical systems of justifying just about anything, including how to evade the rigors of moral law. Clever moralists and advocates pointed out that if the confessor made his advances before or after the actual sacrament, it was not technically heretical, even if still sinful.

Furthermore, the general rule was that anything that a priest does should be interpreted as favorably as possible. Embraces were held to be blessings unless proven otherwise, for example. The more rigid theologians opposed such interpretations, but many held that unless the acts were mortal sins themselves, they did not fall under the papal ban.[13]

Such legalistic evasions were countered by extending solicitation to include all sexual propositions by the priest or even indecent talk, for himself or anyone else, before or afterwards, if it was done in a place confessions were heard. But the Spanish Inquisition would have nothing to do with the bull for fear that it would give their power back to the bishops. So Spain was given an exemption. Nor was it accepted in France or Germany.[14]

In fact, Gregory's attempt to block all the loopholes, including indecent talk, merely opened the definitions up to debate. Theologians and canonists, for instance, argued for thirty years whether handing love-letters to a penitent in a confessional came under the ban. In 1661, the Roman Inquisition decided that giving praise or presents to a penitent threw everything into doubt. It all then depended solely on the confessor's intention. Some reasoned that expressions of love, arranging meetings, or even giving advice to the woman to murder her husband might be innocent of lust. Thus, it wasn't solicitation and did not justify denunciation thereby.

The decisive opinion as ultimately expressed by St. Alphonsus Liguori was that the sacrament itself was the key thing. Unless it could be proven to have been used a direct instrument of seduction, the sin was not heretical. This in effect lifted solicitation right out of the moral arena of the relationship between the penitent and confessor. It became a technical offence unrelated to morality. The letter of the law completely sucked the life out of its spirit.[15]

One thing left out of Gregory's decree was any reference to the customary practice by soliciting priests of absolving their victims. Apparently, it was considered too dangerous to even mention in his ban. Neither jurisdiction nor faculties were to be denied to such priests.

Those confessors caught were told to secretly advise their penitents to repeat every confession they had made ever since as they were invalidated, and they themselves were "to consult their consciences as to the irregularity of celebrating Mass" while being punished.[16] Once again, the fear of scandal ruled supreme.

Another situation left uncovered is one where the priest was not the pursuer, but the pursued. "Passive solicitation" occurs where the penitent is the temptress. Theologians were very much at odds how either party should be treated, though its occurrence was actually quite uncommon. Women were denounced by their confessors to the Spanish Inquisition in a few rare instances in its entire history. In 1661, the Roman Inquisition decided that the confessor should be denounced when solicitation was mutual or if he yielded out of fear. But nothing was said about his partner, and one cardinal asserted she was not liable for denunciation.[17]

Flagellation was a somewhat related abuse of the confessional. It was a traditional ascetic discipline much indulged in by certain sects mainly during the period of the Black Death, as well as a punishment for grievous sin. Penance was delivered as a whipping, either self-administered in his presence or by the confessor himself. Such practices still exist, most notably among the Penitentes of New Mexico, whom will be dealt with further on.

Since the penitent would be at least partially stripped and the lash applied to any sinful part, it gave opportunity for all manner of erotic brutality. It wasn't always necessarily sadism, either. One friar, Francisco Calvo, for instance, denounced himself to the Inquisition in 1730 for having caused himself to be flagellated, presumably because he enjoyed it. Cases of these kinds continued right up until the final end of the Spanish Inquisition a century later.[18]

There were even a few rare cases involving mutual flagellation, where confessor and penitent lashed each other under the guise of misplaced mystic ardor. As always, theological novelty interested the inquisitors far more than any sexual kinkiness involved.[19]

Benefits of clergy

Despite the fact that women were not the targets but victims and sole witnesses, the all-male tribunals were strongly prejudiced against their testimony. If a woman chanced to mention her affair with a confessor while confessing to another, she was to be denied absolution until she denounced her seducer to the Inquisition. In fact, after 1571 in Spain, if a woman did not denounce, she was excommunicated. This was one of the few effective ways of getting female victims to come forward.[20]

Under the Roman Inquisition in 1624, the rule was set that neither penitent nor confessor were to be questioned as to her willingness, and that such information was not to be entered into the records. The Spanish did not follow until almost the end. As late as 1750, the inquisitors were instructed to inquire into and record every nasty little detail.[21]

In any case, once they had the name of a soliciting priest, inquisitors would then ask other tribunals if they had any records concerning the accused. If nothing came up, her accusation would be filed away until another denunciation of the man appeared. The woman was left in the dark with the impression that her defilement was too unimportant to require action.

Meanwhile, the perpetrator would be free to continue assaulting others. If he was not denounced again until after his first accuser had died, he was given another respite. In many cases, second denunciations did not come for ten years or more. In some, further complaints did not surface until as much as forty years after the first, and some contain multiple denunciations because the earliest victims had already perished.[22]

Things were easier for priests after their arrest, too. Instead of being held incommunicado in the Inquisition's secret prison during trial as ordinary heretics were, clergy accused of solicitation were left at liberty to devise their own defenses. Occasionally, this led them to further crimes. One priest threatened to kill the confessor who had sent in a denunciation unless he wrote that the women accusing him had withdrawn the charges. Another attempted to evade justice by persuading several women to denounce him and then retract.[23]

And unlike ordinary accusations of heresy, the accused cleric in cases of solicitation was usually immune from torture, no matter how many witnesses there were. This was based on the comparatively realistic idea that the penalties incurred did not justify its application. If, however, heresy had led to solicitation rather than the other way around, the inquisitors would not hesitate to apply their most merciless methods.[24]

Convicted clerics

Once convicted, the penalties for a soliciting priest were generally far more lenient than for any other heretical activity, especially if he voluntarily confessed at any point. He might get away with just a severe reprimand.

Several cases, however, show that a peculiar kind of immunity could sometimes arise from timely self-accusation. One priest from Seville, Hilario Caone, fled to all the way Rome in 1653, probably on the news that he was about to be exposed. There he confessed to the Inquisition that over the years he had solicited some forty women, usually successfully. He was required only to renounce his sins, visit St. Peter's, and say some prayers every week for three years. From a similar case the same year, such a sentence does not appear unusual.[25]

If duly remorseful, even the worst might be involuntarily banished to some distant colonial mission or committed to a monastery of strict observance. Though some abbeys were notorious hotbeds of homosexuality, many of the cloistered inmates in the most austere houses were actually disgraced clerics seeking redemption by anonymous lives of harsh penance under constant surveillance. A medieval gulag of such convents was once scattered throughout Europe. For many, the prospect of voluntary exile might well have seemed a better alternative.

For priests did get caught. In the mid-seventeenth century, the Roman Inquisition even took down an entire religious order for child sexual abuse. The Piarists, an honored, successful teaching congregation with schools for poor boys all across Italy, had been taken over by a pedophile ring. This was largely due to the founder, St. José Calasanz, perhaps appropriately as the eventual patron saint of Catholic education, covering up abuse. Like so many later prelates, he quietly promoted and transferred the offenders rather than really discipline them. Finally, the misuse became so flagrant that the entire order was put out of business for several decades – despite the ringleaders having most likely having bribed the inquisitors for years.[26]

What got the order first involved with the Inquisition, ironically enough, was their role in exposing one of the most spectacular cases of all time. The Piarists dutifully notified the authorities about a school for poor girls run by nuns in Florence just five years before their own bust. It was being run not only as a prostitution ring but also as a full-blown sex cult.

The sisters' highborn, rich, and well-educated Jesuit confessor, Canon Pandolfo Ricasoli, held the ancient heresy that all things are permitted to the pure. The official record says that he taught that, "All carnal acts between men and women are not only allowed, but meritorious, if one keeps his mind united with God." He claimed Christ with the Magdalene, the Virgin with Saint John, all performed these so-called "exercises of purity" together.

Ricasoli enthusiastically practiced what he preached, too. "Christmas Eve he slept with two girls in order to greet the day with greater devotion." Like a Gnostic libertine of a millennium and a half previously, the abbess Faustina Mainardi, his willing accomplice in all this, even placed his semen-caked handkerchief among the sacred relics in the altar.[27]

The party went on for eight years. Once the Inquisition was informed, however, Ricasoli quickly denounced himself. It didn't save him. He, Faustina, her brother, and seven others were arrested, and some nuns were implicated. At an *auto da fé* on November 28, 1641, attended by the grand duke, the Medici cardinal, and the papal nuncio, Ricasoli, Faustina, and a priest were sentenced to life imprisonment, while others got off with the possibility of parole.

Ricasoli shouted his regrets to the people as he was hauled off. He certainly had time to fully contemplate them, as he lasted almost sixteen years in total confinement, dying at the age of 78. Until the end, he protested that he acted out of ignorance, rather than lust. Despite everything, he was even given a Christian burial. But the inquisitor, Giovanni Mazzarelli, who figured in both the Galileo and Piarist cases also, was reprimanded for this misplaced mercy and quickly replaced.[28]

Though the former confessor and abbess first had to endure public penance in *sanbenitos* "painted with flames and devils," and were then immediately walled up alive forever in the dungeons of the Inquisition, they were not burnt to death but merely declared heretics.[29] Even in such an infamous case, it seems the churchmen could not bring themselves to actually inflict the ultimate punishment on a brother priest for sex crimes.

Faustina had escaped barely excommunication by disavowing her sins. Despite his pleas, Ricasoli was excommunicated anyway and his wealth confiscated. Though never released, he was ultimately absolved, however, and even had some of his fortune restored by the pope.[30]

Indeed, the pair seemingly got off relatively easy, considering that such blatant heresy and public outrage were involved. Undoubtedly, the canon's upper-class connections and great wealth had helped, but perhaps there were also fears of an even wider scandal. For Faustina, a wealthy widow, had been renting her tender charges out to local nobles. It was the confession of one of these young girls to a Piarist priest that led to the cult's exposure.[31]

There still exists a famous portrait by Flemish artist Justus Suttermans of Ricasoli standing erect, regarding the viewer with perhaps the slightest hint of a knowing smile as he confidently holds onto a large crucifix. Daubed in happier times, a small, barely visible devil whispering in his ear was discreetly added to the picture after his disgrace. Hand-rendered copies may be purchased over the Internet.

Irregular regulars

Few culprits, especially monks and mendicants, were so rich, not to mention bold. For members of religious orders were sworn to poverty as well as chastity. Yet, as the records of the Spanish Inquisition show, many more regular clergy were accused of solicitation than parish priests.

One expert thought this was because secular priests usually possessed greater wealth and freedom and so were able to satisfy their passions in less dangerous ways (as with prostitutes, for instance). Ironically, it is therefore the most rigid and austere orders that have produced the greatest number of offenders throughout history, including modern times.

Many of these orders were given special powers to absolve most cases reserved to Rome for judgment – including Dominicans, Franciscans, Jesuits, Augustinians, Carmelites, and Servites. This added greatly to their attraction, which was further increased by the fact that for centuries they were the only allowed alternative for confession to one's own parish priest.

The regulars were given numerous exemptions. As closed associations with widespread networks involving frequent travel between outposts, they were much more liable to successfully cover for each other. Thus, the decrees authorizing the Inquisition to pursue soliciting priests carefully specified their powers over religious orders as well as the secular clergy. This was long resisted, ultimately futilely. But an analysis of some 3,775 cases shows how necessary it was. It turned out that religious orders provided nearly three-quarters of the offenders. That's three times the numbers of propositioning parish priests, vicars, and canons.[32]

All orders futilely struggled to stay free from the Inquisition, which was relentless in its pursuit of jurisdiction. In 1587, two Jesuits found guilty and quietly helped to escape Spain were hunted down and imprisoned, for instance, with two others who had helped them evade the edict. But the Jesuits had powerful friends in Rome, and Pope Sixtus V quickly took those cases to personally decide.

He threatened the Inquisitor General with losing his job and cardinal's hat, which got the desired result. The Jesuits were encouraged and fought to obtain exemption for all orders. The struggle was prolonged, but to no avail. The pressure of the Spanish Empire triumphed in the end, and in 1592, the jurisdiction of the Spanish Inquisition over religious orders was declared exclusive in that realm.[33]

Yet even after conviction, clerical perpetrators, regular or secular, were still protected by the incessant fear of scandal. Unlike all other victims of the Inquisition, clerics condemned of sex crimes were shielded from public exposure and the disgrace that would forever stain their families. Clergy sex offenders were never paraded before the mob in an *auto da fé* along with ordinary lay heretics, blasphemers, bigamists, and sorcerers.

From the beginning, sentences for sexually offending clergy were read privately, discreetly out of sight behind the closed doors of chapter houses and churches. The only witnesses allowed were priests from nearby parishes or members of the culprit's own order. Most often, the sentence involved heavy penance, seclusion, suspension, and for those in an order, being last in the choir and the refectory, and the loss of voting or speaking rights in chapter. Regulars might also even be scourged. Along with also losing privileges such as hearing confessions, secular priests having greater access to funds were commonly fined instead or occasionally exiled. But as time went on, all punishments for soliciting priests generally became more lenient.[34]

In 1869, Pope Pius IX wrote a bull ordering excommunication for women who did not denounce their seducer within a month of the offense. Only by forbidding absolution when they chanced to confess to another priest could victims be induced to do this. The bishop was to keep no copy, but forward the denunciation to the Roman Inquisition and burn all leftover paperwork.

Yet, victims could get dispensed from the onerous duty from the bishop, the Inquisition, or Rome, due to danger to life, possessions, reputation, or because of kinship, friendship, and other reasons.[35]

The Church never really seemed to "get it," however. The power the confessor wields along with his intimate knowledge of the victim makes such misuse of the sacrament an utterly horrific betrayal. Yet, solicitation in Confession has never been considered so heinous an offense that it could only be forgiven by the pope or his special representative. Instead, any confessor can conveniently forgive even the worst lecheries of his fellow confessor, no questions asked. Instead of the welfare of the penitent, the most important thing is that the secrecy of the confessional be preserved.

The great nineteenth-century historian who delved deeply into the histories of celibacy, confession, and the Inquisition, Henry Charles Lea, concluded:

> *Morals, in fact, have nothing to do with solicitation as viewed by the Church. The priest can indulge his passions with his penitents in safety, so long as he commits no technical offence and so long as the danger of scandal is not incurred. The Church sees nothing specially sinful in solicitation itself, notwithstanding the vehement rhetoric of papal utterances... The Holy See has never reserved to itself the sin of seducing a penitent in the confessional... The consequence of this is that absolution can be given by any confessor, and the culprit is told that he need only confess to simple fornication, without mentioning that it had been with his spiritual daughter. He therefore obtains pardon from God on the easiest possible terms, his conscience is clear, and he is ready to repeat the offence. This forms a strange contrast with the excommunication directed against the victim who fails to denounce her seducer, for this is reserved to the Holy See, and... the censures of the bulls are directed against her, and not against him. May we not attribute all this to a callousness engendered by the prevalence of concubinage among a celibate priesthood, where the woman must in almost all cases necessarily be the penitent of the priest and thus be his spiritual daughter?[36]*

CHAPTER VII:
CRIME AND PUNISHMENT

Triumph of propriety

In any case, centuries passed before the reputation of the clergy recovered. Lack of morality long continued to inspire derisive laughter. During the Enlightenment, scholastic theology also became regarded as amusingly quaint by the new scientifically minded intellectuals. For instance, Jean Meslier, a well-regarded pastor, was discovered after his death to have written a scathing atheistic testament against religion, *Superstition in All Ages*. Though authorities tried vainly to suppress it, Voltaire gleefully had the book published anyway.

But the rampant corruption in the Church grew alongside skepticism. It was well illustrated in the lives of notorious characters like the Marquis de Sade. His uncle, also called by that title, a priest whom he lived with for a time, kept a mother and her daughter as his mistresses at home. The elder Marquis introduced the young man to sex in the rectory, and was finally arrested in a Parisian brothel. It has been speculated, however, that de Sade had been initiated into what he is forever known for – sodomy, bondage, and sexual cruelty – as an adolescent by his Jesuit masters.[1]

The ostentatious wealth and decadence of the First Estate, the high clergy in France, fed smoldering anticlericalism that helped ignite the purifying flames of the Revolution. That conflagration generally chastened clergy all across Europe. Bloody revolt apparently accomplished what reform had failed to achieve, though at a great price.

Soon after, during the Victorian era, however, tales of lecherous priests began to fade away like a bad dream. The ever-increasing secrecy imposed since 1622 probably accounts for the continued repression, and the well-known prudery of the times for much of the rest.

Many simple souls assumed that the grace of chastity must automatically follow a priest's ordination. Maybe it did sometimes, for certainly new nineteenth-century priests, though warned of temptations they would face in the world, were completely unprepared for the actuality. Counseled against both the wiles of women and the danger of "particular friendships" with their fellow seminarians, the main tool against lust and loneliness they were given was prayer and more prayer, particularly to the Virgin Mary.

Young, virile, and in the prime of life, new priests had been isolated during their formative years in the seminary and unused to feminine companionship. Yet these men found themselves suddenly alone and thrust into the most intimate, demanding relations with the most alluring but utterly forbidden creatures.

Moreover, the women they comforted were taught from earliest childhood to regard priests as having the supernatural powers of heaven or hell over them and that they had to share with them their deepest and most shameful longings. Doubtless, many priests overestimated their self-control, especially since similar desires in themselves were only made stronger by long years of repression and denial.

The American historian of the Latin Church, Henry Charles Lea, quoted above and used throughout this work, carefully noted the Spanish and Roman Inquisition's roles. He had written massive studies of Confession and the Church's struggles with sex through the ages as well. Yet, somehow, he could not fully understand how the secret system could continue to be so successful in his own day.

"In Ireland, for instance," Lea wrote in obvious puzzlement, "we rarely hear of immoral priests, though such cases would be relentlessly exposed by the interests adverse to Catholicism ... In the United States, also, troubles of this kind only come occasionally to public view."[2]

Perhaps Lea was unaware of Ireland's so-called "blushless press." Long before the scandals, it was said that, "Roman Catholic Ireland's law and custom have long forced Irish newspapers to adopt one of the most rigorous self-censorships of any free press in the world."[3]

In nineteenth century America, however, there were fiercely anti-Irish and anti-Catholic movements, called "navitists" and "Know Nothings." Eagerly seizing on sensational stories of baby-murdering nuns from alleged escapees from convents, it seems logical that they would have gladly broadcast other examples of priestly immorality if they knew of them.

Yet, little can be found in the public record. Perhaps the lack is somewhat due to straitlaced editors staunchly supporting any civilizing power in the wild new lands. Or maybe they dared not stand against threatened or imagined boycotts. The quiet cooperation with the Church by secular authorities who didn't want to bother with sensational cases if that could be avoided also doubtlessly helped.

Society in general, however, has historically seemed quite determined to protect the good name of the clergy no matter what. James Porter, whose exposure provided early notice of the coming disaster, admitted that the Roman collar protected him so he could molest hundreds of kids. "Now there is no shield," he regretfully wrote in his letter to the pope asking permission to leave the priesthood, "if I become familiar with children, people would immediately suspect me."[4] And so they did.

Savaged sisters

The modesty of Victorian victims probably stifled as many of the most outrageous tales as social suppression. "Maria Monk," a woman who escaped the convent after becoming pregnant, for instance, could barely bring herself to mention the multiple and repeated rapes by three priests that she alleged happened on the very night she professed her solemn vows. She minimized it in a most embarrassed fashion, just as later victims would. This, for example, is all she had to say about what happened after the ceremony:

> *Nothing important occurred till late in the afternoon, when, as I was sitting in the community-room, Father Dufresne called me out, saying, he wished to speak to me. I feared what was his intention; but I dared not disobey. In a private apartment, he treated me in a brutal manner; and, from two other priests, I afterwards received similar usage that evening. Father Dufresne afterwards appeared again; and I was compelled to remain in company with him until morning.*
>
> *I am assured that the conduct of priests in our Convent had never been exposed, and it is not imagined by the people of the United States. This induces me to say what I do, notwithstanding the strong reasons I have to let it remain unknown. Still I cannot force myself to speak on such subjects except in the most brief manner.*[5]

Yet, for this, the first North American victim to speak out was nearly universally reviled and disbelieved to this day. Modern revelations about rings of perpetrators and the abuse of nuns, however, show that her story rings true. In fact, several studies in recent years confirm a high amount of sexual abuse of "sisters" by "fathers" around the world.

One such was a four-page paper titled *The Problem of the Sexual Abuse of African Religious in Africa and Rome*, presented by Sister Marie McDonald at the Vatican in November 1998. The problems she reported in Africa are truly universal.

When a sister becomes pregnant, she wrote, she is usually punished by dismissal from the congregation, while the priest is "often only moved to another parish – or sent for studies." Priests sometimes exploit the financial dependency of young sisters or take advantage of spiritual direction and the sacrament of Reconciliation to extort sexual favors. And perhaps worst of all, the AIDS pandemic caused nuns to be seen as "safe."[6]

With such horrors having been brought forward by the orders of consecrated women themselves and proven in courts of law, the claims of rampant abuse and crime by Maria Monk do not sound so wildly extravagant anymore. Even the charges of infanticide, which moderns find so distasteful, might look entirely different to those women who lived in medieval gloom before the invention of contraception.

After all, the Catholic Church opposes abortion partially because it believes the soul of the infant, if left unbaptized, will not be allowed into heaven. At least, the nuns might say in self-justification, their babies, being brought to term and baptized, were guaranteed an eternity of happiness, unlike today's aborted fetuses forever doomed to Limbo, whatever that means nowadays. Their sins, they might claim, were thereby the lesser.

In any case, Maria Monk never claimed *all* nunneries were corrupt, but only spoke of her own personal experiences. But hers was not the only one so debased, and conditions have not necessarily changed for the better.

In 1993, at a national conference for clergy abuse victims at which the author was present, for instance, an elderly woman softly told her story. At her quite advanced years, she claimed she had recently quit a wealthy, influential convent related somehow to the Benedictines and Sisters of Mercy that is situated on an island off the East Coast.

Among other things, she said that the order stole land, duped recruits and supporters, and led by several shady confessors, advocated Eucharistic meditations for the sisters that were overtly autoerotic fantasies. Her complaints to the ecclesiastical authorities brought no relief but only harsh discipline for herself, and so she was forced to leave in protest. The Vatican later investigated the place and ordered reforms.

A century and a half ago, Henry Lea speculated that some sort of a "don't ask, don't tell" accommodation had evolved outside the convent. He felt that parishioners might be somewhat less critical of a priest with a live-in maid or a young "niece" if it kept him safely away from their own daughters.

Concubinage, he believed, had become so accepted as to be almost not worth mentioning, at least in the more sophisticated areas of Catholic Europe. Some sort of tacit living arrangements were certainly possible to some extent, at least in cynical France and Italy. Like many, however, including those in charge of the secret system, Lea appears not to have fully appreciated that most clerical offenders have multiple victims. Getting away with it in one instance usually only encourages them to try in others.

Lea was aware of the Roman Inquisition's continuing role in his day, however, even citing recent decrees. Curiously, he did not ascribe much importance to it, placing most of the blame on celibacy itself. Nonetheless, he was quite cognizant of the role of secrecy. He was even aware of significance of the secret archives, which will be dealt with in detail later.

> As formerly, scandal is the one thing dreaded. All other considerations are of minor importance, and the subject is treated on the basis of the principle... 'Nothing is to be done that creates scandal... to avoid scandal the rigour of ecclesiastical law often yields.' To this end, the proceedings in all cases are conducted with the most impressive secrecy from the beginning to the end. When a priest [is delegated to receive an accusation] he is sworn in the presence of his bishop to perform the duty faithfully and to observe inviolate secrecy... on the gospels and not by merely touching the breast, as is customary with priests. All names are to be scrupulously suppressed, and what testimony is shown to the accused is to be so carefully disguised as not to give him an inkling of any witness. All papers are to be kept by the bishop in a special cabinet to which even his vicar-general is debarred access, the accuser is kept in ignorance of the result, and when the case is ended it is to be buried in oblivion. Under these circumstances it is impossible even to guess what may be the frequency of either the crime or its detection.[7]

In any event, Lea clearly understood that society had greatly changed over the centuries. Victorian repression and refinement in general made sexual topics of all kinds taboo. Moreover, since the Reformation, the Catholic Church had become too embarrassed by the sins of its clergy to speak with anything at all like the coarse candor freely used in the Middle Ages.

> In modern times, however, when an external veil of decency is to be maintained... when scandal is of all things to be avoided, and when the proceedings of ecclesiastical bodies are carefully revised at Rome before they are allowed to become public... only the most guarded allusions can be made to such subjects, and these only when the case is urgent.[8]

Other means of control

The terror of the Inquisition is but the most extreme method the Church has used to keep its clergy in line. Gentler means are more the norm, including piety, obedience, and poverty.

Prayer is the primary duty of the clergy. They are immersed in a world of it, swimming in a sea of doctrine and liturgy. Many entered out of their devotion to God, and for Catholics, that means devotion to the Church. All religious swear an oath of obedience to the hierarchy as part of their profession of faith. Those in the various orders of priests, monks, and nuns may take additional vows, but all are equally bound to obey their superiors.

In exchange, the Catholic Church promises to support them economically. This, however, gives the hierarchy even more power over them. The Church makes very large investments in training its clergy, and it does not like to see it wasted. A priest is highly trained specifically for his job. Unless he has acquired other skills, a man might find seeking adequate employment difficult outside the Church. After all, there's sadly little demand for theologians in industry – or most anywhere else.

Many priests started in seminaries as young teens. They would have little experience in the outside world to begin with. Moreover, the Church controls their education. Certificates, licenses, and even degrees earned in Catholic universities by those who later dissent have occasionally been revoked. For career academics, such actions would be devastating.

In addition, because the Church provides food, housing, and other supports, the wages of most parish priests are puny by worldly standards. Regulars who have sworn oaths of poverty lack even that. It would be difficult for most clergy wanting to leave to accumulate sufficient funds without dipping into the collection basket.

Getting out would be just the beginning of their problems, especially in Catholic countries. For instance, the Lateran Treaties of 1929 between Mussolini and the Holy See had not only made Catholicism the state religion of fascist Italy, it gave immense power to the Church over the entire educational system. Decisions of Vatican courts concerning religious were to have "legal effect" by civilian authorities, also.[9]

Therefore, in Italy for much of the twentieth century, ex-clerics could be legally denied employment as teachers or even as public clerks. They were also forbidden to hold public offices. Yet, arrested ecclesiastics were to receive preferential treatment by the authorities, including private trials, just like in the old days.[10]

This cozy arrangement lasted until 1984 when the agreements were finally modified. Catholicism was then disestablished as the sole religion of the state and lost many privileges. In Ireland, the Catholic Church, while not a state religion, occupied a "special position" in the Republic until the Irish Constitution was amended in 1972.

More daunting to a priest, perhaps, is the psychological price of leaving the only life he's ever known. With their long preparation, often beginning in parochial school, and continuing uninterrupted through college-level seminaries, clergy is thoroughly indoctrinated by the time of their ordination.

The Catholic Church's attitude has long been "no salvation outside the Church." Before the Second Vatican Council, to voluntarily seek liacization for almost any reason was to expose oneself to total ostracism. Anyone who left was branded as an apostate and shunned as a traitor to Christ.

Rumors would often be spread among a priest's former associates about his moral depravity in order to explain such abandonment. The gossip was not limited to clergy, either. Whispering campaigns could make an ex-cleric's life miserable, if not unbearable. Sometimes the rumors would follow them wherever they went, too, like some kind of mark of Cain.

Yet, if problem-causing religious chose to stay, their bishops or abbots retained complete control over them. As one former priest asserted shortly before Vatican II, "the power of the bishop over his clergy is as unlimited as that of a monarch in the Middle Ages. Only the right of capital punishment is denied him."[11]

In the 1940s, alcoholic priests were treated somewhat leniently, if they admitted their problem, sent to a retreat house to sober up and then be reassigned. Sexual offenders might be sent to a monastery or even expelled. "For all practical purposes, there was no way for a priest to get out without jeopardizing his immortal soul."[12]

This put clergy entirely at the mercy of their superiors, who are supposed to be guided by canon law with its own independent system of punishments and censures. Even though the clergy have certain rights under the 1983 *Code*, bishops and abbots still reign as virtual monarchs within their own domains. Often formal means to discipline do not need to be applied.

Abbeys served the medieval world as hospitals, hotels, libraries, schools, and research centers. But they were not always full of those voluntarily seeking sanctity. They took on the additional role of religious prison quite early. The most austere, such as the Trappist monasteries, seemed particularly well suited for locking up clerical criminals. According to one former Trappist monk of 24 years who cared for such men, "'wayward priests' were still sent to there 'to do penance'" even as late as 1989.[13]

Though many may have found monastic rigor edifying, the long-term presence of men with no real vocation or desire to be there was inevitably corrupting. It actively contributed to the loss of esteem that monks suffered leading up to the Reformation. Decay like this of a religious order by its own members occurred repeatedly, and would still be a significant aspect in the clergy abuse scandals of the late twentieth century.

In modern times, there were far fewer abbeys to which to exile the most difficult. So before "treatment centers," another convenient option was to send them to Catholic-run sanatoria or mental hospitals. There unruly priests could be kept out of sight or undergo "therapy" until they submitted. Often insubordination or a desire to get married was the real problem, but such ideas were considered crazy when they occurred to clergy.

Retreats, however, proved to be the most attractive option. The Church could apply whatever spiritual remedies deemed appropriate in a private, confidential setting. Nothing would ever appear in the priest's records. Best of all, if the priest got into trouble again, the providers would have no liability, unlike givers of custodial care.

The Inquisition in the Twentieth Century

In 1908, the now-Universal Roman Inquisition was re-christened, this time as the Holy Office, but retained all its powers. By the 1920s, however, any knowledge of its interest in sex abuse was deemed too scandalous. New rules were written, covered in the darkest secrecy, which have only recently been revealed. Nor is it known what specific events might have happened to trigger this.[14]

By then, however, the role of the Inquisition that Lea had described had been completely forgotten again. It remained unsuspected until the early years of the new millennium. Then, in 2003, a curious document was discovered among the diocesan papers during the Boston scandals that had led to a broad public awareness of the crisis.

Known generally as *Crimen sollicitationis*, "Crimes of Solicitation" was a typed English translation of instructions from the Holy Office. Secretly sent to all the world's bishops over forty years previously with permission of

Pope John XXIII mere months before the opening of the Second Vatican Council, it revealed an entirely unsuspected aspect to the crisis.

It was nothing less than a how-to-do-it-yourself guide for bishops on handling secret clerical sex crime trials. Though reassuring them that troubling cases could always be sent to Rome, the manual detailed a set of systematic instructions on holding covert hearings just like the Inquisition. These clandestine tribunals were solely for clergy charged with sexual solicitation in the confessional and "the worst crime," that is, homosexual sex. Almost as an afterthought, sodomizing children and bestiality were thrown in for good measure.

Rigorous secrecy was its overriding concern, with virtually every page repeating dire warnings of automatic excommunication for anyone involved in any way in the trial who revealed the proceedings, including victims and families. The document itself stipulates that it is to be stored under lock and key in the most secret archives of the diocese, accessible only to the bishop and certain approved priests, but not even listed in the index of documents. Much like modern anti-terrorist legislation, this blanket order even covered anyone who found out about the trial, wittingly or otherwise.[15]

Initially denied, then grudgingly admitted by authorities, apologists claimed that few bishops even knew of the instructions. Perhaps, though it seems unlikely that secret orders of the Inquisition would be treated so heedlessly. Conceivably, it could have been deliberately forgotten in time – or at least conveniently until needed.

Regardless, this was the first sign of interest in recent times of the Church's thought police in the sexual sins of the clergy. When it was discovered, the world had no idea that the policy had apparently been pushed aside shortly after it was written. Neither was it imagined that the result of doing so had been the explosion of sex scandals around the globe that had already been going on almost two decades.

Ironically, those scandals would be an unanticipated effect of a great effort intended to reform the Catholic Church. This attempt to modernize the faith came about due to the largest meeting of prelates ever assembled, the Ecumenical Council history knows as Vatican II.

CHAPTER VIII:
REVOLUTION AT THE COUNCIL

Throwing open the windows

Why *Crimen sollicitationis* was issued is not known. Perhaps it was prompted by the advent of civil reporting laws or maybe it was felt that the bishops needed a refresher. But it was strong, if soon neglected, reinforcement of the traditional system of secrecy.

On March 16, 1962, the prefect of the Holy Office, Cardinal Alberto Ottaviani, probably brought it himself to the Apostolic Palace for Pope John XXIII's signature. It's easy to picture them chatting pleasantly over tea or coffee as old friends. Perhaps they didn't even discuss the document, mainly a reissue of the old rules anyway, but rather the grand upcoming council.

Ottaviani was to prepare the proposed agenda intended to guide and shape the council's discussions. Neither man had any reason to suspect that this historic assembly to revitalize the Church's image would quickly slip out of their control, its wild hopes prompting a strong reactionary backlash. Nor could they guess that it would set the stage for a mass exodus of priests, brothers, and nuns, followed by seemingly endless sex scandals.

But no sooner had the great gathering begun in October than significant opposition against the Vatican's agenda appeared. On the very first working day, Cardinal Josef Frings of Belgium, the chief spokesman for the progressive camp, spoke out against the proposed plans of the curia.[1]

Ottaviani replied the next day in a classic exchange, both men old and nearly blind yet orating in perfect Latin. But the members were clearly not on the prefect's side. He sat down baffled and hurt as his proposals were spurned. As *Time* magazine said in his obituary, "His power seemed to evaporate in one humiliating and dramatic day."[2]

Out of pique, the cardinal then boycotted the event for several weeks. The unexpected absence of the head of the Holy Office proved critical. It gave the council fathers the time, freedom, and confidence needed to form their own opinions. The curia's hopes for a tame rubberstamping of their proposals were quickly dashed. There would be real debates and the hopes of liberal Catholic onlookers everywhere began to rise.

The first enormous change was signaled by Pope John's issuing of his final encyclical, *Pacem in terris*, or *"Peace on Earth"* less than two months before his death. In a long list of human rights was included freedom of conscience in worship. Man, it said, had the God-given right "to profess his religion both in private and in public."[3]

The statement seems harmless enough, but it threatened the fundamental principle that no one could achieve salvation without the Catholic Church. Before, freedom of religion had always meant the freedom of Catholics to worship according to the means provided by the Church, the sole possessor of revealed truth, without State interference. Previously, the freedom of pagans, infidels, and heretics to worship according to their own beliefs had been grudgingly permitted only out of political necessity at best.

With this acknowledgement in a single world-shattering paragraph, all the dire anathemas ever uttered evaporated; every inquisition undertaken was suddenly recast as a tragic, embarrassing mistake. Poof! All the heretics who had been burned – and Martin Luther, too – were miraculously transformed. They were no longer necessarily damned enemies of God but possibly, just possibly, repressed innocent victims of conscience.

Such dangerous thinking could not be tolerated for very long. A little over two decades later, a strong conservative reaction set in under Pope John Paul II. That pontiff would slowly and deliberately undermine many of the provisions of Vatican II – without ever admitting it, of course, and even citing it at times. Like most official documents, John's encyclical had contained enough careful qualifications and conditions that the Vatican could back away from it without actually seeming to contradict anything.[4]

But at the time, however, *Pacem in terris* seemed nothing less than revolutionary. It must have felt like the beginning of a Catholic Age of Aquarius.

Frings, naturally, had not acted alone. He had the guidance of a trusted team of liberal theological advisors. These radical young lions included Hans Küng, Karl Rahner — and a Bavarian named Joseph Ratzinger. Due to his impaired vision, the cardinal was especially dependent on them. For them, however, wresting the agenda from the enfeebled grip of the curia was just the beginning. Ratzinger, already a rising theological star, wrote the speech that would deliver the fateful blow.

On November 8, 1963, just two weeks before a Catholic president across the sea would be murdered, Frings rose again to confront the prefect. Undoubtedly largely composed by Ratzinger, his speech firmly denounced the Holy Office and its medieval methods, calling it a "cause of scandal to the world." Loud applause and cheering broke out among the assembly – itself unheard of. "No one should be judged and condemned without being heard," Frings declared, "without knowing what he is accused of, and without having the opportunity to amend what he can reasonably be reproached with."[5]

He sat down to a noisy ovation while Ottaviani's impassioned but impromptu reply was greeted with stone cold silence. The confrontation, as John Allen, a highly respected analyst, put it, "became in some ways the defining moment of the entire council and the question of the Holy Office's future became symbolic of everything else at stake."[6] That night, the new pope, Paul VI, personally called to congratulate Frings: the reformation of the Holy Office would proceed.

The council still had a long way to go, however. The most contentious issues – even more than birth control – were those surrounding the clergy. Celibacy, lifestyle, and training were all questioned. The documents were argued over until the end of the very last session. When it was done, a single easily-overlooked paragraph buried in the "Decree on the Life and Ministry of Priests," *Presbyterorum ordinis*, proclaimed the enormous change:

> *Finally, … priests should realize that they are obliged in a special manner toward those priests who labor under certain difficulties. They should give them timely help, and also, if necessary, admonish them discreetly. Moreover, they should always treat with fraternal charity and magnanimity those who have failed in some matters, offer urgent prayers to God for them, and continually show themselves as true brothers and friends.[7]*

Hard to imagine, but this coded bit of pious banality may actually be the long-sought smoking gun of the Catholic sex scandals. But there was more. The decree then made the astounding admission that celibacy "is not demanded by the very nature of the priesthood." This was to reassure Eastern-rite priests – who could legitimately be married – that nothing would change for them. However, celibacy would still be demanded of Western clergy.[8]

This must have been a bewildering double blow to clerical morale. Roman Catholic clergy had constantly been assured that celibacy was somehow vital to their role in salvation, exalting them above all other men. Now, Latin-rite priests had been informed in essence that the greatest sacrifice of their lives was not only unnecessary but even irrelevant. Yet, though total sexual self-denial was still mandatory, the men would no longer be punished as before for failing to live up to it.

Thus, the Church's stringent demand for the absolute chastity of its priests was abruptly revealed as both wholly arbitrary and ultimately unenforceable. It's hard to conceive of a more confusing or damning confession.

For sexually abusive clergy, this could be nothing other than a license to act out. Other unhappy clerics, though, saw it as the writing on the wall. In the following years, a trickle of reactionary traditionalists departed amidst a greater flood of discouraged progressives.

Nothing in the decree made it any easier for disgruntled clergy to actually get out, however. It took Paul several more years before he reluctantly bowed to the growing pressure. Finally in 1967, he wrote an encyclical that gently tried to back away from that damning admission about celibacy, claiming it was actually "virginity" that was not required for the priesthood. But despite this, the pontiff grudgingly waived most obstacles of the Holy Office to voluntary liacization and the flight began.[9]

Of course, the intention of Ratzinger and his allies at the time was doubtless simply to protect freedom of discussion among theologians. It surely was not to turn clerical sex predators loose. But the guard dogs of the Holy Office had indeed been muzzled. The signal came on the very last day of the council when Paul changed the name of the Holy Office to the Sacred Congregation for the Doctrine of the Faith (often referred to as the CDF); in effect, a kinder, gentler Inquisition. It was the greatest victory of the liberals.

The pope said he wanted the department to continue its good theological work but not in quite such a punitive manner as before. The secrecy of its inner workings would be finally ended along with the *Index of Forbidden Books*, and accused priests would have rights of appeal and judicial representation. Bodies of consultative experts would be employed.

Ominously but largely overlooked at the time, however, the CDF would henceforth be given a say over all issues that touched on faith and morals. This extended even to those concerns traditionally reserved to other Vatican congregations. The clause was intended to ensure that all curial departments lived up to the reforms. But for all intents and purposes, it gave the CDF the supreme power of judicial review over the entire Roman Catholic Church. Later, in Ratzinger's now-conservative hand, this whip to enforce the decrees of Vatican II would serve to sharply rein them in.[10]

Thus, the Second Vatican Council planted the seeds for the worldwide clergy sex scandals. But by giving the CDF a means of ultimately restoring its power, it also provided for their conclusion. Yet, the signs that the council had inadvertently mishandled perpetrator priests would not become apparent until a generation later, when the bitter tree bore its first fruits.

The building storm

It happened first in Louisiana where a priest named Gilbert Gauthe had molested altar boys for years, quietly being reprimanded and transferred to a new parish each time he was caught. Finally, in 1984, the parents of one victim were not willing to settle and hired an attorney. The local diocesan officials botched the attempt to cover everything up. Gauthe was convicted and the family awarded a million dollars.[11]

Meanwhile, news agencies picked up the story. Other local abusive priests soon became known. The first of many scandals was off and running in a pattern that would become all too familiar in the following decades. But since Gauthe had stayed in Louisiana, so did most of the news.

Before long, the lawyer hired to defend him, Ray Mouton, called for help. Two priests became involved: Michael Peterson, a psychiatrist who had recently founded what would become the preeminent treatment center for priests, St. Luke's Institute, and would eventually die of AIDS, and Tom Doyle, a Dominican canonist who had been working in the Vatican's Washington outpost keeping Rome abreast of American developments.

Knowing of many other cases, these men were soon worried and rightly so. They sensed a volcano of litigation rumbling to life, an eruption of lawsuits to come. Alarmed, the trio created a bold proposal for a new policy for the American bishops to avert the crisis they foresaw.

Their proposal was called *The Problem of Sexual Molestation by Roman Catholic Clergy: Meeting the Problem in a Responsible Manner*. It's widely known by several names, but most simply as *The Manual*, which may hint that it was not, as is often claimed, generally disregarded. Among other things, it called for a "crisis control team" of medical, legal, and Church experts to be established. Like the Inquisition of yore, they would act as a top-notch mobile emergency intervention squad, flying into hot spots when and wherever needed to extinguish scandals and limit damages.

However, as in almost every action the Church has ever taken in regards to clergy sexual abuse, there were few if any real concerns displayed for the victims, especially compared to the rights of accused priests. Secrecy and the prevention of scandal remained the primary priorities.[12]

The proposal was first presented to the bishops at a June meeting in 1985 in Collegeville, Minnesota. Ironically, this was the same place where an important national victims' conference would be held eight years later in blithe ignorance of the previous proceedings. In any case, the problem remained on the bishops' agenda every year thereafter. Little officially came of it.

Why the proposal died is still a mystery. Rumors of personal vendettas and cliques of bishops persist. Certain initial supporters such as Cardinal Bernard Law of Boston, later revealed as a prime mover in the cover-up, puzzlingly abandoned it.

Yet, the failure of *The Manual*, if nothing else, stands as mute testimony of the ability of the secret system to protect not only itself but also powerful prelates from exposure.[13]

In such circumstances, having been proven prophetically correct is probably not much of a consolation. To this day, Doyle remains adamant that their efforts were completely misunderstood and misrepresented. The man has doubtless paid a heavy personal price, too. He left parish work and became a military chaplain the year after *The Manual* was presented.

Later, Tom Doyle became a leading expert and fearless advocate for victims, testifying on behalf of many. If he has rightfully earned their esteem as a lone representative of the Church trying to do the right thing, he has also occasionally suffered their misplaced anger as well.

However, any bad feelings among the bishops towards him have probably been well earned. Doyle consistently holds them responsible for the mess, although as a proper Dominican, in the author's view, he tends to minimize the importance of both pope and inquisitor in his writings.

A confusion of bishops

But there had been, as one perplexed canon lawyer has admitted, for some time "an almost total breakdown of the canonical system. Rather than face a canonical process for their crimes, priest perpetrators were coddled, sent off to some of the most expensive treatment centers in the nation many of them Church-run." The "small number of bishops" who "managed to stymie" the national conference were aided by Rome not wishing to act.[14]

This expert, Nicholas P. Cafardi, blames much of the confusion on the revised *Code of Canon Law*. Bishops, who could remove priests without a church trial under the previous version, found their hands tied by the 1983 reforms. For one thing, a clause forbad priests with mental illness from being so disciplined. Plus, John Paul, trying to stem the tide of priests leaving to get married, had made it all but impossible to laicize a priest against his will.

The final irony was that *Crimen sollicitationis*, although still in effect and capable of resolving the situation, had been so secret that it was completely forgotten by then.[15]

Though doubtless a sincere, good faith effort, *The Manual* posed the bishops with a real dilemma. On the one hand, some were already deep into the cover-up, so how could they do anything? Yet, how could they not? They probably felt it far too dangerous to admit any culpability and with good reason, as events have since proven. So the only alternative was to brazen it out, pretend the need to study the situation, and just hope it would go away.

However, if *The Manual* had been effectively implemented, it just might have worked. The horrific revelations of the last two decades would likely have been greatly muted if not averted. For victims and their parents all along have largely just wanted the Church to take care of the problem as they were promised. Most would have been content to have the damage acknowledged and the offending priest prevented from molesting again.

Just as in the Middle Ages, however, the problem is by no means confined to the lower ranks of the clergy. Richard Sipe, a noted expert on celibacy, relates that when one bishop was asked on the record why the American episcopate was having such a hard time with the problem, the man repeatedly and emphatically responded, "Undoubtedly part of the problem is that some of the bishops are, themselves, abusers."[16]

Events have sadly borne this out. As will be shown, this correlation is particularly apparent in the case of one the first prelates to resign in disgrace, none other than the archbishop of Santa Fe. But he is far from being alone. As of this writing, Robert Sanchez has been joined by over 19 American bishops and even a cardinal who have been accused of the sexual abuse of minors or its concealment.[17]

But the cover-up is even more extensive than that. As testimonies have consistently revealed, time after time bishops assuaged outraged parents with exactly what they wanted to hear. They pledged that the priests would be taken care of, perhaps never be allowed around children again. Coast to coast, decade upon decade, and the same script was soothingly repeated countless times that the offending priest would be given treatment.

This is such a frequent refrain that it is easy to imagine that the bishops were all reading from the same playbook. Perhaps they were. Though no written policy, official or otherwise, has ever surfaced, the uniformity of complaints and language is highly suspicious. If the bishops did know all about the problem then, it is totally incomprehensible how so many could claim, repeatedly, that they did not – unless, perhaps, the policy itself was so highly secret that lying in its defense was justified by the Vatican.

If that is the case, it seems likely that the legal counsel for the NCCB at the time, an attorney named Mark Chopko, had a hand in it. In his dismissive response to *The Manual*, Chopko claimed that the bishops' council was already aware of everything in the report and had already taken "appropriate action," though what was never specified. The plan Doyle and his colleagues proposed was not deemed suitable and the lawyer criticized it as a moneymaking scheme.[18]

Whether or not the bishops had common directives or not, however, the result was often the same. Usually they shipped the offending clergy off somewhere else with no explanation or comment to the parishioners and no outreach to victims and their families.

That "somewhere else" depended greatly on the severity of complaints against the priest and the potential for scandal. Often another parish in a nearby town would suffice, in more extreme cases, another diocese or even country would be necessary. For the worst cases of all, somewhere else was still often a Church-run treatment center.

By the early 1980s, there were a growing number of these places. Some were administered by an order of priests called the "Servants of the Paraclete." The most important was their original monastery, a secluded motherhouse set in the distant mountains of New Mexico. It would become a major epicenter for the crisis to come.

CHAPTER IX:
A REFUGE IN THE OUTLANDS

Mountains of secrets

In the upper part of New Mexico, due north of the major city of Albuquerque and west of Los Alamos where the atomic bomb was born, sits a sleepy village. Jemez Springs lies scattered amid stands of cottonwood trees along the bottom of a picturesque ochre-walled canyon cleaving the southern ramparts of majestic, pine-clad mountains.

This little all-American town is charming, with a small park and playground, a single bar but not even a gas station. Today, it's more a touristy art colony than anything else. Nowadays, the town also boasts a Zen Buddhist meditation center. Blessed with volcanically heated baths, impressive ruins, and inspiring canyon vistas, the village mainly serves as a major entrance to the Jemez Mountains.

The Jemez range, formed out of the now-slumbering remains of North America's largest supervolcanic crater, has long given refuge to those with explosive secrets. The mountains, with the immense grassy Valle Grande in their center – now a national preserve – and especially the great dome of Redondo Peak looming over all, remain sacred to the Pueblo Indians.

Centuries before the white man arrived, the Native Americans built towns around and in the mountains, complete with sacred semi-underground ceremonial chambers called kivas for their own secret religious ceremonies. They concealed powerful spiritual objects in mountain caves; some so important legal battles have been fought over them. Carved sacred figures, the legendary stone lions of Bandelier, for instance, were so holy they were re-hidden in the mountains by helicopter in modern times.[1]

Originally, Jemez Springs was the small pueblo of Giusewa, one of several inhabited by the Jemez people. The Franciscans started a mission there, San José de los Jémez, in the 1620s. A huge church with 8-foot-thick walls of fieldstone was constructed but later burned. Now a state monument, its massive walls and octagonal bell tower still brood over the town, an enduring reminder of both the power and limits of faith.

In the early 1940s, Dr. Robert Oppenheimer visited a boys school on the opposite side of the mountains from Jemez Springs. Los Alamos became the site of the greatest and most secretive operation of the entire Second World War, the Manhattan Project, which developed the first nuclear weapons. An entire hidden city quickly sprang up on pine-covered plateaus extending out towards the Rio Grande. Only a single guard tower remains from that era, but its culture of secrecy still largely endures, complete with concealing conifers screening the city's streets.

But the mountains shielded other visitors also wanting to avoid attention, too. Before Oppenheimer came, they had already served as an occasional vacation spot hideaway for none other than the infamous mobster, Al Capone.[2] Then at the end of 1946, half a year before something strange fell from the sky down south near Roswell, a Catholic priest arrived in Jemez Springs from back East. Like Oppenheimer, Father Gerald M. C. Fitzgerald was on a mission. He, too, sought an isolated location with just the right facilities to launch his own secret project.

What Fitzgerald established in Jemez Canyon would be an abbey unlike any other. It would become a covert laboratory of the spirit. In a way, the holy monastery in the valley was like a strange reflection of the unholy atomic workshop on the hill across the mountains. For just as in Los Alamos, though of course in a different form entirely, dangerous clandestine experiments would take place. Little thought would be given of their widespread toxic and irrevocable consequences. Powerful forces would be unleashed that would change the world.

The Archbishop of Santa Fe, Edwin Byrne, had generously offered several potential sites. Fitzgerald was given a choice between a run-down monastery in the mountains near Pecos, east of Santa Fe, or an old tourist hotel in Jemez Springs, to the west. He instantly chose the Jemez Inn, and on January 5, 1947, celebrated his first Mass there.

Rumors to this day persist that the hotel itself was actually owned by Capone, who died less than three weeks later. Supposedly, it was given to the Church in exchange for allowing the Chicago gangster a Christian burial in a Catholic cemetery. It's also said that Fitzgerald had to clean a massive amount of filthy pictures, liquor, and gambling equipment out of the place before he could use it.[3]

Was this an omen of the corruption that would eventually spoil his ambitious enterprise? In any case, the deal would prove to be a Devil's bargain for all concerned. In due course, there would be Hell to pay.

A prophet for priests

Fitzgerald's order was to be called the "Servants of the Paraclete" – "*paraclete*" being a Greek term for the Holy Spirit as Consoler and Comforter.

It was not a bad choice. The order's compassionate mission was to care for, and if possible, rehabilitate alcoholic priests, and they would be aided by an order of nuns, too.

Pious legend already building about the man states that helping fallen priests had long been Fitzgerald's dream. One chilly night during the Depression while still a parish priest, he gave a beggar some food and a coat at his Boston rectory. As the man disappeared back into the darkness, he acknowledged that he, too, had once been a priest.[4]

The incident left a powerful impression on Fitzgerald, one that stayed with him ever after.

A classmate of the future Cardinal Cushing, Fitzgerald was ordained alongside him in 1921, worked as a parish priest for a dozen years before joining the Congregation of the Holy Cross, and became rector of their seminary. During the war, at the age of 48, he had volunteered to become an Army chaplain and served as secretary to head of the Catholic chaplains' corps, Cardinal Francis Spellman.[5]

Spellman had already approved Fitzgerald's first book of inspirational letters before the war, even writing a brief note of introduction. It's not known how deep the priest's friendship was with either cardinal; however, having the ear of several of the most powerful men in the American Catholic hierarchy certainly couldn't have hurt. Spellman even charitably gave him $25,000 in seed money to start his new ministry.[6]

After the war, Fitzgerald began to actively pursue his new calling. The timing was right. Though few negative stories had been allowed into the news media during the global conflict, the Church hierarchy had been deeply shocked by the wartime conduct of some priests. Thousands had been involved in the conflict on both sides as chaplains, as leaders, and sometimes even as combatants.

The stresses of war had greatly increased the number of clerics facing serious psychological problems. Since priests were required to drink wine as part of their daily Mass and lived generally solitary lives, alcoholism proved to be a widespread and persistent difficulty. Homosexuality fostered by the masculine environment of the military also was a big concern.

Yet, since clerics claim a right to support, the institutional Church was obligated to take care of them, no matter what. And with so much time and money invested in their training, the hierarchy was eager to get as many drunken clerics sobered up and back on the job as possible.

Even before the war was over, Fitzgerald wrote to Cushing and Spellman about a mission to help old chaplains and other priests, especially those in spiritual difficulties. Spellman invited him to start work in his diocese, but Fitzgerald went back to the Holy Cross Fathers in Boston when he was released from the military.

Instead, with the pope's blessing, letters were sent out to bishops around the world.[7] Fitzgerald traveled extensively the next year seeking an isolated place to begin his work. But the only bishop anywhere to respond to Fitzgerald's inquiries with an offer to help was Archbishop Edwin Byrne of Santa Fe. Fitzgerald jumped at the chance.

The two men shared many of the same ideals, and Byrne agreed that the place would be used as a retreat house with "purely spiritual activities."[8] In thanks, Fitzgerald often referred to his superior as his friend and co-founder of the order.

New Mexico was, as Oppenheimer had doubtless earlier noted, sparsely populated with vast tracts of unoccupied land that made it ideal to hide large projects. Yet, being crossed by a major transcontinental railroad, the state enjoyed relatively easy access to the population centers of the coasts.

Of particular importance to Fitzgerald's scheme was that its inhabitants was largely Catholic, although many were poor and uneducated. It seemed like an ideal match. He probably had no clue whatsoever of just how diabolically perfect a fit it would be.

A Catholic backwater

There is but one basic reason why New Mexico was such a superlative site for Fitzgerald's vision to become real. It's probably also why the danger took so long to be recognized once those plans went wrong.

This reason shaped the intertwined and complex secular and religious history of the region. The simple fact is that New Mexico has always been in the remotest outlands of empire. Though established a decade before the Pilgrims landed in New England, the tiny, insecure colony formed the furthest thrust into North America of New Spain.

This seclusion had a number of effects. Primarily it resulted in a culture that, though mainly Catholic, has a surprising tolerance of religious secrets. People here are still remarkably unquestioning of diverse, even forbidden, private spiritual practices – and with good reason.

For in New Mexico, unlike most of the country, the Spanish Inquisition had been active for centuries in all its ruthlessness. Yet, somehow, the native population openly retained much of their ancient pagan religions. Both Jews and heretics, possibly even witches, also somehow survived.

To this day, New Mexico's isolation and indifference has made it attractive to sects of all kinds. Renegade Mormons, Bible-shaking fundamentalists, occultists of various flavors, even the suicidal Heaven's Gate cult have all hidden out here at one time or another. Every year or so, it seems, another one comes to notice. The latest would-be Messiah, Wayne Bent, was tried and convicted for lying naked with two female teen devotees in a supposed religious rite even as this was written.[9]

But Catholicism has been the central faith in New Mexico ever since the first Europeans arrived. In fact, the salvation of souls was the primary excuse employed by the Spanish for colonization. Nowhere else in the United States has the Catholic Church enjoyed such a long, profound presence, lasting influence – or suffered such numbers of bad priests. And not just in modern times, either.

Long a mission territory, for centuries the New Mexican people have been continually desperate for more ministers of grace. The missionaries included both saints and sinners, and great power and freedom encouraged both. Life on the frontier made all laws optional depending on the closeness of authority, an attitude still frequently found among residents today.

The Church feuded with the State from the very beginning, and won more times than it lost. Even today, the Roman Church retains the unrivaled dominance in local culture and politics that it has enjoyed since colonial days. The invasion by the Anglos (as all European Americans are usually called) in the mid-nineteenth century did little to overturn that balance.

The centuries have seen a cavalcade of colorful Christians and miraculous tales, too. There was the mysterious "Blue Lady" whose visionary visitations from her convent in Spain supposedly helped convert the heathen Indians of the eastern plains. A learned wandering hermit, Juan Maria de Agostini, lent his name to Hermit's Peak, which looms over the town of Las Vegas (not to be confused with its more famous namesake in Nevada), where he lived for a while in a cave. A chapel in Santa Fe boasts a wooden spiral staircase legendarily crafted by Saint Joseph. And divine vengeance in the form of a fatal bear attack ends one widely published cautionary true tale from colonial days about the price for mocking clergy.

Probably most important touchstone of devotion remains the living shrine at Chimayó, where there is an ancient sacred hole in the ground. From it, hundreds if not thousands of the faithful make a long pilgrimage on foot every year during Holy Week to draw forth healing dirt. A room full of crutches and votive folk objects testify to the abiding power of their faith.

Missions for pope and king

The Church has always vigorously defended its missionary efforts among the Indians. The second archbishop of Santa Fe wrote, "The Catholic religion was not forced on the Indians. The first step to be made by the missionary... was to introduce himself, cross in hand, and to explain as well as he could, the meaning of this sign. The priest alone in the tribes, and far from the soldiers, was, as a rule, received... by people eager to catch the ideas he tried to convey to them."

Not knowing the language, the padre had to use other means to teach. "First of all, the naked cross was planted... before it knelt the missionary, crossing himself... and inviting the persons around to do the same." He would then use pictures and sing prayers to introduce them to the faith.[10]

A pretty picture, but there was quite a bit more to it. After the initial Spanish beachhead was secured in Mexico, friars were indeed sent in pairs, alone and unarmed, on initial scouting missions into the wild unknown beyond the frontiers. It was cheap and "it was known that religious, with their poor habit, and with crucifix in hand, could penetrate everywhere, better than soldiers with war apparatus."[11] However, they went first not as evangelists but rather as spies.

Missionaries rarely established formal contact with native tribes without the full backing of a Spanish military detachment. The bearded Europeans in their shining plate armor, mounted on equally-armored warhorses, came equipped with plumes and banners and above all with steel swords, lances, and guns. Large retinues of Indian slaves and allies, and long wagon trains pulled by mules or oxen accompanied them.

The conquistadors completely overawed the natives. Theirs was a display as literally out of the Indians' world as an invasion by space aliens would be. The tribes' initial shows of resistance, if they dared to offer any, were usually easily overcome.

The soldiers entered as swaggering subjugators, supremely confident of their superiority in all things. The conquistadors were motivated by a modern extension of the crusading spirit; noble ideals mixed with brutal avarice. But their victories were not as much for the Spanish crown as the pope. Religious zeal was not merely a rationalization, but their entire justification.

The Spaniards would erect a cross first, rather than plant the banner of their king. This demonstrated that the land now belonged primarily to Christ. As the cross is also a sacred symbol in many Native American religions, including that of the curious Pueblo Indians, this probably did not alarm them. It likely reminded the Indians of the ornamented prayer sticks they themselves used. Indeed, friars wrote touching reports of simple natives decorating the recently raised crosses with flowers and feathers.

Then the situation got serious. A document would be read aloud to the doubtless now puzzled aborigines. The *requerimiento* related how God the Creator had delegated his authority on Earth to the pope, that "Admirable Great Father and Governor of Men." The pope, they were informed, in turn had given the Americas along with the native peoples to the king of Spain.

Thus, natives must first acknowledge the sovereignty of the Church as "ruler and superior of the world, " followed by the pope, and finally by the king. They must consent to have the faith preached to them, but they would not be compelled to turn Christian. Their conversion, however, would be rewarded with certain privileges and exemptions.

If they refused, it concluded, the Spanish would make war on them, and "shall subject you to the yoke and obedience of the Church and of their highnesses." Their wives and children would be enslaved, goods plundered, and disobedience severely punished.[12]

The conquistadors meant exactly what they said and ruthlessly proved it, too. It's little wonder that so many friars they left behind paid the price with their blood. Of the 239 Franciscan missionaries counted by the aforementioned archbishop during the colonial period, the Indians killed 32.[13]

During the first Pueblo Revolt, 21 clerics died on a single day and the Archdiocese of Santa Fe later boasted of 50 martyrs in full.[14] Oddly enough, just as the total number of missionaries is a little less than the number of priests employed by the archdiocese just before the sex scandals, the number of martyrs exactly equals those later accused.

Conquest and "pacification"

New Mexico is generally a stark, albeit beautiful, desert region. Pleasant valleys are watered by summer thunderstorms and the melting snowfall from distant blue-hued mountains scattered on every horizon. Portions of it even reminded nostalgic invaders of their distant homelands around Seville.

But it was far from empty. Relations with the inhabitants would be crucial from the start, barely a generation after the fall of Mexico. One of the first regions of the future United States to be invaded by Europeans, in 1540, Francisco de Coronado brought friars with him on the first military scouting expedition to the far north seeking a "new Mexico."

He dreamt of the legendary "seven cities of Cibola" covered in gold that had been supposedly founded long before by Portuguese bishops fleeing the Muslims. But if not other Christians, the conquistador at least hoped to find another native realm of wealth and sophistication like that of the Aztecs they had so recently seized. He and many others would be sorely disappointed.

It wasn't just the soldiers. Franciscan missionaries came along to provide guidance and morale. Early comers to the New World, they soon shut out their old rivals, the Dominicans, out of many mission territories, including New Mexico. Their new rivals, the Jesuits, who would create a virtual theocratic kingdom in the wilderness of South America, would be confined to Sonora and Arizona in the north.

But the popes had granted religious orders the right to minister to the faithful as well as Indian converts. The first governor, Don Juan de Oñate, in his initial act establishing the colony, confirmed the Franciscans' total monopoly on religion. He gave them sole jurisdiction over the missions forever. The friars would repay this generous concession by constantly fighting against any efforts to rein them in thereafter.

The gray-robed missionaries, drawn by the prospect of winning souls for Christ, soon had their first martyrs. The first priest certainly murdered within the future state was Juan de Santa María. In 1581, he was returning to old Mexico to fetch more friars when locals killed him while he slept by dropping a rock on him. Tellingly, this ignominious method of execution was one the natives reserved especially for evil sorcerers.[15] He would not be the only Catholic cleric so dispatched.

The Spaniards had entered a land populated by around 100 sovereign city-states speaking at least eight different languages.[16] However, they were not technologically highly advanced. The Indians used pictographic signs but true writing was unknown, along with the use of draft animals and most metals. The only gold to be had, the disillusioned invaders soon discovered, was the yellow corn the Indians grew.

Still, that was enough. The Indians' humble, compact, yet largely unfortified earthen villages, the pueblos, were quite poor compared with the majestic carved pyramids and floating gardens of metropolitan Tenochtitlan far away to the south. But the people at least wore clothes and farmed. They were civilized enough to be taxed for maize, beans, nuts, blankets, and especially the tanned hides which served almost as cash.

The demand for these goods and especially the labor of the Indians would repeatedly set secular and civil officials against each other, sometimes even physically. Governors would be excommunicated and friars arrested. On several occasions, it led to a virtual civil war among the invaders while the pueblos watched and waited, biding their time. Ultimately the conflict between Church and State helped create the greatest disaster of all, a successful native rebellion.

Land of disenchantment

Serious colonization of New Mexico began in 1598. Under Don Juan de Oñate y Salazar, the Spanish took over with their usual efficient brutality much as they had their earlier colonies. Once firmly established, early growth was rapid. By 1617, a dozen years after the founding of the capitol of Santa Fe, there were already eleven churches.[17]

But Oñate's oppressive rule proved disastrous. Even most of the missionaries abandoned their posts. Their leader, Juan de Escalona, begged the viceroy in Mexico for help. He wrote, "we cannot preach the Gospel now, for it is despised by these people on account of our great offenses and the harm we have done them." [18] That initial damage, compounded repeatedly, has not been forgotten or forgiven even to this day.

The purpose of "pacifying" the land was to spread the faith. Perhaps as few as 60 to 600 or so Indians had been baptized. The viceroy in turn begged the king not to abandon the enterprise. Even if there was but "one lone Christian," they were obliged to save him.

What saved the faltering enterprise was a lie by a religious, perhaps the first, but definitely not the last that would ever be uttered by a churchman about New Mexico. An enterprising friar just returned from the colony, Lázaro Jiménez, gave the viceroy just what he needed by suddenly asserting there were actually 7,000 baptized natives.[19]

Doubtless, this was a huge exaggeration, but the pious claim saved face for everyone involved. And so, the colony was not given up but reinforced with royal status. The Franciscans were also regulated but always sorely undermanned, and their numbers diminished over time.

Despite any dark pasts, the padres suddenly found themselves with great prestige in their new home. In the new land, they served not just the ministers to the faithful, but were the sole teachers and among the few colonists who could read and write. Moreover, the mission system gave them unparalleled authority over the natives.

The friars ran their missions as landed estates, built and maintained by the local population as payment for the "enlightenment" they brought. They often could command the labor of their reluctant disciples without pay. The Franciscans (now wearing blue in honor of the Virgin) were often accused of gouging Indians and colonists alike for their services.

The missionaries were kept busy with teaching, building, and the sacraments. As newcomers to the faith, the Indians were exempt from the Inquisition, but the missionaries were empowered to administer punishments that were almost as cruel. However well meaning they were, the Franciscans rarely succeeded in truly converting the natives.

Starting with very harsh policies in the beginning, such as filling in kivas with refuse and burning the sacred kachina masks, the missionaries slowly became more tolerant. They were repeatedly criticized for never learned the Indian's languages, however, or even successfully teaching the natives Spanish. Natives, it was said, only confessed on their deathbeds – if then – as they could only talk through interpreters.

This was probably not entirely the priests' fault. They complained of often being transferred before they could grasp the local tongue. Moreover, it seems that the Indians were as reluctant then as they remain today about handing over the master key to their culture to outsiders.

The chief Franciscan, the "*custos*," or custodian, clashed with the governor almost instantly over who had more right to exploit the Indians. Though later fights were largely due to the rapacious greed of tyrannical and corrupt officials, a friar started the first. Isidore Ordóñez, ambitious and arrogant, actually forged letters making him the custodian. He even had the governor arrested by the Inquisition, accused of being a secret Jew. The priest then ruled the colony for years as a theocratic despot, excommunicating anyone who disagreed with him. It was a very bad precedent.

Likewise, the Inquisition also ruined a later governor's term of office. Diego de Peñalosa was humiliated by being forced to appear as a penitent in the *auto da fé* of 1668, for "indiscreet words about priests and inquisitors and expressions verging on blasphemy."[20]

The friars used the Inquisition at first chiefly as a weapon against the governors in their feuds. Later, however, it would occasionally be turned back against them with charges of solicitation in the confessional and other crimes once the Holy Office in Mexico City tired of their constant political intrigues.

But the Inquisition took awhile to take root. On January 25, 1625, the Edict of Faith was read for the first time in Santa Fe. Its minions pursued the other usual suspects, such as petty sorcerers, gamblers, and even bigamists, of which there were a surprising number on the frontier.

It even affected geographical names. One of their victims, a German by the name of Bernardo Gruber, was arrested for writing charms on paper to make a person immune to bullets and selling them to the Indians. After waiting in jail for over two years for a decision, he escaped.

Gruber's murdered remains were later found in the barren desert far to the south near Socorro, in a desolate shortcut named thereafter in his honor: the "*Jornada del Muerto*," or "Journey of the Dead." The name proved ominously prophetic, as it was there in 1945 that the first atomic bomb built in Los Alamos was exploded at a spot called Trinity Site.

Revolt and Reconquest

Isolation also made the colony vulnerable to revolt. Native resistance, evident from the first forays, steadily grew. Apache raids further complicated years of drought and famine. Their attacks began, however, as revenge for Spanish slaving expeditions on the plains. Trainable Indian youths, Pueblo or nomad, Christian or heathen, were prime commodities throughout much of the colonial period. Governor Vargas, who reestablished the colony, even curried favor with the Franciscan custodian by promising him the best of the boys.[21]

Pressed to the limit by famine, sickness, and oppression, the Pueblos finally launched the only successful revolt against a colonizing power that ever took place within the future territory of the United States. Under a native tactical genius, a shaman called Popé, the tribes managed to secretly organize themselves despite informers, traditional hatreds, and language barriers to accomplish this unparalleled feat.

The missions provided a prime target for the Indians, and indeed, fortified churches served as refuge for the surprised and beleaguered colonists. The Indians brutally massacred every Franciscan missionary they could seize, often piling their corpses inside the desecrated churches. The aged Juan de Jesús, the friar stationed among the Jemez, was stripped and ridden like a mock horse before being killed.[22] The Jemez, who had been badly treated by Ordóñez, were in fact major participants in the Revolt. They would also be deeply involved in later resistance.

The friars left behind tales of lost or buried church treasures in their wake. Many of the missions were burned, the hated bells that had called the Indians to pray and labor smashed to pieces. Over half the clergy were martyred along with nearly 380 other colonists slain.[23]

Desperate colonists beat off the siege of Santa Fe. Survivors were allowed to depart the devastated colony for El Paso. But the Pueblos' victory was seemingly for naught. The Spanish returned a mere dozen years later, virtually unopposed. Once again, the Catholic monarch could not in good conscience abandon Christian Indians left behind. There were also imperial fears of the French coming in from Louisiana to fill the void.

The natives had fallen out in the meantime. So, the celebrated Reconquest under Don Diego de Vargas was bloodless, although the resettlement period that followed was not. The initial success was in large part due to the governor's personal courage and wise policy of moderation. His shows of good faith paid off during a second rebellion in 1696. Though 21 colonists died this time, it failed due to warnings and support given by Indian allies. Five missionaries were murdered, however, including the one at Jemez Pueblo, who was called out to confess a dying person and clubbed to death.[24]

Failure of the missions

A somewhat more moderate arrangement was worked out after the Reconquest. In time, Pueblo and Hispanic villagers traded with each other, occasionally intermarried, and above all made common cause. Repeated epidemics and raiding Comanches and Apaches, now armed with guns on horseback, forced them to work together for their common survival.

Friars and governors still quarreled, but somewhat more reasonably. The missionaries' importance waned once their wagon trains were no longer the sole lifeblood of the colony. In the middle of the eighteenth century, the bishop of Durango even visited on several occasions. The friars opposed his authority and prevented him from inspecting the missions at first, for good reason. The bishops were shocked and highly disappointed by the Franciscans' greed and failure to instruct the Indians.

Their blunt criticism led the Franciscans to inspect themselves with an even more damning critique. Out of 29 friars, Atanasio Domínguez, one of the first Europeans to visit the Grand Canyon, wrote in 1776 that eight were ill, old, or blind, two were drunks, one was living openly with a woman, and five were scandalously trading or getting into trouble with the Indians. Only thirteen padres, less than half of the overextended missionaries, it seemed, were living blamelessly.[25]

The bishop sent a vicar to Santa Fe, the first secular clergy in the territory. He even went so far as to have a list of fair prices for marriages and funerals and other services posted in the capitol but it was soon ignored. But henceforth, the power of the friars would inevitably decline.

After the Revolt, the Franciscans were grudgingly accepted again into the pueblos, carefully watched, and limited by the elders. Women cooks were expressly forbidden in the missions. Missionaries remained a mixed bag, however, as the history of one locale in particular vividly demonstrates.

The important pueblo of Pecos was a rich trading center a day or so east of Santa Fe. It was the gateway to the Great Plains. Through the colonial period, however, Pecos slowly declined and was finally abandoned by the American conquest. But it thereby later became one of the most well-studied and documented missions of all, both textually and archeologically.

Of the one hundred Franciscans associated with Pecos during two centuries, several were agents of the Inquisition but another wrote a satire that outraged the whole colony. Two were accused of soliciting sex and two others were notorious drunkards. One friar who also fought witches in Abiquiu, Juan José Toledo, was himself denounced to the Inquisition for saying that fornication was no sin. The governor charged another one for abusing the Indians. At least eight died violently.[26]

But the real amount of sexual and other abuse in the missions through the centuries remains unknown and unmentioned, to outsiders, at least. Though the tribes doubtlessly watched the missionaries carefully, their power and isolation certainly provided some opportunities for mischief.

A few must have been exceptionally outrageous. Resentment among the Hopi Indians, for example, stayed so strong it manifested itself in myth. One of their sacred protective powers is known as Yowé, the Priest-Killer. Like all kachinas, he is shown as a masked and feathered dancer. Uniquely, however, he often carries a cross and a bloody knife, or sometimes a severed head.

The story was that the priest stationed at the Hopi town of Oraibi in what is now Arizona had stolen the kachina's girlfriend. Bloody revenge had been taken during the Pueblo Revolt. Yowé killed the priest and grabbed at the girl but only succeeded in tearing off an earring, which he often wears.[27] The exact historic basis of this legend is unknown, but curiously, an apocryphal story about José de Espelta, the actual missionary at Oraibi at the time of the uprising, says that he was not immediately martyred. Rather he was kept alive for years as a slave, a reviled object of mockery and abuse.[28]

Save for Oraibi, all the Hopi towns had given the token submission demanded by Vargas. But the Hopis even annihilated one of their own villages, Awátovi, after the people there consented to allow the Franciscans to return. And so, of all the pueblos, only those of Hopi have no missions.

Such figurines and stories were doubtless pointed warnings that missionaries ignored at their peril. However, the silence that was finally shattered in the Anglo and Hispanic communities during the scandals of the 1990s remains unbroken to this day among the Pueblo Indians, Apaches, and Navajos. They have learned to keep their own secrets. Who knows what sleeping serpents might yet stir within their tight little communities from such disclosures?

In Canada, lawsuits brought against the churches and the government over horrific and virtually genocidal abuses of native peoples in the residential school system have bankrupted one Catholic order and threatened the entire Catholic and Anglican churches there. But as far as is known, no tribal members anywhere in the American Southwest have ever filed a single clergy abuse lawsuit.

In any event, relations between the Pueblo Indians and the Church were substantially different after the revolts. The friars were much more careful not to antagonize their charges too much. Where they had previously built bonfires of kachina masks, they now protested the government's efforts to do the same, disarm the pueblos, and make them conform. They wisely pointed out, for instance, that the governor could hardly forbid Indians from wearing paint and feathers to church when Spaniards wore them, also.[29]

To prevent further violence, the humbled missionaries even encouraged the traditional dances after the government banned them. Thus, the friars essentially gave up. The Indians had successfully preserved much of their old ways under the cover of the veneration of saints and literally underground in the kivas. Now they could practice their traditional religion as openly or privately as they wished, to the delight of those future anthropologists, artists, and tourists privileged to witness.

The Indians weren't the only group who kept a contrary faith alive despite the Church, either.

Secret witches and hidden Jews

New Mexico was just about as far away from the authorities, royal and religious, as one could get. Various groups came to the frontier to do just that. Among them were likely a few secret Lutherans, boatloads of bigamists, and maybe even some *brujas*, "witches."

Though the Spanish Inquisition generally regarded witchcraft as superstition, a genuine witch panic brought in from France did infect northern Spain in 1610, complete with mass burnings. The Inquisition called for a crusade, but indecisively hesitated before launching it. After receiving the skeptical report of the friar assigned to handle confessions, however, prosecutions for witchery in Spain all but ceased.[30]

But half a century after the English colonists in New England suffered witchcraft trials, so too did the Hispanic colonists of New Mexico. The Franciscan priest, Juan José Toledo, who got into trouble on his own with the Inquisition, launched trials lasting a decade. He believed a group of Indians living in the area of Abiquiu had bewitched him and made him sick.[31]

It's impossible to know how many practitioners of herbalism or other occult arts fled Spain or where they went. However, though there had been no reaction the first time, inquisitors carefully noted popular consternation over the condemnation of charms and powders when the Edict of Faith was read again in Santa Fe in 1631.[32] Whatever the case, a lively *curandera* folk-healing tradition based on herbs still flourishes in the state.

Another group still living secretly are the crypto-Jews. Descendants of Muslims and Jews were forbidden in Spain's colonies, so many *"marranos"* – a derisive term for the descendents of the converts or *"conversos"* from the word for "pig" – illegally came to the colony in disguise.

The very first attempt to settle in 1590 was unlawful and also quite irregular: tellingly, they brought no priests with them.[33] Gaspar Castaño de Sosa, the leader, as well as most of the settlers, were likely on the run from the Mexican Inquisition.

He was lieutenant to the governor of Nuevo León, where the Inquisition had located a hotbed of *marranos* not long before. It started when Luis de Carvajal the Younger, a nephew of the governor, rediscovered his Judaic roots. He lived openly as a Jew and also enthusiastically attempted to spread his ancestral faith among other *conversos*. The governor was arrested and died in his cell. Carvajal himself was tried and burned with great ceremony in an *auto da fé* in Mexico City on December 8, 1596. The affair shocked the colonies.

Those of Jewish descent who fled to New Mexico often bore names such as Salazar and Rael, which are still quite common today.[34] Many remain in hiding. Perhaps 1,500 still pretend to be Christians, mainly Catholics, in the state while secretly carrying on Jewish practices. One scholar believes some may yet meet in their own clandestine synagogues, completely isolated from the mainstream Jewish community that came in with the Anglos.[35]

Some crypto-Jews changed their cover religion to Protestant, especially Seventh Day Adventist, during the last century. Other families have entirely forgotten their origins. The rest remain mainly in the villages of northern New Mexico, privately practicing their inherited religion just like their Indian and Penitente neighbors.

Brothers of light and darkness

As early as 1630, one missionary who had established nearly a dozen churches returned to Spain to plead hopefully for Santa Fe to become the seat of a diocese. But it was to no avail.[35] As Spanish colony, Mexican province, or American territory, the region long remained an ecclesiastical backwater.

With the freedom of distance and great importance in their own vicinities, however, the few existing local clergy acquired fearsome reputations. Some padres, like Antonio José Martínez of Taos, a farmer, publisher, and influential politician as well as parish priest, were ruling as virtual lords when the Yankees came. Others also kept wives or mistresses with impunity.

With the revolt of Mexico from Spain, however, the Spanish-born Franciscans were thrown out. Since the new province had but a small handful of diocesan priests, the bloody sect of the Penitentes grew up to fill the spiritual void. This fraternal religious brotherhood seems to have evolved out of the Third Order of St. Francis, which Governor Vargas established after the Reconquest. Led by priests, it was intended for laymen to act as a sort of prayer auxiliary for the friars. But once re-organized by Martínez, they began to go their own way free from ecclesiastical oversight.

The Penitentes based their devotions on harsh medieval penitential practices. Their roots go back to the Flagellants who whipped themselves across Europe during the era of the Black Death. The Brotherhood meets in their own small private chapels called *moradas,* much like aboveground kivas. There, painfully masochistic rituals led by their own hierarchy keep a gory version of the faith alive, well illustrated in the crude folk renditions of the bleeding savior by the *santeros*.

On certain rocky hillsides on Good Friday, Jesus' own ordeal would be relived by specially chosen members, sometimes even down to the Crucifixion itself. It is believed the last using nails happened nearly a century ago, although there some have been reported since.[37]

For a long time, the official Church condemned the Penitentes as heretics. The second archbishop, John Baptist Salpointe, in particular fought them, forbidding clergy to say Mass in their chapels or administer the sacraments to any whom publicly flogged themselves or carried a cross. This only led to deeper secrecy but their bloody devotions had to be tolerated in practice, as there were few priests available to fill the void.

In 1947, Archbishop Byrne formally recognized the Brotherhood, claimed the Church had absolute authority over it, and even appointed a Penitente Pope of sorts, the *Hermano Supremo*. By 1960, there were an estimated 2,000 to 3,000 brothers organized in 9 districts with 135 *moradas*.[38]

Finally in the 1970s, during the reign of the first native Hispanic New Mexican archbishop, Robert Sanchez, the Penitentes were fully accepted when he joined in public processions with them. Their violence has virtually disappeared, at least in public. However, there is little doubt that in some of remote backwoods towns in areas like the Sangre de Cristos – the "Blood of Christ" Mountains north of Santa Fe – the ancient self-discipline is still administered.

A bishop in Santa Fe

In any case, the Santa Fe Trail, and later, the Yankee invasion which took Santa Fe almost 166 years to the day since the Pueblo Revolt, brought New Mexico into the American empire. There it would remain despite a failed revolt a year later in Taos. In 1850, Pope Pius IX declared New Mexico prime mission territory, and sent a French bishop, Jean Baptiste Lamy, as his apostolic vicar to straighten things out. He was named Bishop of Santa Fe, the city of Holy Faith, and his name, like his successor's would be, was Anglicized.

Originally, the Diocese of Santa Fe also included the area of Utah, Colorado, and Arizona, which further stretched the new bishop's scant resources. In time, those regions would be split off and further divided, along with the western and southern parts of the state. Santa Fe, by being the "mother" ultimately to seven other dioceses, thus became an archdiocese in 1875, with Lamy as the first archbishop.

But he and the other French clergy found little to admire in their new territories, including the native adobe mission style. These primitive churches, built from mud and decorated with crude local copies of baroque devotional art, would be treasured by later generations and exalted by architects like John Gaw Meem, photographers including Ansel Adams, and painters like Georgia O'Keefe – but not by Archibishop Lamy.

Instead, he began building a sandstone Romanesque-style cathedral in honor of St. Francis. Interestingly, the Tetragrammaton, the sacred name of God in Hebrew, was carved discreetly above the front entrance, framed within a triangle. Commonly thought to be an acknowledgement of the contributions of the Jewish merchants of Santa Fe, supposedly that story has no basis in reality.[39] Though it is a common enough Christian symbol, considering the many crypto-Jews in the territory, its appearance in such a prominent spot is curious, like a subtle gesture of recognition.

The archbishop did not get on with everybody, though. He struggled for power with Padre Martínez, excommunicating him without much effect. Horrified by the Penitentes, he strove to limit the excesses of their zeal and reestablish ecclesiastical supervision. Lamy's companion and immediate successor, Salpointe, thought it had become unrecognizable. They were groups of "simple credulous men, under the guidance of some unscrupulous politicians" who used them chiefly for political ends.[40]

Archbishop Lamy faced as great a challenge as any churchman had since the founding of New Mexico. "In a population of 70,000… there are fifteen priests, and six of these are worn out by age and have no energy. The others have not a spark of zeal, and their lives are scandalous beyond description," another of his companions wrote in 1851.[41]

The pathetic spiritual state of the land by that time was well recognized and recalled in later fiction. In Willa Cather's classic novel based on Lamy's life, *Death Comes for the Archbishop*, one missionary oracularly sums up the stakes at the time of the American conquest:

> *This country was evangelized in fifteen hundred, by the Franciscan Fathers. It has been allowed to drift for nearly three hundred years and is still not yet dead. It still pitifully calls itself a Catholic country, and tries to keep the forms of religion without instruction. The old mission churches are in ruins. The few priests are without guidance or discipline. They are lax in religious observance, and some of them live in open concubinage. If this Augean stable is not cleansed… it will prejudice the interests of the Church in the whole of North America.*[42]

Lamy and his successors tackled this Herculean labor as best they could, but it seems it was too great. After several hundred years, corruption had deeply infected the region's culture. But the archbishops heroically recruited clergy and nuns from Europe and back East nonetheless, establishing churches and schools across the land.

The Franciscans, this time in the brown robes of a German branch of the order, finally returned to the Indian missions around 1900, bringing nuns to help teach. At Jemez Pueblo, they also served as postmaster and local bee-keepers. One friar would even become the sixth archbishop.

All that was insufficient. The people still cried out for Catholic priests, any priests, and few questions would be asked. So it was to New Mexico that Gerald Fitzgerald came, to accept the only offer he had received from any bishop anywhere.

He unknowingly arrived in a land steeped in ages of Catholic power, religious violence, and stubborn independence. It was an ancient place fully accepting of both sacred mysteries and dissolute priests. A ratline of clergy with dark secrets would silently snake behind in his footsteps to take full advantage of the waiting opportunities. They would be welcomed also.

It was a match surely made in Hades.

Fitzgerald only sought to provide relief and refuge for those troubled shepherds. What ultimately happened was never intended at the start. Supposedly, providing a client with "psychosexual difficulties" for a ministry in the archdiocese or anywhere else as a "supply priest" was never anticipated at first, according to one of his successors.[43]

But such practices – along with actually recruiting some of their clients into the order itself – would have a toxic effect on the ministry. They would drag Fitzgerald's young order squarely into the very crosshairs of the controversy and permanently tarnish its reputation. Not to mention wrecking the lives of children, locally and elsewhere in the country in the meantime, thus contributing much to the greatest crisis in the modern Church.

Of course, none of that was Fitzgerald's aim. He prayed his endeavor would be a divine blessing to the people. But in time, powerful forces beyond his control would unravel his tight restrictions. His beloved spiritual sons, like so many idealistic orders before them, eventually became victims of their very success. Instead of a blessing, they would prove to be a curse.

CHAPTER X:
MINISTERS TO THE FALLEN

Mission of mercy

Fitzgerald must have liked what he found. He moved quickly, acquiring 2,000 prime acres at several sites along Jemez Canyon as well as the old hotel. In time, it would grow into a complete modern monastic complex. There would be a number of residences, a church, infirmary, even sports and other facilities.

Future leaders would set up a halfway house called Pius XII Villa (long since sold) in Albuquerque's South Valley, and other centers were established in St. Louis, Vermont, Minnesota, Ohio, and even in Italy, England, France, and other places, too.

Across the road from the ruined mission in Jemez Springs, Fitzgerald built an impressive motherhouse atop the remains of the old pueblo. Offices faced the road next to a large white church surmounted by a towering, abstract metal sculpture of Mary and the dove rather than a cross. Behind these, several rows of individually roomed dormitories stood. Next door, an equally spacious convent housed a sister order of burgundy-robed nuns with white veils, the "Handmaidens of the Precious Blood." The women were to support the priests by constant prayer, service, and sacrifice.

Once approved in April 1948, the male order wore a gray tunic, since simplified. A former novice said it was modeled on Confederate Army uniforms, complete with holsters for 15-decade rosaries due to Fitzgerald's affiliation with lost causes and the military. As head, he and his successors took the title of "Servant General," which apparently also played to those affectations. For according to the same source, he divided the order much like the Knights Templar had been into priestly "officers" and "enlisted" lay brothers, assigning various military ranks such as "Major" to his underlings depending on how they were doing to build up morale.[1]

His sense of chivalry and love of overblown martial metaphor was already evident in his devotional writings of the pre-war period with chapter titles such as "Under Fire." One typical piece, "Brother-In-Arms," like most, is addressed to a "Dear Brother in Christ." He calls him "a brother-in-arms in the Most Glorious of Causes," and talks of how they "sit at desks rather than bestride restless chargers, and wield frail pens *in lieu* of gleaming blades and beflagged lances," battling in the service of "the Leader, Our Captain," Christ.[2]

He played other verbal games besides writing pious purple prose, too. Fitzgerald liked giving places and things names of his own – the monastery itself was called "Via Coeli" – the "Way to Heaven," for instance. He often referred to Jemez Canyon as the "Canyon of the Blessed Sacrament." He took the name "Fr. Gerald of the Holy Spirit, s.P," the initials at the end indicating his new order.

The man was gifted with a poet's agile imagination and Irish blarney. It served him well, for he was also a tireless promoter, as he had to be. Fitzgerald regularly lobbied bishops and cardinals for money to continue and expand the operations, even treating them to guided tours of the facilities.[3] Articles were even placed in Catholic magazines. So there's no doubt that many bishops knew about his mission.

For a while, the Paracletes even ran a sponsorship program for individual priests. At one point, a novice posing as an order priest, would regularly send out begging letters and progress reports, and apparently played the part of a spiritual guru too well. He had to discontinue the effort when he was finally caught by an admiring mother superior.[4]

"Father Gerald," as the founder was usually called, was certainly an odd, intense character, like many saintly types. Strong mystical tendencies evidenced by his writings were coupled with an equally powerful determination to establish them in reality. Fitzgerald was practical enough to found two orders and win the support of the hierarchy. Yet, his impracticality with money apparently annoyed many of his brethren, threatening to drive the order into bankruptcy. It likely played a major factor in his downfall.

Indeed, the devout tales that began to accumulate around Fitzgerald even during his lifetime betray a compulsive charity. Often it went annoyingly beyond even the Gospel counsels. Early stories of his giving away his own and an extra suit belonging to his pastor without permission to bums during the Depression match later tales of donating food, clothes, and even land to local people in the Canyon who had helped him. Apparently, some of his followers considered this behavior almost pathological, and a definite threat to the order and its purpose.[5]

Not surprisingly, Fitzgerald's spirituality and approach was thoroughly, even radically, traditional. Not only believing passionately in the hierarchy of the Church as God's conduit, he also had great faith in free will and the unlimited power of prayer to change the souls of men.

He was confident that mere exposure to the divine radiance flowing from a displayed Host could have an effect on moral reform. So, Fitzgerald spent at least an hour a day in meditation in the chapel and required the same of all residents. His devotion to "Mary, Mother of Priests" was so deep that he named the place after her. He also said fifteen decades of the rosary daily, and strongly recommended the practice.[6]

Fitzgerald's attitude towards the priesthood can perhaps be described kindly as "medieval." He was an ardent, unashamed clericalist. His faith in the inherent power and dignity bestowed by Holy Orders was unshakeable – the real problem in the Church, he felt, was creeping secularism. "The priesthood is God's greatest gift to man," Fitzgerald proclaimed. "Its faithful fulfillment is man's greatest gift to God."[7] So glad was he to be a priest that he wrote that after every wedding he performed, he would slip behind the altar to privately kiss the tabernacle in gratitude for belonging solely to God.[8]

As his hagiographer put it, Fitzgerald believed priests were united in a "blood relationship of grace that has no human counterpart."[9] They were like chalices themselves which might become bent and tarnished when fallen into vice and despair but with time, grace, and tender care given by their brother priests could be repaired and restored to gleaming service.

This unshakable belief in the awesome power of the priesthood was based entirely upon the Eucharist. The special men who daily bring God down to Earth give hope and salvation to the world. They were not only themselves elevated by this wondrous work; they were an essential part of the Divine Plan. Therefore, Fitzgerald said in all seriousness that the soul of one priest was worth those of a thousand laymen to the Devil.[10]

The utter sincerity of his faith in this conviction is shown by the fact that the Servants of the Paraclete have never demonstrated any appreciable concern for victims of priest abuse. No apologies for their mistakes have ever been made. It appears from his letters that Fitzgerald may have privately worried about the children of the village, but even that seems to have been primarily with an eye to preventing talk.

Once the scandals actually enveloped them, the Paracletes fought vigorously against victims' lawsuits, blamed their seeming negligence on bad advice, and complained bitterly about how media misunderstanding had forced them to move their programs beyond the canyon. When they decided to settle, however, they did so quickly.

The motto Fitzgerald left his spiritual sons was "Every priest is my brother."[11] The Paracletes' mission has never wavered from charity to their comrades in trouble. This left many observers with the impression, not altogether erroneous, that they simply coddled abusive clergy. Fitzgerald was unwilling to throw anyone out, no matter how resistant they were to change.

He believed that priests whom fell did so chiefly out of pride. Disregarding their prayer lives and especially the Holy Eucharist caused them to neglect their ministry. Even if their flock never discovered their sins, the people would fall away as their shepherds' own faith ebbed.[12] Thus the problem was spiritual, demanding a spiritual solution.

Fitzgerald was determined to save their vocations by restoring their connection to God at almost any price. On one occasion at least, he even supposedly allowed himself to be beaten by an enraged resident without offering any defense or resistance.[13]

In any case, for Fitzgerald, keeping priestly secrets was all-important. As Jesus did not reveal Judas at the Last Supper although he knew of his imminent betrayal, and since a priest "can go to the altar in mortal sin and God will not betray him," so too, the Paracletes had to take great care with the "humiliating failures" of priests. It spared Christ embarrassing reminders, and would win the Servants divine mercy for their own sins, also.[14]

For what Fitzgerald's spiritual sons would do as soon as they put their father out of the way, mercy was what they would surely need.

A hidden sanctuary

From the outside, the gradual shift of Via Coeli from retreat and priestly prison to psychiatric treatment center went unnoticed even as more and more clerics were sent for help. And as clergy began to desert in droves after Vatican II, the Church became ever more anxious. The transition, however, was not without major internal conflict.

Alcoholics were the most important focus to begin with. Fitzgerald, however, privately derided the Alcoholics Anonymous program with its acceptance of the disease model of addiction. Believing firmly in the traditional concepts of sin, grace, and free will, he had little use for anything that diminished human responsibility.[15]

But later, when things changed after Vatican II, along with the first psychologist the order hired, his superiors authorized a 12-step program. Perhaps out of spite, Fitzgerald then ordered everyone to participate, alcoholics or not, order members and clients alike.[16]

The original program the Paracletes developed was strong on traditional spirituality and practices. It relied heavily on the ancient monastic disciplines of lots of group and private prayer, an assigned hour of Eucharistic contemplation each day, and spiritual direction. In the beginning, it was a retreat program where those undergoing the process were to contemplate their own failings and privately reform. If therapy was deemed necessary, priests were sent to hospitals and psychiatrists in Albuquerque on a contract basis. Only later were more aggressively challenging modern psychological treatments added to the course.

The Paraclete program included good old healthy exercise like hiking in the pinewoods, attention to diet, intellectual stimulation with arts and crafts, and so forth. The scheme was far removed from the punishing austerities of the "monasteries of strict observance." When all this was finally revealed, however, to many victims it seemed like the "guests" as they were called, were being given a treat for their sins, not "treatment."

Life at Via Coeli wasn't all sweetness and light, however. The narrow canyon far from any big cities with but a single road twisting through it allowed a certain degree of control over comings and goings. Many guest residents were closely monitored, even perhaps confined, grouped together according to their problems. Some escaped anyway.

At one time, there was even a high observation place called the "Crow's Nest" where a novice would keep watch for attempted escapes and hit the alarm when he saw one. If a priest got out and into trouble in the village or even down in Albuquerque, the police would call and a special squad of Paracletes would be dispatched to discreetly fetch the offender.[17]

Unhappily, many of the priests' women would come to town to try to rescue their lovers. Though Fitzgerald approved of gradually weaning the men away, the rest of the order detested the women, referring to them as "Jezebels." Since the priests considered them all whores anyway, these unfortunate women would sometimes be given money to go away. The Paracletes comforted themselves with the thought, real or not, that many of these ill-fated ladies wound up as prostitutes in Albuquerque.[18]

Like Los Alamos, Jemez Springs was a "company town." The order soon dominated the area as the major landowner and presence in the community. The Servants employed about 50 of the town's residents. For a while, they even ran the town's telephone switchboard and post office, while the Hand-maidens provided a medical clinic for the villagers and one in Santa Fe as well. They hired the mayor and even took over the local parish. Fitzgerald never did get the social center of the town and source of temptation, the still-popular Los Ojos Bar and Grill, replaced by a bowling alley, however.[19]

Fitzgerald did not just serve as a money-raising figurehead, either. Though a General Council supposedly ran the order, he actually controlled everything. As the resident head of Via Coeli, he took an active day-to-day role in their guest's treatment programs, too. He also heard their sacramental confessions, so he felt he alone was able to make accurate judgments as to their progress.[20]

The goal was to restore the men's shattered self-esteem and thus their vocations. Or if that was too much, provide a sanctuary for them. But the often-reluctant guests kept raising sexual issues in counseling sessions. It soon became clear to Fitzgerald and his colleagues that alcohol abuse, insub-ordination, and loss of faith were not the only problems their charges faced. Homosexuality, pedophilia, or maybe just the simple desire to get married challenged the vocations of many priests.

Something more was needed. Therapy might help the majority, but for the worst offenders, incarceration should have been required, and Fitzgerald well knew it.

Lost islands of the Paracletes

From the start, the first Servant General did not want to have anything to do with child molesters. As far back as the 1957, he was begging his "dear Cofounder" for approval "for the sake of preventing scandal that might en-danger the good name of Via Coeli" to "not offer hospitality to men who have seduced or attempted to seduce little boys or girls."

Fitzgerald said they were "devils and the wrath of God is upon them and if I were a Bishop I would tremble when I failed to report them to Rome for involuntary liacization." This implies that the traditional system enforced by the Holy Office was still intact at that time, but the bishops themselves were impeding its proper functioning.

Fitzgerald then indicated that if the bishops considered these men too dangerous for their parishes, he was not justified in receiving them in Jemez Springs, either. "It is for this class of rattlesnake I have always wished the island retreat – but even an island is too good for these vipers." He reluc-tantly admitted he thought such men were damned, and promised that he would speak to the Pope the next time he saw him to get them "ipso facto reduced to laymen when they act thus." [21] In other words, what Fitzgerald really wanted was for child-abusing priests to be automatically reduced to lay status the instant they even attempted to touch a child sexually.

It was a bold albeit impossible idea. Not since Pope Gregory the Great, thirteen centuries before, had such dire penalties been seriously proposed for any sexual sins of priests. But by the time Fitzgerald actually got his private audience, there was a new pope, John XXIII. This pontiff, who would issue the secret rules for prosecuting sex cases several years later and set into motion the abortive revolution of Vatican II, officially approved Fitzgerald's order. However, he apparently preferred the island prison alternative.

Fitzgerald was well aware that he was never privy to all the Vatican's policies, though. Pope John's successor, Paul VI, also gave the Servant General an audience. They discussed releasing priests who were already civilly married over a year before Paul actually issued his encyclical that let them leave. Afterwards in a letter to a bishop, Fitzgerald wrote, "I am certain there is a secret directive to Bishops permitting – under what conditions I know not – something along these lines. I surmise it is so new a development that Bishops have been slow to exercise it."

Interestingly, Fitzgerald was not worried about this causing a "landslide," naively thinking that priests who left would soon advise their former comrades who were thinking of leaving, "'In God's name, don't be a fool.'" Rather, he was far more anxious about growing homosexuality among the clergy. He claimed it was a "practically unknown rarity" before World War II. When he began ministering among priests, he said alcoholism was the biggest problem ("eight out of ten") but by the mid-1960s, the ratio at Via Coeli ran 5:2:3 – that is, 5 alcoholics to 2 heterosexuals to 3 homosexuals. In other words, the clergy was decidedly turning gay.

"Bishop," Fitzgerald implored, "do not quote me because this is given in strictest confidence, but we know of several seminaries that have been deeply infected and this of course leads to wide infection."[22] His outlook for the future of the priesthood was presciently pessimistic. Now it is estimated that almost half of all Catholic priests are homosexuals, and the majority of them actively so.[23]

Though it was later said he started looking in 1963, obviously Fitzgerald had been thinking about the "priest prison" for quite some time. He again wrote begging letters to the bishops. This time the bishop of San Juan, Puerto Rico, James Peter Davis, responded with an offer of the island of Tortola. But it was inhabited and had no facilities that could be adapted so it was abandoned by 1961.

In 1965, at Davis' suggestion, Fitzgerald arranged to purchase an inhabited island called Carriacou near Barbados in the diocese of Grenada with an abandoned, burnt-out hotel. He put down $5,000 out of a total purchase price of $50,000. The place was used briefly but supposedly never as a penitentiary for sexually abusive priests.[24]

For "Paraclete Island" was apparently not to be. Reasons for its rejection are obscure. Instead, a more risky but less expensive plan of rehabilitation would be attempted. Its dismal failure would be an immediate cause of the crises, not just in the state, but also across the entire country.

Fall of the founder

What is known is that the year before, 1964, six months after Byrne died, the bishop of San Juan, James Peter Davis, had been appointed Archbishop of Santa Fe, curiously enough. Why he was chosen, and if the decision had anything to do with the Paracletes or not, is anyone's guess. Byrne also had been a bishop in Puerto Rico before Santa Fe, so perhaps the assignment was just due to presumed familiarity with Hispanic culture.

But Davis' relationship with Fitzgerald was more formal, less friendly, cooler, and quite different than that of his predecessor. He was said to be "more business oriented" and concerned with finances, including those of the Servants.[25] Perhaps he was ordered to keep Fitzgerald on a tighter leash.

At that time, the congregation was still under the control of Santa Fe. Before long, the new archbishop curtly ordered that the island be sold. Fitzgerald followed these commands with extreme reluctance. This all seems most peculiar, for Davis was the one who had advised Fitzgerald to buy an island in the first place. Most probably, the new directives came down from John XXIII's successor, Pope Paul VI, who was already busily dismantling the Holy Office's ancient penitential system.

Officially, Fitzgerald said that due to the "growing popularity" with tourists, the privacy required was no longer available and so they were withdrawing from the project.[26] The Servants claimed during the lawsuits, however, that the Paracletes' psychological advisor at the time, Dr. John Salazar, had recommended instead that priests with "psychosexual difficulties" should not be segregated, but rehabilitated.[27]

Whether he did or not has been much disputed. In any event, the new policy did not take long to go into effect. It was now deemed more compassionate to mend offenders in hope of returning them to ministry than condemning them to permanent exile. After all, restoring vocations had always been their prime goal. Public service had long been a key part of the Servants' program to rebuild the sacred commitment of their guests.

In fact, by this time, they were already sending out guests to local mountain communities to offer Sunday Mass in private homes during the summer.[28] Within a few years, formal deals would be cut, first with Santa Fe and then with other dioceses to place supposedly rehabilitated guests into parish situations. However, this was done with minimal supervision and no notification to the parishioners. In a few instances, the results would be disastrous.

But there might have been a more immediate trigger than Fitzgerald's generosity and resistance to change. About a month before the end of the Vatican Council, a young man named Roger Allen LaPorte set himself ablaze in front of the United Nations building in New York City. Inspired by the self-immolation of a Buddhist monk, he, too, tragically chose a fiery means of protest against the Vietnam War. He died of his burns some thirty hours later, just before the great Northeastern power blackout began.

Though identified in the newspapers as merely belonging to the Catholic Worker movement, LaPorte was actually a fellow member at the novitiate in Vermont according to a former Paraclete novice. This source claims that Cardinal Spellman ruthlessly intervened to immediately squash that information, and everyone's silence was ordered.[29]

Perhaps this event somehow heralded Fitzgerald's downfall by sparking an internal conflict for control. One report said that he resigned in disgust in 1965 after losing a battle over assigning a residence hall at Via Coeli for pedophile treatment.[30] In any case, for some reason, a crisis brewed within the order. It resulted in the founder being effectively stripped of power by the end of 1966, but not of his title.

By then a new generation of Paracletes had risen with modern ideas. Seeing deficiencies in the program, they had been trained in psychology and therapy. Moreover, the same reforming spirit that enthused the great Council in Rome found its way even to the distant mountains of New Mexico. These young monks felt their order could no longer afford their revered founder's impulsive charity, fiscal irresponsibility, or antiquated methods.

Fitzgerald had acted as if his order were a dashing, elite papal police force with a worldwide reach and pontifical authority. Perhaps to some degree it was. In any event, he apparently had little problem in accepting new challenges. He had a tendency to constantly overreach and apparently was blithely unconcerned about burdening his order with debts. By this time, the founder was an old man and may even have been going senile.[31]

Moreover, Fitzgerald's antiquated piety was deemed insufficient to deal with the growing numbers of priests with modern "psychosexual difficulties" in the post-Vatican II world. Scientific therapy would be the new solution for saving priestly vocations from personal aberrations, which might range from a simple desire for matrimony to extreme perversions. So, under the next few following Servant Generals, each serving a six-year term, the program would greatly expand to accommodate the ever-rising need.

In any case, though there is no sign in the official history, an intense power struggle was fought over the idea of lay treatment plans. Fitzgerald distrusted outside psychologists, leaving such matters largely up to a guest's superior, and strongly resisted the introduction of Alcoholics Anonymous. Conflict grew with the archbishop over those issues as well as finances. By August 23, 1965, Davis had had enough. He wrote the letter ordering the sale of the island, along with the promotion of those seeking to introduce AA and other programs, and that Fitzgerald accompany him to Rome.[32]

Thus, Father Gerald was discreetly removed from daily management of the monastery, although his struggle for control of the order escalated. Eventually, Fitzgerald went too far. He threatened Cardinal Ildebrando Antoniutti, prefect of the Sacred Congregation for the Religious and Secular Institutes, with giving the Archdiocese all the Paraclete's property and taking his order out of New Mexico.

The agreement that was worked out in October 1965, appeared to favor Fitzgerald, but in reality, his gambit backfired. Davis had won the support of the cardinal to implement treatment programs, and Fitzgerald was never again permitted to reside at Via Coeli.[33]

The now-displaced founder died at the ripe age of 75 while giving a retreat to lay teachers in Massachusetts. His earthly remains were returned to Jemez Springs to be buried in the Servants' small private cemetery at Lourdes House in on the Fourth of July, 1969, with full military honors. Several dozen Servants and guests now rest there with him, too.

One of his successors, Liam Hoare, boasted that by then, "His little canyon retreat was now known throughout the world. In the Catholic Church, Jemez Springs had become a by-word for 'healing.'"[34] Perhaps so, but over a generation later, some would curse the name as a term for "cover-up" and "enabling."

Yet, well before Fitzgerald passed on, the die had been irrevocably cast. On March 23, 1966, three months after the end of the Second Vatican Council, Antoniutti wrote another letter. In the typically innocuous sounding language of the Vatican, this one gave the official blessing of the Curia to the brave new era of psychiatry:

> *Insofar as you can, please see what can be done in regard to the methods of rehabilitation of the guests, retaining, by all means, the primacy of the spiritual renewal, but striving also to effect a wise selection of those mental and physical means which help the workings of grace.*[35]

A daring experiment was about to begin. Modern psychology and ancient spiritual discipline would be combined together in an attempt to save men who could help save others.

If it succeeded, the noble dreams of the reformers of Vatican II for a more liberal Church, open to the possibilities of science and the modern world as well as the "workings of grace," might yet come true. The stakes could not have been higher.

CHAPTER XI:
THE OPERATION OF ERROR

Come the revolution

Fitzgerald's replacement, Joseph McNamara, soon had the Paracletes' version of the sexual revolution already well in hand. Dr. John Salazar, a clinical psychologist, was brought in to advise on the rehabilitation effort as an alternative to the island. The new plan would involve a "Graduated Step Rehabilitation Program for Impaired Priests" requiring a six-month stay at Via Coeli followed by two years supervision and therapy.

By 1967, the new programs were in place.[1] Yet; Via Coeli would not be formally called a "treatment center" until 1976, when they opened what was "perhaps the first program in the world designed to treat psychosexual disorders in priests."[2] As they were now actively trying to change men, rather than invite them to reform themselves, the Paracletes' responsibility for their charges should have been correspondingly higher.

What happened then has been the subject of much dispute. The Servant General claimed that Salazar advised them that segregating priests with "psychosexual difficulties" would be "counterproductive to rehabilitation." He says that Salazar and other psychologists told the Servants that such men could be "treated and cured of their problem." The Paracletes, he emphatically snorted, did not originate "the notion" of sending pedophile priests into parishes for supply work.[3]

Salazar was blamed for bad advice, and even accused of giving the victim's attorney information on the program for cash.[4] In his counter-lawsuit against the Servants, Salazar put the fault squarely back on the Paracletes, stating he advised them not to send the men out. He felt he was being scapegoated by the order in suits some of the most notorious offenders.[5] Dismissively, albeit quite accurately, the psychologist pointed out that patients with sexual problems could be "better controlled in Jemez Springs than in New York City."[6]

During his public feud with the Paracletes, Dr. Salazar made a number of interesting statements. Claiming he recommended that pedophiles should not be released for parish work, he had only been allowed to see them for six sessions. He resigned in 1968. He mentioned the island but said he had advised against it, that it would result in an "organized den of iniquity." Salazar even admitted to experimenting with electroshock to decondition priests' erotic responses.[7]

In his own defense, Salazar spoke of "an unspoken conspiracy of silence" to cover-up aberrant sexual behavior by clergy. He blamed "a self-protective network that forms within the clergy and tends to preserve the opportunity for priests to continue their deviant sexual behaviors."[8]

As will be seen, evidence suggests that the Paracletes' foundation, by providing a refuge, actually allowed some pedophile priests to network, enable each other, and even protect fellow predators far beyond Jemez Springs.

In any case, those guests who passed the Paracletes' assessments would be sent back out into the world virtually unmonitored. Whatever really happened, it is indisputable that there was far too little communication with the parishes or the bishops, insufficient supervision, and far too much trust.

At the height of the ministry, according to their own internal documents, up to 88 guests at a time could be housed in the order's five residences scattered along the Jemez Canyon. Later they claimed only half that amount.

The men were often grouped according to their needs. To keep confidentiality, a system of secret notations in the men's records indicated exactly what problems they were there for. By 1963, the Servants had so many pedophiles that they were using "Code 3" to identify them.[9]

But among the Paraclete wardens themselves, an informal but restricted list was rumored. Supposedly, this ranked the ten most notorious offenders currently resident who needed the closest watching. These were privately referred to as the "Sons of Perdition."[10]

Along with ancient monastic devotions, modern science was now brought to bear. Some techniques, however, might have been at home in the Inquisition. To accurately determine sexual attractions, for example, guests would be strapped into a device called a penile plethysmograph – a "petermeter." By measuring their involuntary erections while the clerics were read or shown different scenarios and photos, the men's true erotic preferences could be determined despite any evasion, denial, or rationalization.

Another psychologist who performed such evaluations for the Servants said that the images were quite varied and included deviance and violence, including sex with children. Various treatments tried in other offender programs involved aversion therapy where the negative consequences of acting out were contemplated, or even masturbating until it became painful.[11] Such techniques may have been tested on the Servants' guests as well.

In any case, regular therapy sessions were to be scheduled; but the record is unclear how extensively therapy was actually employed. According to complaints from one of the worst offenders who molested well over a dozen altar boys while supposedly in treatment, sometimes there was no therapy, nor even evaluations. Doctors and psychiatrists would prescribe medical treatments, including feminizing drugs like Depo-Provera to diminish sexual attraction.

However, patients and Paracletes often ignored many other medical recommendations, which was confirmed by one nurse who quit in protest.[12] Combined with the guests' gripes, it appears that the Servants' facilities and programs had been constantly on the verge of being overwhelmed by the ever-growing demand from the start.

More radical techniques were tried. The electroshock treatment already mentioned that was tried out by Salazar bordered upon mind-control experiments. It used meditation to decrease desires as the subject was shown pictures while given a mild shock on the wrists. Despite reports to the contrary, he insisted that the pictures were not pornographic but from the mainstream media, and the technique was tried not only for sexual compulsions, but overeating and alcoholism, too.

"I had some equipment built for me to use that, and I was doing research work with it," he testified. Salazar called the therapy "new and novel," but "I did not feel the success was that great." He never published anything on it.[13]

This may seem right out of *The Manchurian Candidate* or *A Clockwork Orange*. However, there are dark whispers of an even stronger method, called "SANGRE." This was allegedly used once upon a member of the order to successfully prevent him from leaving at another, secret location for a month.[14]

Some guests who seemed to do well in treatment were sent unsupervised to parishes. The pastors had not been especially warned. Very few parolees, though, actually caused problems. One pastor of a remote southern parish admitted he had used over a hundred recovering alcoholic priests sent by the Paracletes and never had any trouble, except with one.[15]

That one just happened to be David Holley, a serial predator who should never have been let loose in the first place. He molested altar boys again during his weekend assignments as soon as he was given the chance. Holley would not be the only guest to do so.

But the tragic mistake of putting unreformable perverts back into parishes was already being set up on a much larger scale. Children across New Mexico and elsewhere would pay the price for it.

Wolves among the sheep

On February 13, 1967, at that fateful disputed meeting between Salazar, the Servants, and the Archbishop, a formal agreement was signed between the Servants of the Paraclete and the Archdiocese of Santa Fe to send certain guests into specific parishes. Sixteen of Albuquerque's 22 parishes were listed; nearly all with schools, plus all churches in the state capitol of Santa Fe save for the cathedral itself. Two rural parishes were also included. Many of these churches had names that would become quite familiar once the scandals broke.[16]

Other priests were sent to a halfway house, Pius XII Villa, south of Albuquerque where they had even greater freedom. It was originally a posh hacienda owned by a prosperous trading family. Located in a rural area by the Rio Grande, it sat near an archdiocesan retreat house for priests and another run by Dominican nuns. In the heady days after Vatican II, the scene was popular with many in the young "guitar Mass" crowd.[17] Yet it was alleged that some of the most serious offenders, like Holley, were kept down there, and one priest even formed his own private cult-like devotional group.[18]

Not only that, but an unknown number of priests wishing to avoid ecclesiastical sanctions had successfully escaped from Jemez Canyon over the years. They slipped back into the general population, totally unsupervised and free to find their own way. Though Servant General Hoare claimed they were trying to track dropouts, many were still too "embarrassed and/or angry" to stay in touch.[19] Numbers and identities of such escapees remain unknown.

Despite all this, Hoare, also gifted with a bit of Irish blarney, once proudly referred to the Servants as the "M.A.S.H. unit of the Catholic Church. We get the casualties."[20] Other people had different names for the Paracletes' programs. Locals joked about the "Center for Boozy Priests" and even some of its more cynical inmates referred to it as "Camp Ped."[21,22] Yet even in Fitzgerald's own time, the program's effectiveness was seriously challenged – and the first voice raised belonged to none other than the town's own parish priest.

In a letter to American bishops in September 1966, F. John Murphy strongly objected to gay guests making advances on the town's youth. Even worse, he claimed that some members of the order had their own serious, untreated problems with alcohol, drugs, and sexual issues.

"Homosexual solicitation in my parish is a matter of grave concern to me," he indignantly wrote. "When I reported to the superiors of Via Coeli such an incident occasioned by one of the resident of Via with that problem behavior, he disclaimed all responsibility for the conduct of the guest in relation to the civil community."

He accused the Paraclete community's superiors of often being drunk or on barbiturates. "Inactive priests have been roused from stupor and sent on active duty assignments." Murphy also complained of a lack of "mandatory therapy for alcoholics, homosexuals, neurotics" and prophetically that "there is no recognition of the responsibilities imposed by civil law on institutions housing behavior problems."

Fitzgerald had responded to a similar earlier letter from Murphy to the archbishop, saying that the most of the charges were untrue and that troubled priests were getting proper treatment. "If a priest is unwilling to admit his mistakes and refuses to make a determined effort to change," he wrote, "then Via Coeli becomes for him a house of refuge... By being here, the chance of occasioning scandal in and for the Church is minimized. This is no small service to the Church, and Via Coeli has provided it from the beginning."

In any event, Murphy's predictive protestations were useless. Widely regarded as a "nut" by Fitzgerald and the hierarchy, a Paraclete priest soon replaced him. He died in 1981.[23]

But Murphy was essentially correct. The Paracletes often described Via Coeli and the Villa simply as "retreat houses." In such a setting, a person's improvement was entirely up to him. Calling the place a retreat was a convenient pious fiction that lent the Servants, their clients, and the bishops who funded the operation ideal cover. The guests, whatever their problems, were spared any embarrassment. Meanwhile, both the order and their sponsors evaded any responsibility for any shenanigans the guests involved in while they were there – or any time later.

This was bad enough when the Servants were simply counseling alcoholics. Unfortunately, their attitudes and policies did not seem to stiffen once they started treating more difficult cases. The Paracletes let criminal sex offenders out on assignment without apparently even the slightest checks, restrictions, or warnings that would be imposed if the men were on parole from jail. This carelessness crossed the line into active enabling. They became not part of the solution but a significant contributor to the problem, and a source of grave scandal.

Meanwhile, difficulties were apparently brewing beyond town, too. For suddenly, at the height of their success during the "mid-1980s" according to one newspaper account, or perhaps later, the Paracletes destroyed most of their old files – supposedly on the advice of the bishops to save space – and advised the archdiocese and others to do the same.[24]

In fact, correspondence shows that they were still shredding evaluations of guests up until 1990, allegedly to preserve client confidentiality. At that point, they finally deleted the standard language in their correspondence requesting destruction when their attorney advised them to stop, to avoid the appearance of destroying evidence.[25]

What possibly triggered this could have been an unintended consequence of *The Manual*, though it had warned about the danger of "sanitizing or purging files."[26] Yet, the document also contained much anxious discussion of how to keep everything secret, including the proposal itself. The actual record destruction, however, had been ordered by the bishops' conference, which funded the whole enterprise.[27]

"Ecclesiastic prison"

The initial cracks in the wall of silence had been around for a good while already, though, had anyone cared to notice. Just seven years after the center had been founded, an American ex-priest, Emmett McGloughlin, first mentioned the forbidden in his own exposé. He was a former Franciscan, a highly successful hospital administrator from Arizona who left because of the jealousy of his superiors over his innovative minority training programs.

"It will come as a surprise to most Americans," he wrote in his 1954 autobiography, *People's Padre*, "to know that there are institutions in the United States to which priests are sent without any trial ... One is in Oshkosh, Wisconsin ... Another, supported by the hierarchy, is in Jémez Springs, New Mexico, near Albuquerque. The 'crimes' for which priests are sent to those institutions are generally alcoholism, insubordination, or lapses in the realm of celibacy."[28]

This was the first public revelation that has been located of an "ecclesiastic prison," as he called it, anywhere in modern America. It was already a growing concern. In 1951, the Paracletes reported that they had "sheltered 200 priests within the first four years," in 1956, 488; and 900 "priest-guests" had come to the New Mexico monastery within the first dozen years, according to a later Servant General. Still later figures indicate a total number treated of around 2,000-2,100 to date.[29]

The figures indicate a growth from 50 to 137 guests per year by 1959, but if the later figures are to be believed, only averaging around 35 guests every year until the program officially closed in 1994.

But this completely contradicts what is anecdotally known about the radical expansion of their rehabilitation programs, especially during the 1980s. Of course, there are natural limits to how many bodies they could handle. Their own handbook for guests indicated that at most 88 beds among 5 residences were available in Jemez Springs. Given a six-month program, that indicates a maximum possible number of 176 guests could be treated there each year.

It wasn't cheap, however, one source claiming it cost $4,500 per month. Total cost, including Depo-Provera, therapy and the priest's subsidy for the first year was estimated to $48,740.[30] The Servants themselves priced their services, however, at $5,400 a month, just as the crisis was beginning in 1992, but claimed no one was turned away for lack of funding.[31]

Eight months later while trying to bolster their bad image, more details were provided. The Servants said that they had 44 guests in residence staying an average of 6-7 months. 98 went through their full program each year. 96% returned to active ministry. Only 3-4 pedophiles were admitted each year. Since 1981, they required a full year of sobriety before admission, and those with severe disorders or custodial needs were taken elsewhere – where was not mentioned.[32]

That so few pedophiles were admitted may be as deceptive as calling the place a "retreat." Not all sexual abusers prefer pre-teens, those who go for teenagers are called "ephebophiles" and there are those who target adults instead. Nor does the category necessarily include those who have not been diagnosed or who exhibit multiple conditions. Neither did they mention the other psychosexual problems the center treated. Dr. Salazar himself listed pedophilia, but also voyeurism, sadism, and masochism, as well as transvestites and those with sexual fetishes.[33]

Like other claims the Servants have made over the years, their numbers simply cannot be relied upon. These discrepancies likely reflect the critical difference in the way the order wished to be seen before and after the scandals. Whatever the true amounts were, the figures given all mean the same

thing, however: The substantial investment made in the facilities was justified by a large number of priests who needed help. Just how many will likely
never be known.

"The sexual affairs of priests in the U.S. are more closely guarded secrets
than the classified details of our national defense," McGloughlin prophetically claimed in a later work.[34] He related few stories of clerical abuse but
they show that times were changing. One involved a Fr. Dukind, who had
first informed McGloughlin of "alcoholic rehabilitation centers for priests
only." The FBI nabbed Dukind in 1960 living in Phoenix with a 17-year-old
girl he had abducted from Wisconsin. He appealed to McGloughlin for help.
Dukind fully expected to be packed off to Jemez Springs and was quite dis-
mayed to be hauled back home to face criminal charges instead.[35]

Some knowledge of Via Coeli did leak out into the surrounding New
Mexican Catholic communities in the meantime. Devout mothers would
whisper to their young children, who were not at all sure who these "Para-
keets" were that people were talking about, to "pray for the poor alcoholic
priests" when passing old men tottering along the road in Jemez Springs.[36]

But it wasn't until the furor surrounding a former guest broke decades
later that the Paracletes began to be noticed when his stay at Via Coeli was
revealed.

CHAPTER XII:
THUNDER IN THE DESERT

The troubles begin

The Gauthe case in Louisiana was the first one to achieve wide attention, though it too was soon forgotten. For years afterwards, while the bishops ineffectively debated *The Manual* and other proposals, other scandals surfaced and vanished without a ripple. All such news, as would continue through most of the scandals, generally stayed confined to local communities. It would take an explosive affront on the national stage to finally break the silence and seize the attention of the country.

The one that decisively did so was the infamous James Porter case in the summer of 1992. The man who struck the match was a Massachusetts victim named Frank Fitzpatrick. He had been abused as a 12-year-old altar boy and now was a private investigator and needed answers. Two years previously, he had finally tracked down his abuser to Minnesota and taped his confrontation over the phone.

Porter actually admitted his abuse with a slight chuckle, showing no remorse whatsoever. He initially claimed that he had stopped molesting children back in 1967.[1]

Fitzpatrick was furious, and from that righteous indignation sparked the greatest crisis in the modern history of the Church. For James Porter was not just a one-time priest with an unfortunate mistake or two in his past. The private eye had exposed a genuine monster: a depraved serial child molester with a seemingly endless appetite and absolutely no qualms whatsoever. Moreover, this man got around. This scandal could not and would not be confined to a single region.

While most of these predators have definite preferences, Porter was thoroughly ecumenical in his tastes – gender and age seemingly made little difference. If young enough and Porter could get him or her alone, he would sexually abuse the child any way he could. The priest left a wake of several hundred broken boys and girls trailing behind him.

Soon the meaning of the year Porter mentioned became clear: it was when he was sent from his original posting in Fall River, Massachusetts to Jemez Springs. But his assertion was an outright lie. He had soon molested three altar boys in a southern parish, and sodomized another at the Albuquerque church of St. Edwin. Incredibly, he was then sent out on yet other temporary assignments, including one to a parish in Houston, Texas, where he acted out yet again.

Unbelievably, the Servants then gave him a clean bill of health and recommended he be accepted in Bemidji, Minnesota, with the inevitable results.

By 1970, somehow consensus had finally been reached that he should leave the priesthood. Four years later, it was ultimately accomplished. He then married, fathered four children, and within a decade was abusing their babysitter in Minnesota. Convicted for 30 years at the end of 1992, he died disgraced in prison in 2005. James Porter managed to outlive most of the scandals he helped set ablaze.

In time, it would be revealed that Porter had voluntarily left the priesthood at his own request, with the pope's permission. He was neither forcibly laicized nor ever canonically punished in any way for his sins by the Church. If anything could be considered proof that the secret system had indeed broken down, this should.

In any case, the story first went national on July 2, 1992, when ABC News' *PrimeTime Live* featured a segment on the case. Three weeks later, they followed it up in a big way with an update given by journalist Diane Sawyer with more background. She even bravely faced Porter down in public. There was an electrifying confrontation where the former cleric turned on the cameraman with a snarl like a trapped animal. In the meantime, some 60 victims had come forward. It was an omen of the end for Porter, and the start of decades of scandals.

Looking back, what is most surprising is how many core elements of the crisis were already laid bare by these initial revelations. Not only was the predatory priest exposed, but also the collusion of the bishops and the enabling role of the Paracletes were all in plain view right at the very beginning. Understanding how it all worked and fit together would take another sixteen years and not all questions have yet been answered. But the basic outline was clearly visible from the first.

At the time, the Servants of the Paraclete suddenly found themselves faced by the one thing they didn't want – the glare of media attention. The fuse was now lit to scandals in their Southwestern homeland and beyond. In the Land of Enchantment, because of the concentration of pedophile priests in the state, however, the worst blows would come hard and fast.

Some scandals were already smoldering in New Mexico already but had gone largely unnoticed until then. A then-anonymous woman filed a lawsuit in August 1991 against an unnamed priest whom she claimed had molested her for years starting when she was 15. Another involved a former teacher now in trouble in Kentucky who had abused seminarians in Santa Fe.

Meanwhile, other clergy abuse victims, including the author, were busy dealing with recovered memories or just quietly trying to get by. For as everywhere else, shame and secrecy ruled until Fitzpatrick's exposure of Porter shattered the silence like the trumpet of doom.

In New Mexico, the crisis simmered quietly until the fall. An early indication that events were moving came when Richard Olona, the chancellor of the diocese, was quietly replaced at the beginning of September. The new man, Ron Wolf, 55 when it all began, was a tough-talking canonist who had previously served on the marriage tribunal. Born in Wisconsin and trained at a seminary in Indiana, he came late to the priesthood. He was ordained at St. Therese in Albuquerque in 1986. In spite of his relative inexperience as a pastor, however, his doctoral dissertation had been about sex abuse from a priest's perspective and canonical processes to deal with it.[2]

Wearing thick silver-framed glasses and slicked-back black hair, Wolf had a quick temper but passionately loved the Church. Early on, he admitted that the scandal was a "volcano waiting to happen," yet vowed, "Priests who hurt children will not work in a parish as long as I am chancellor." He even promised free counseling for victims.[3]

Wolf was noted for his fairness and above all, his frank speech, which would get him into trouble. Nonetheless, he would serve thanklessly as point man throughout the worst part of the crisis.

The new chancellor was soon put to work. At the beginning of October, it suddenly became clear that the crisis would not be confined to the past when a 16-year-old altar boy fled the rectory in the small town of Questa, north of Taos. He told police that the pastor, Vincent Lipinski, 31, had bought him alcohol and molested him.[4]

The priest was sent to the Servants for evaluation, and legally got off lightly with probation. When he returned from treatment, however, Wolf took the unusual step of writing a letter to be read at all Masses the next Sunday in Questa. It demanded that parishioners stay away and not communicate with the popular young priest. It also asked other victims to come forward, causing considerable resentment among villagers. He was not allowed to wear his Roman collar, represent himself as a priest, or say Mass publicly. Lipinski was also ordered to avoid contact with parishioners, and was publicly reprimanded by Wolf when he disobeyed.[5]

Perhaps the reason for this unusual action was due because it was not the first time Lipinski had been accused. Years later, it would come out that anonymous allegations had first come to the archbishop's attention in the summer of 1989. While serving at Our Lady of Fatima in Albuquerque, it was alleged he had gotten a volunteer for the youth ministry drunk and the young man had woken up in bed with the priest in the rectory. Sanchez and his chancellor then, Richard Olona, confronted Lipinski half a year later and were apparently impressed by his sincerity. "I would never compromise my priesthood or the reputation of the church," Lipinski had firmly maintained. "I only go out with other priests."[6]

Due to his vigorous defense and the informality of the accusation, his superiors didn't feel inclined to investigate further, or even to ask his pastor, Clarence Galli, anything about it.

Other than that, by forbidding him to dress or act as a priest, Lipinski was at first given what became the standard punishment reserved for those who were considered guilty of causing scandal at the very least. Time after time throughout the scandals, such ecclesiastical restrictions would be handed out like parking tickets. In many cases, they would serve as the only acknowledgement that the archdiocese considered accusations to have some weight or feared further shenanigans.

The missing monsignor

Such limits would be ineffective when applied to the next major case, however, as the accused priest could not be found. Arthur J. Perrault, 54, suddenly vanished at the beginning of a sabbatical. His fall was as swift as his disappearance was dramatic and mysterious.

Given "The People's Choice Award for Favorite Clergy in Albuquerque" just the year before, Perrault was a highly intelligent, admired priest who had served in four of the biggest parishes in town. Among other things, he had been the head of a department at St. Pius X High School, a colonel in the Air Force Reserve chaplains' corps as well as the archdiocesan director of liturgy and communications and coordinator of worship for the Western United States for the bishops. He did TV Masses and wrote columns for the archdiocesan newsletter he edited.[7]

He was also widely known to be close friends with Archbishop Robert Sanchez. Ironically, they had both taught Ethics around the same time at the high school.

At the end of September, Perrault had resigned his pastorship of the city's richest parish, St. Bernadette, to go on a sabbatical earned by a quarter-century of service. Several weeks later, he arranged with a real estate agent in Denver to rent a condo to live in while he pursued scriptural studies. He would never even pick up the keys.[8]

A police detective in Lakewood, Colorado, Michael Harris, whose work involved children, had already heard about what Fitzpatrick had done. Inspired, he went public and accused Perrault of having tried to molest him in the rectory of an Albuquerque church in 1971. The first article appeared on October 9 in the *Albuquerque Journal,* the local morning paper. The accusation against such a prominent figure in the archdiocese sent shockwaves through the community. It was already too late.

By this time, Perrault had made a clean getaway. He had gone to Vancouver in Canada "on vacation" – via a one-way ticket. Although adamant he was not at the Paracletes, Wolf would deny knowing his whereabouts, though he admitted to having several phone conversations.[9] But Arthur Perrault has never been spotted again.

The pastor had more than sufficient cause to take flight. Within weeks, seven people would sue him and the archdiocese. Ron Wolf admitted that he had taken calls from 25.[10] Wolf also confessed early on that the priest had been disciplined once for sexual misconduct but the case had been settled. The chancellor soon instituted a hotline for victims to handle the load of calls and announced an Independent Commission to review the overall situation and propose solutions.

The details that gradually emerged about the missing monsignor were hard to believe. Perrault was by all accounts a bold and opportunistic perpetrator. One of his victims had committed suicide. He abused not only two brothers who were servers, but also a talented young graphic artist hired to help him with the church newsletter, Elaine Montoya, and tried to molest her brother, Paul.

Elaine had only recently returned to the state and had been astonished to find Perrault still in ministry. It was not until she disclosed her abuse to her brother that he admitted the priest had attempted to assault him as well.[11]

Another man also spoke out at the same time. Conrad Jiron, 41, alleged that Perrault had abused him at the archbishop's own home back when Davis was still in charge. He also had sex with Jiron "almost every day in the archdiocese offices."[12] Privately, Jiron said that Perrault would even take him with him on visits to Jemez Springs, where he was allowed to roam the grounds of Via Coeli unquestioned while the priest was busy.[13]

The victims' lawyer, Bruce Pasternack, arranged these dramatic disclosures. He was a handsome, sharp-dressing, sharp-tongued attorney, only 42 when the scandals began though his hair was already frosted with silver. His high-powered style contrasted strongly with the state's famous laid-back *"mañana"* or "worry about it tomorrow" attitude.

Though several other lawyers took up clergy abuse cases, Pasternack made it something of a personal crusade. He and Wolf often locked horns in the media with suits and counter-suits, but the counselor got things done. He filed over 180 claims against clergy and turned down many more. But without Pasternack's energy and determination, very few victims would have gotten anything at all.

From such revelations, the monsignor's sexual activities appeared to be almost an open secret. Throughout the fall, even more disquieting information about Perrault's history trickled out. The Montoyas had met with the chancellor at the time, Ronald Starkey, back in 1985. He admitted he had seen complaints, told them Perrault was in counseling and he would be transferred to a church where he would have no contact with children.

Significantly, Starkey admitted to the Montoyas that Perrault's activities had been going on for 25 years and "nothing could be done." In a letter, he also said that Perrault had the maturity of a 9-year-old.[14]

Marlene Debry-Nowak, the mother of the two abused boys, had also been told Perrault would be kept away from kids by the archbishop. The priest himself had molested one of her sons even while she was in the kitchen preparing dinner.[15]

Other embarrassing disclosures followed. Perrault had written a letter to Harris' mother blaming his actions on the shock of having been diagnosed with incurable lung cancer. It was a bald-faced lie.[16]

Archbishop Sanchez admitted he had given his friend "two or three chances." He placed Perrault in therapy for eight years in the early 1980s, and assigned him to the chancery, or to a parish "far away from temptation."[17] Not nearly far enough, it seems.

Even the police acknowledged that they had investigated the popular pastor around that time, but had insufficient evidence. They again launched a criminal investigation, but found no victims within the statute of limitations. The district attorney sought a grand jury criminal indictment against Perrault and failed.

Ordained in Hartford, Connecticut, it was soon discovered Perrault had been reassigned to Santa Fe after a stint at Jemez Springs. The Paracletes' one-time contract psychologist, Dr. Salazar, admitted Perrault had been his patient, but refused to say much more save that he had recommended a high school or college teaching job, not parish work.[18]

In time, those suits against Perrault and the archdiocese would be settled without much argument but with the usual secrecy clauses. No criminal charges were ever filed, but the man's fast rise through the ranks, his close association with Sanchez, and how he was able to get away with his crimes for so long left many with an uneasy foreboding. The timing of Perrault's sabbatical and his easy escape especially raised eyebrows. The once-admired archbishop even found himself being asked by a clearly embarrassed reporter on TV if perhaps he should resign.

Two more monsters

Another guest of the Paracletes who was surely a Son of Perdition was exposed around the same time. His case focused even more attention on the Servants. Jason E. Sigler was a former priest ordained in 1966 in Edmonton, Alberta. Or perhaps Winnipeg – he apparently got into some kind of trouble with one bishop or the other. In any case, during the 1970s, he was a guest of the Paracletes from the diocese of Lansing, Michigan. Finally, it was agreed that unspecified charges in Lansing would be dropped on the condition he never return.

So he stayed in New Mexico, where a friend of his whom he met at the Paracletes, Robert Kirsch, recommended him his as assistant pastor in Abiquiu. Sigler soon racked up at least 17 more victims in four parishes and was twice returned to the Paracletes. In 1982, he left the priesthood and pled guilty for one offense. He was busted again the next year, though the sentence was deferred. He must have been quite persuasive, however. Clarence Galli, his pastor, was used as a reference in a résumé, and gave the police a letter that claimed he was giving Sigler "extensive psychotherapy."[19]

Later during the scandals, Sigler's own defense attorney allowed that he had hired the former priest to do office work. This continued even while lawsuit after lawsuit was filed by former altar boys – there were at least 22 and Pasternack thought there could be as many as 100.[20] More lawsuits and criminal charges would continue to pursue Jason Sigler into the next millennium, 45 at latest count.

Another of the worst offenders that made the news was the aforementioned David Holley. Ordained in Worcester, Massachusetts in 1958, he was sent to Jemez Springs in 1970. On temporary assignment in the small southern town of Alamogordo, near White Sands, at a church across the street from a junior high school, he managed to abuse 10 boys.

The pastor reported him to the Paracletes. Back at Pius XII Villa, he roomed with several other priests, one very old, another who was a foreigner, and an alcoholic. He claimed he was never given any more therapy beyond being told to try his hand at painting. As one lawyer claimed, they had been put out to pasture, dumped like nuclear waste. The Paraclete lawyers, though, claimed at that time the Villa was not a treatment center but just a retreat house.[21]

Whatever the case, Holley was active again soon enough. He acted out in an assignment in El Paso and wound up as a chaplain at an Albuquerque hospital. Finally, in early 1993, after his retirement, he was arrested at St. Luke Institute treatment center in Maryland – the exclusive priest-care center founded by one of the authors of *The Manual*. It had been his fourth time in custodial care.[22] Though his presence there had been denied repeatedly by staff, sheriffs finally found him hiding beneath a stairwell.[23] Apparently the Servants weren't the only caregivers soft of disciplining perpetrators.

Extradited back to New Mexico, Holley was convicted up to 275 years in prison. In his career, he had claimed between 20-25 victims, if not more. He, Porter, and Sigler were perhaps the worst offenders, but there would be plenty more to follow.

From victims to survivors

That fall and through the winter, victims and their supporters began to come together. One woman whose sons had been abused started a support group in connection with a group meeting for the first time in the Midwest that October. A victim's mother also began a branch in Albuquerque. At first, it was called "VOCAL," for the "Victims Of Clergy Abuse Linkup." It was a most unfortunate choice. The acronym had already been claimed by a group supporting people allegedly wrongly accused of child abuse. The clergy organization quickly changed their name to the "Survivors of Clergy Abuse Linkup" or simply "the Linkup." [24]

Under the leadership of Tom Economus, an Independent Catholic (i.e., non-Roman) priest, the Linkup became the largest and most influential victims advocacy group in the nation throughout the 1990s. Sometimes called "the poster boy of the Survivors Movement" due to his looks and eloquence, Tom actually had been one. His priestly perpetrator had literally used him as such on posters and in person to solicit funds for a place called "Sky Ranch for Boys." He flew both Tom and the boy's brother around the country while abusing them until he killed himself in a plane crash.

Tragically, Economus died of cancer in the spring of 2002, just as the Boston scandals that led to the resignation of Cardinal Law were taking off. A great voice was silenced just when it could have done the most good. And he just missed out on getting the recognition that he so deserved.

The author would play a small but significant background role in publishing the Linkup's journal. In New Mexico, the local founder soon dropped out for the sake of her kids, and while a friend of hers ran it for a while, it served mainly as the seed for a small group of victim activists, to which the author also belonged. Elaine Montoya, Conrad Jiron, and the woman who had filed the first suit, Susan Sandoval, were also members, as were several who preferred anonymity.

They gave the group the grandiose name of the "Alliance for Justice" and would be in evidence over the next year demonstrating against the archdiocese and providing support for other victims – as well as a steady stream of criticism in the media. This was accomplished despite certain psychological problems, sometimes severe. Combined with the stress of lawsuits and slanders by parishioners, these forced several members into the hospital on suicide watch at different times. Close relationships were put under severe strain also, and some broke. Another person, claiming to be a victim, but not directly associated with the group, even had a restraining order put out for her death threats against the chancellor at one time.

Legal processes themselves were long and difficult for victims. Public accusations triggered the shame that their perpetrators had often used to control them. Depositions themselves were often traumatic, especially when the accused priest was allowed to be present. If the news media showed a certain restraint, comments by the faithful rarely did.

Ironically, because of the way the legal statutes of limitations worked, few victims got generous settlements, even with proof. It all depended on when they first recognized the damage that had been done to them. Usually this was determined by when they had initially told anyone at all about it, which set the clock running. If they did not promptly sue within a year after that, later three years, they were out of luck. And the archdiocese's promises to pay for therapy were rumored to limit victims to Church-approved therapists who would report to the chancellor.

For most victims, suing priests was hardly winning the "Catholic lottery" as one psychologist scornfully put it during the public meeting of the Independent Commission. Those few victims who did receive large amounts of cash generally quickly disappeared from view. Most often, their lawyers got half of it anyway.

Yet, despite the financial burden, monetary settlements were a good deal for the Church. Actual amounts paid out were usually kept secret and frequently a gag order was imposed on the victim. Unlike what happened later elsewhere in the country once victims got wise, few plaintiffs in New Mexico at the time thought to include a mandatory release of records as a condition in their agreements. Thus, even in seeming defeat, the secret system was preserved.

Civil v. criminal

Most victims had sued out of desperation because there seemed to be no other way to get justice or the Church to change. Criminal charges for the most part seemed rather futile. Again, Arthur Perrault provides a case in point. Of the 20 suits filed against various priests early on in the crisis, only a single victim, one of Perrault's, had actually complained to the police.

The district attorney, Robert Schwartz, wanted to prosecute and took the case to the grand jury. He said, "You're talking about this being the only victim who apparently has tried to treat what happened to him as a crime instead of a cash register." But Schwartz placed the blame for this mainly on the lawyers who didn't inform victims of their options.[25]

Considering how much attorneys such as Pasternack made off these cases, he had a point. However, Schwartz' indictment attempt failed due to the criminal statute of limitations. As O. J. Simpson's murder trials vividly demonstrated, criminal cases are generally much harder to win than civil suits due to differing standards for evidence. So the attorneys pursuing lawsuits were not just padding their pockets, they probably saved many victims needless grief and expense. Their cash winnings provided the closest thing to real justice most would ever see in this world.

Apart from Lipinski, few other priests would ever be criminally charged in New Mexico. Most of those cases would be dropped due to insufficient evidence.

The same Hispanic heritage that accepted the presence of corrupt priests also made it harder for victims to speak out. It was a male-oriented *macho* culture, deeply respectful of the clergy, and decidedly not friendly to gays. Many New Mexican victims stayed as anonymous as possible to keep their shame secret from their own family. This is yet another reason that the true numbers of abused children in the state will never be known.

Catholic culture can be especially cruel to those who criticize the clergy. Many family relationships were ruined among those victims who did come forward and not because of gold diggers, either. Not a few had come from alcoholic or otherwise dysfunctional and broken homes, which had made the perpetrator's efforts so much easier to begin with. Virtually all their families were extremely devout, flattered to have priests devote so much attention to their children.

That devotion was often the first thing victims lost, usually never to be recovered. As Pasternack said, Catholic victims of priests "lose the faith, but never lose the fear."[26] "Healing Masses" by the archbishop, prayers by the faithful, even apologies, were largely futile in getting them to return to the fold, though such things made good press.

For all too many victims, the mere sight of a Roman collar was enough to make them vividly relive their ordeal. This rarely has prevented Catholic clergy anywhere from wearing theirs to meetings with victims, or from often starting those meetings with a prayer.

All victims had been traumatized by their abuse in some way. The damage varied depending on their age and natural resilience, circumstances including the brutality and psychological manipulations of the perpetrator, and the amount of time the molestations lasted. What happened when victims finally disclosed the abuse was also critical.

Many of them were left with severe, even crippling, emotional injuries. Some form of addiction often masked the pain. To say that their lives had been wrecked is not an exaggeration. Some even passed the damage on by physically or sexually abusing their own family members.

Years of psychological counseling were usually needed. Many times there were large ongoing medical expenses, too. Victims had paid with bitter tears during their abuse; most would pay again during their recovery as well. Those who made it through the ordeal and had not succumbed to suicide, drugs, alcohol, sexual obsession, crime, or various diseases along the way had truly won the right to call themselves "survivors."

But both victims and all 275,000 or so Catholics in the archdiocese were about to be severely shocked, faithful or not. The scandals were about to blow up in a huge way that no one could have expected.

CHAPTER XIII:
DOOM COMES FOR THE ARCHBISHOP

Fall from grace

"Robert Fortune Sanchez" is an auspicious sounding name. Born on March 20, 1934 from the union of two prominent families in Socorro – "Fortune" being his mother's maiden name – the future archbishop was set early on a path that did indeed seem most providential. He already knew he wanted to be a priest as a young boy. He entered the seminary in Santa Fe in 1950, finishing his studies as the prestigious North American College in Rome. This was a rare honor and a sure sign that he was destined for an important post. Ordained there at the end of 1959, he returned to the Archdiocese of Santa Fe where he served in a variety of positions.

In 1974, he was abruptly and unexpectedly plucked from his pastorship of the city's oldest church to become the tenth archbishop of Santa Fe. His installation on July 25 was such a joyous celebration that it had to be held in an outdoor stadium due to the immense crowds. His pal Perrault served as one of the master of ceremonies.

Sanchez set some precedents: the first Hispanic archbishop in the country and the first priest in the state to be so elevated straight from a parish. But most importantly, Robert Sanchez was the first native New Mexican to become its archbishop. His people loved him for it.

The new prelate was only 40 at the time, extremely young for such an exalted position. He was slim, dark, and handsome, his black hair touched with silver, and customarily wore silver-framed aviators glasses. A gentle soul with a surprisingly soft handshake, Sanchez seemed universally well liked. Most of his reign went peaceably right up until the scandals. A serious car accident as he was rushing between engagements on Christmas in 1983, however, left him with brain injuries. This would turn out to be unexpectedly fortunate by providing him with a ready excuse for memory problems when the time came.[1]

That point arrived a decade later, during the winter of 1993. Cold questions had been raised by the still-simmering scandals, particularly in regards to Perrault. Sanchez, however, had promised support for victims, appointed Wolf, and said all the right things.

Then in the first week of March, a small article in the newspapers heralded the end soon to come. It alerted people to the presence in the state the weekend before of Mike Wallace, the well-known reporter for CBS News. He had apparently gotten into trouble confronting a group of pilgrims hiking to the healing shrine at Chimayó. The rumor was he had been physically rebuffed trying to confront Kirsch. Wallace only admitted to the media that he just wanted to talk to the archbishop about sex offender priests at the Servants of the Paraclete.[2]

The subject would be dealt with on an episode of the news magazine *60 Minutes* to be broadcast in several weeks. As the state waited, rumors, anxiety, and leaks steadily grew. Every newscast seemed to have more. It soon became clear the story involved Sanchez more than Kirsch. Wolf was said to have been talking to the Vatican, which was investigating something.[3]

Several members of the Alliance for Justice called for Sanchez' resignation as gossip about him spread. It was revealed that the archbishop was going to be accused personally. Soon, a name leaked. Judy Maloof was a college professor in the Midwest and a member of a wealthy Catholic family who were staunch supporters of the archbishop. Along with four other women, it was said that she had accused Sanchez himself of sexual abuse.[4]

Ever more troubling information boiled over. Dr. Salazar said that Sanchez went to Rome to talk about leaving the priesthood before becoming archbishop and was talked out of it. And he mentioned he had treated one of Sanchez' lovers as well, whom he declined to name.[5] In court, the archdiocese tried to get a restraining order on Pasternack. It was claimed he had met with Sanchez and Wolf in January with evidence of the archbishop's affairs and threatened to release it unless other cases were settled. Pasternack denied the accusations.[6]

Sanchez released a statement apologizing and asking for forgiveness, but neglected to specify what for. The chancellor said he had personally confronted his boss who had admitted his sorrow, but would not give a straight answer.[7] Wolf would later clam up about it, claiming priest-penitent privilege, and for months doggedly stonewalled attorneys and the press as to Sanchez' location. All that was known was that his boss was supposedly someplace on retreat "out of state" – though many suspected he was actually holed up in Jemez Canyon.

On Friday, March 19, the sandal dropped. From wherever he was hiding, Robert Sanchez resigned as archbishop. Wolf sadly read his boss's letter to the pope aloud to the media. The chancellor initially said he too would quit, but he remained loyal and very much in charge. Despite his own personal disapproval of his superior, Wolf soon threatened to suspend a parish priest who had criticized Sanchez from the pulpit.[8]

With a touch of truly divine irony, Sanchez' fifty-ninth birthday fell the very day after he did. No wonder his supporters were concerned about his mental state.

But Robert Fortune Sanchez was spared setting one historical precedent: he was not the first American prelate in the country to resign in utter disgrace due to an affair. Archbishop Eugene A. Marino of Atlanta, as luck would have it, the nation's first African-American archbishop just as Sanchez was the first Hispanic one, claimed that dishonor several years previously.

Sanchez' secrets

The archbishop's supporters held a prayer rally and hundreds more attended a Mass for him at the holy shrine at Chimayó. It was too late to do much immediate good. For that Sunday evening, the other sandal finally fell with the long-awaited broadcast of the CBS News report.[9] Exceeding the people's worst fears about their beloved leader, it was not so much an anticlimax as a grim confirmation of the terrible mess their Church was in.

Victims' mother Marlene Debry-Nowak led off, telling how she had complained to Sanchez three times about Perrault. Her sons had revealed many more additional instances of abuse that occurred even while she was present in the house, and six more kids were molested later. She unhesitatingly blamed Sanchez for failing to protect them.

Attorney Bruce Pasternack batted next, saying there were several hundred victims in the state. He claimed that other bishops had even warned Sanchez about the situation. New Mexico had so many because it had been "the center for the accumulation of the world's pedophile priests." He placed the responsibility squarely on the Servants and their policy of allowing priests to work in the archdiocese after treatment. Citing Sigler, who had molested six boys while in treatment, Pasternack mentioned that on Sigler's first assignment afterwards, he was placed in charge of the altar boys.

Wallace then talked to Kirsch's victim, Susan Sandoval, who said that she was sure Sanchez knew about it. Kirsch was a friend of the archbishop; he had introduced her to his boss. The reporter's dramatic confrontation with Kirsch on the road involving a bit of pushing and shoving by pilgrims was then shown. When asked about the allegations, the priest mumbled that her attorney must have put her up to it.

Finally, three of the five women, including Judy Maloof and state politician Patricia Madrid, told their tales with remarkable calm and dignity. Maloof had been swept away in college by the handsome cleric, shortly after she had graduated from high school and not long after he had become archbishop. The affair lasted five years, only ending after Sanchez returned from a trip to Rome. He had taken both her virginity and her faith.

The stories the other two women told were remarkably similar to each other's. They had not had intercourse, but the archbishop had groped one and kissed the other both on the same night during a camping trip. Perhaps most disturbing of all, he had later said to one of them, "If only your father knew what he was missing."

For the grand *auto da fé*, Wallace put Ron Wolf in the hot seat. The priest angrily demanded to see the evidence. So, the reporter obligingly showed him a tape of Maloof's statement. It was a true gallows moment as the chancellor was filmed uncomfortably watching it and then having to admit the seriousness of what he had just seen.

Mike Wallace calmly concluded the segment noting that they had talked to other alleged victims, including one woman who claimed Sanchez had raped her the year before he became archbishop, and she had been given $25,000 for therapy.

All said, it was a stunning tour de force, a thoroughly devastating piece of journalism. The sour taste left behind was that if the situation was out of control it was because the archbishop himself was too busy fooling around.

This intuition was right, though just how accurate would not be known for a while. Over three and a half years later, after a legal battle hard-fought all the way to the state's Supreme Court, the world was finally told something about what the tenth Archbishop of Santa Fe knew and did about clergy abuse. The simple answer was: Not much.

The archdiocese's lawyers had bitterly contested those of the local news media up until the very last minute. When his 760-page deposition was finally released, a judge had heavily edited it. More than a quarter of the testimony was deleted for "privacy concerns." At least 35 names of accused priests that have never been made public were also removed.

The deposition, taken over four days in January 1994, concerned what Sanchez knew about pedophile priests in the archdiocese in general, his own history, and specifically how it all related to cases involving Sigler and Perrault. Continuing legal action by local media got other parts and another deposition released later. Much of his testimony remains secret still.[10]

From the transcript, it would appear that Sanchez didn't know very much at all about what was going on and cared even less. He did demonstrate great loyalty to his friends, or possibly, he himself was being blackmailed.

In a later lawsuit against Sabine Griego, accused various times but treated remarkably leniently by Sanchez, Pasternack claimed that the priest knew of Sanchez' acting out with "young girls" as late as 1992, even as the archbishop was aware of Griego's attraction to altar boys. After Griego was caught molesting children as pastor in Las Vegas, New Mexico, Sanchez assigned him to Queen of Heaven in Albuquerque. There, the lawsuit alleged he molested the plaintiff, starting when the boy was 9 or 10 years old, for five years.[11]

Then the archbishop sent Griego to Southdown, a Canadian treatment center that was not run by the Paracletes, for ephebophilia, or attraction to teens. Sanchez even visited him there.[12] Perhaps the archbishop felt that Jemez Springs was too close to home for such an intimate associate who knew so much.

Sanchez would keep him close, too. Once Griego was released, he moved into the archbishop's residence as his roommate. In another lawsuit, a different plaintiff said that Griego took him to the house, and gave him wine, making him "tipsy" in the archbishop's presence, even though he was only 15 at the time.[13]

Griego was then made chaplain at a local Catholic hospital but this new assignment didn't last long, either. Wolf soon restricted him from saying Mass publicly. He told the press that the priest had been under investigation for months. He also innocently made an honest but career-killing admission that since Sanchez had sent Griego away for treatment, the archbishop must have known of his condition.[14]

None of that, however, was apparently known or mattered to law enforcement. Griego's last known job was as a psychologist at a state prison, which he quit as soon as his past surfaced. The state Department of Corrections said they had hired him because he had successfully passed an FBI background check.[15] But, the priest seems guilty of something. The last lawsuit against him was settled in 1995 when he assigned rights for $1.5 million from the insurance policy to the victim.[16]

During a discussion on TV immediately following the *60 Minutes* broadcast, Pasternack speculated that because Sanchez had failed to be celibate, he had been caught in a "theological gridlock in his own mind" that prevented him from acting effectively when informed of an abusive priest.[17]

Perhaps, but it seems likely that something more must have been involved with both Griego and Perrault. Both men were intimately associated with the archbishop and steadily advanced in their careers despite being repeatedly accused and even sent to treatment.

Was it extortion or friendship? In his deposition, Sanchez emphatically denied that Perrault was his friend. If true, it makes sense – real friends do not blackmail each other.

In fact, Arthur Perrault was the very first priest whose abuse Sanchez had to deal with.[18] In 1976, the man, with his lawyer present, personally admitted molesting kids to the new archbishop, describing it in language Sanchez found shocking. Sanchez sent him to treatment and then, despite having said he would never be around children again, gave him several more "chances."

By far, the most remarkable feature of Sanchez' testimony was the archbishop's many memory lapses. His deposition made it painfully clear why so many of the lawsuits were directed against him personally and the archdiocese as well as the accused priest. Repeatedly, Sanchez could not recall being told allegations or warnings about clergy.

Incredibly, in the case of Perrault yet again, he was told of the man's activities by at least 15 people at different times: four priests, two nuns, five parents or concerned adults, and four victims. Not to mention that there were several negative psychiatric evaluations and even direct admissions of guilt by the offender himself.

Yet, Sanchez didn't blame his forgetfulness on brain damage this time. He confessed that it was "possible" that he might have put information out of his mind because it was painful or that he was too busy with his duties. He did speculate, however, that Alzheimer's might be "an affliction that hits all archbishops" but not, as Pasternack cynically suggested, "only when they're sued." Perhaps not, but this and other depositions with forgetful prelates would easily give that impression.

The archdiocese had good reason to want the testimony kept secret. Sanchez was revealed as a man simply too involved and compromised by his own sexual acting out to effectively deal in any way with the sins of his priests. He confessed his own sexual activity with eleven women, all in their twenties, over the span of 18 years that supposedly only began after he became archbishop.

Lying, brain damaged, or senile, the leader who had charmed so many came off as an incompetent administrator and an even worse pastor. Throughout the deposition, Sanchez admitted repeatedly that he had asked no questions, sought no information, and never looked at anyone's personnel files. Not even once had he tried to minister to victims, victims' families, or any parishes where accused priests had been removed. He had taken notes on just two cases that had come to his attention during his nearly nineteen years on the throne.

The only time he ever spoke to civil authorities was on the sole occasion when they called him. Claiming he never received any instructions from the Vatican on the subject, Archbishop Sanchez simply felt he had no responsibility whatsoever to report anything to anyone. "The Church is not an institution that initiates investigations," he defensively declared, somehow even forgetting the Inquisition, too.

The former ethics teacher swore that he had not realized until 1990 that pedophilia was incurable and that sexual abuse was a crime that one was legally obliged to report. Sanchez said he was informed at the one seminar for bishops he had attended on the subject that the first two concerns when allegations arose should be to protect the rights of the accused priests and to get the lawyers involved. He had never resorted to outside psychologists because that would be interfering with the Servants of the Paraclete.

As for the reasons he never told parishes why priests had been removed, Sanchez cited the need for privacy, canon law, and a desire to avoid scandal and divisiveness in parishes.

Under close questioning by Pasternack, the archbishop finally had to admit that ultimately it rests solely on the shoulders of an abused Catholic child to disclose molestation at the hands of a man the whole community reveres.

As his testimony chillingly confirmed, the sacrament of Confession can easily be twisted to conceal crimes. The archbishop stated under oath that the "forcible rape of a child" is far less a sin for a priest to commit than breaking the seal of Confession by reporting hearing about it to his religious superiors, the police or the child's parents, even if forgiveness is denied in Confession.

Only the pope can forgive such a serious transgression as telling secrets of the confessional — as a "reserved" sin, it ranks right up there with physically striking a priest. But the ex-pastor verified that any priest can forgive anyone, including another priest, for raping a child and then must keep it secret forever.

As expected, Sanchez showed little understanding of the victim's point of view. His concern for children never extended to the point of asking even self-admitted pedophiles (or anyone else for that matter) if there were any more victims. He even wrote a nice letter to Jason Sigler, whom he knew had abused children, when the man left. It expressed thanks for all his service, "out of courtesy." This was a greater kindness than the boys Sigler had molested ever got from their spiritual shepherd and guardian.

Sanchez' final statement released along with the deposition showed the same oddly passive indifference. "Out of respect for the rights of individuals to privacy, I have chosen not to speak out publicly. If my silence has been misleading or has given offense, I ask your forgiveness."[19] He did only slightly better on a second try after another deposition was later released.

So it was that the most beloved archbishop of Santa Fe fell into shame, dishonor, and oblivion. For a while, he was thought to be living in seclusion in Phoenix. Then in 1998, a television station in Albuquerque said he had been living with nuns in a small Minnesota town.

It was reported that Sanchez had been seen with the Sisters of Mercy in Jackson, but their spokeswoman said that Sanchez no longer lived with the nuns who have two farms there. She said Sanchez had lived there only because the nuns were hospitable. He had held no formal job but may have served as their chaplain. Not quite a monastery of the strict observance, but to some it might seem punishment enough.

It was also discovered that he had led a retreat for priests in Tucson that October in spite of his disgrace.[20] He visited his old haunts in 1995, and he was rumored to have returned briefly in 2008 for his successor's celebration of twenty-five years as a priest. Robert Sanchez' current whereabouts and activities remain unknown.

CHAPTER XIV:
AFTER THE FALL

Texas arranger

Sanchez' replacement was not long in coming. In early April 1993, several weeks before Easter, Pope John Paul II formally accepted the archbishop's resignation and named Bishop Michael J. Sheehan, the first bishop of the brand-new Diocese of Lubbock as apostolic administrator. Despite his Texan origins, Sheehan was almost as eagerly embraced by the faithful as his predecessor had been. He claimed he had nothing in his "very dull closet" except shoes, though that turned out to be not entirely accurate.[1]

Sheehan, affectionately called the "boy bishop" by Texan Catholics, was 53, not quite so young as Sanchez had been when selected. Born in 1939, he too attended seminary in Rome like Sanchez, being ordained in 1964. As he called Sanchez his friend, perhaps they had met there. He was also friendly and outgoing, slim and wore glasses, but had much more gray in his hair.

He later served as pastor, the head of a seminary, and received a degree in canon law.

Despite his infectious enthusiasm for building up the Church out on the arid plains of the Texas panhandle, not everything there had gone smoothly. In 1988, three charismatics claimed to be receiving messages from the Blessed Virgin. As many as 22,000 people had shown up to witness visions that may or may have not happened. In any case, Sheehan silenced the pastor and shut the whole thing down.

Then, in December of 1992, a New Orleans TV station exposed Rodney Howell. He was a pastor in O'Donnell, who with his brother and fellow priest, Gerard, had molested children in Oklahoma and Texas. Howell, 60 at the time, was still serving in West Texas but died the following month.

Sheehan called a news conference, established a victims' hotline and offered counseling. Praised for his quick actions, it turned out there was more to the story.

In 1986, a family in Anton had accused Howell of abusing two children in an alcohol-related incident. Sheehan sent the priest to treatment for alcoholism. Complaints about Howell again surfaced a year or so later. This time there was no mention of sex, but there were financial improprieties including his bingo operation and mysterious fires on church property. Sheehan, it was said, had not responded until the later public sexual accusations made it necessary.[2]

But the "boy bishop" rode out the crisis without much problem. Perhaps it was Sheehan's successful handling of the affair, and familiarity with Hispanic culture, that had recommended him for the position in Santa Fe.

More ominously but unknown at the time of his arrival there was another black mark on his record. Sheehan had a small but critical role in the tragedy of Rudy Kos. He had been the rector of Holy Trinity Seminary in Dallas who had admitted Kos.

If indeed a list of the "Sons of Perdition" really existed, Rudy Kos would surely have earned a prominent place on it. Once ordained, he may have had as many as 50 victims. Ten former altar boys and the parents of one who had committed suicide sued him and the Diocese of Dallas. All the boys had been abused hundreds of times, starting with having had their feet used to masturbate him, and progressing later to oral and anal sex.

One victim even openly lived with the priest for two years under the pretense that he had adopted the boy. Another testified that Kos had telephoned him regularly while under treatment at Jemez Springs and that the priest abused him twice while on leave from the place. One was molested both before and after Kos' two-month exile.

In July 1997, after an eleven-week trial, the plaintiffs were awarded $119.6 million dollars, a record civil judgment at the time. It was later reduced to $23 million to avoid forcing the diocese into bankruptcy. Kos convicted to three life sentences and then some. He forcibly laicized by the Church for good measure.

Kos didn't defend himself at trial but later blamed the diocese for making him a scapegoat. He also said that some of the charges were vicious lies. He made himself out to be a "wounded healer" and even a victim, claiming to be not a pedophile but a foot fetishist. However, the evidence presented indicated a long history of serious problems.

Kos had spent a year in a juvenile detention center for molesting a young neighbor. His brothers claimed he had molested them both and would have told diocesan officials that he was unfit for the priesthood if asked.

To get into the seminary, Kos sought an annulment from a previous marriage on the grounds it had not been consummated. His ex-wife claimed he had married her "to make his life look normal so he could molest boys without any suspicion." She testified that she had told a diocesan official that Kos was gay and attracted to boys.[3]

Apparently, no investigation had been made into Kos, but the former head of the seminary had rejected his application anyway. Sheehan conceded under grilling that a top diocesan official had pressed for his acceptance. He yielded and so Kos entered the seminary.[4]

As the trial made abundantly obvious, Sheehan was far from being the only church official that had cleared the way, ignored, or covered-up for Rudy Kos. However, his willingness to go along and seeming lack of concern was all too reminiscent of Sanchez.

The crisis continues

As apostolic administrator, Sheehan said all the appropriate things, apologizing for his predecessor's failures while praising Sanchez' accomplishments. The new man was clever enough to claim to like green chile, the state's most prized crop, and he would often spice his sermons with Spanish, too. The news media were filled for weeks on end with excited pieces about his meetings with parishioners and how the Church was healing. The people had endured an almost daily drumbeat of bad news since the previous fall. They just wanted to put it all behind them.

But the crisis so long in coming would not easily depart. And it would cost plenty to make it all go away. Soon, Sheehan asked his parishes to voluntarily pitch in and they did so with few complaints at first.

Sanchez had set up an Independent Commission to review the problem. Their report at the end of April under Sheehan's new regime contained few surprises. It called for a hotline for victims, screening for seminarians, treatment but no return to parish work for abusers, and a Review Board to study future complaints. The Board would consist of nine members, including two priests, one victim, and a parent of a victim.[5]

All deliberations were confidential; yet, just two pastors were ever publicly accused by it before it was eventually dissolved. However, one of the priests who sat on the Board, Robert Malloy, would be accused much later in the most singularly bizarre scandal to ever become known in the archdiocese – so far.

Other priests were fingered, victims came forward, and more suits filed throughout the spring and summer of 1993. Susan Sandoval, Robert Kirsch's victim who had finally gone public, saw her case thrown out due to the statute of limitations. She ultimately received $6,000 to cover therapy but no other settlement even though she still had his love letters and the Church's lawyers had never disputed what had happened to her.[6] Indeed, this case had prompted the letter from the Paracletes' attorney to stop them from destroying records.[7]

Robert Kirsch was a controversial character right out of the old days. He had been sent to the Paracletes in 1965 and 1989 supposedly for somehow stirring up his parishioners. Trained by the Jesuits, he was from a well-to-do family and a private pilot. Once he supposedly had flown another victim to a remote location for a fake marriage ceremony.

He mounted a novel defense to explain his actions with Sandoval. Kirsch admitted intercourse with her starting when she was 15 but claimed that it was not really sex, as he had not attained orgasm. Moreover, he boldly claimed this was a theological principle called the "reserved embrace" and as such, was nothing wrong.[8]

That might explain her venereal disease, but not how the priest had gotten her pregnant while abusing her over three years.[9] Wolf, as a canonist and chancellor, angrily corrected him in public for this novel theological conceit.

A priest named Barney Bissonette, originally from Norwich, Connecticut, where he had served in various parishes and molested seven boys, was accused in April. Confronted by three brothers, he admitted it and two other occasions and said he had been to the Servants. The oldest brother, Bissonette's own godson, had committed suicide. The brothers reported the abuse to the archdiocese, and were lied to about his status.[10]

Bissonette had served in parishes around New Mexico too. He had also been chaplain at the New Mexico Boy's School in Springer, a reformatory for underage male offenders. In 1978, he was relieved after five years, when at least three boys accused him of molesting them in the school chapel. Sabine Griego, then archdiocesan liaison, informed Sanchez. Griego assumed supervision and assured Archbishop Sanchez that Bissonette would get treatment.

A year later, Bissonette was stationed at St. Bernadette. He was then transferred around the state until late 1992.[11] He retired to Belen, a small town south of Albuquerque, and was forbidden to publicly minister.[12]

In 1994, another, now-deceased chaplain at the Boy's School was also accused of abuse in two lawsuits. This predecessor of Bissonette, Edward Donelan, had been there eight years when he got the idea of a ranch for troubled boys in 1966. He founded the Hacienda de los Muchachos far out on the eastern plains. When the residents' complaints of Donelan's molestations reached the state Department of Corrections, the Secretary notified Archbishop Davis. Davis checked the man's personnel file, reported no homosexual tendencies, and so the inquiry was dropped. The ranch continued to be licensed until Donelan was removed in 1976.[13]

An ex-priest, Ronald Lane Fontenot, from the states of Washington and Louisiana, had been to treatment in Massachusetts. He had also spent two years with the Paracletes. He became a counselor, and was accused of inappropriate touching at several firms in Albuquerque.[14]

A priest imported from India, Augustine Abeywickrema, had a suit filed against him by three sisters, ranging from six to fourteen years of age when he had molested them, settled. He had abused them at his first post, St. Bernadette in the 1960's, and then served around the archdiocese until the suit was filed and he was forced to retire.[15] He also was forbidden to minister, but claimed Sanchez had given him permission to work on a door-to-door job.[16]

But the most significant case that summer was undoubtedly that of Gordon MacRae. Its importance laid not so much in his molestations, but the position he held when arrested. MacRae was a counselor, test administrator, and assistant director at the Paracletes' facility in Jemez Springs.[17]

MacRae became a priest in 1982. By the next year, he had molested three teenaged boys in Keene, New Hampshire. Three years later, he had become a counselor at an alcoholic treatment center. In 1989, after having been found guilty of two sexual misdemeanor charges, he had been sent to Jemez Springs for sex problems. Accusations had involved taking nude pictures of boys, and contacting them when on a visit home from the House of Affirmation, the first treatment center to which he had been sent.[18]

Liam Hoare, then Servant General, confirmed that MacRae went through a six-month treatment program and had been hired as admissions director. But he also claimed MacRae merely worked on the telephone switchboard and not as a counselor. Nor was he an actual member of the order.[19] Yet, even seven years after the sentencing, Hoare's successor, Servant General Peter Lechner, proposed hiring an attorney and setting up a defense fund for MacRae.[20]

After his arrest at his home, MacRae tried to commit suicide and failed. He pled innocent, and was admitted to a treatment center in Hartford, Connecticut with unspecified problems.[21] He even sued officials in Keene for persecuting him.[22] Despite his adamant proclamations of his innocence, however, after being convicted of one count of oral sex with a minor, he pled guilty to two other charges. His victims claimed he had abused them as many as 70 times.[23]

The pope flies by

August brought a welcome new distraction from all this: World Youth Day. First held by Pope John Paul II in Rome in 1986 to reinvigorate the Church's youth, it was to be celebrated internationally every three or four years. This international Catholic love-in soon became a major global event, drawing in hundreds of thousands of young people and their shepherds. In 1993, it was held in Denver, Colorado. The pontiff even loaned various treasures from the Vatican to a museum there for the pilgrims to marvel at. No special indulgences were offered, however.

In New Mexico, plans were soon drawn up for an expedition of busloads of kids to the event. But many hoped that the pope, who would be flying over the state from a previous stop in Mexico, might drop in on his way, or at least say something. The shattered morale of the faithful surely could have used it. But the pontiff did not change his plans. Disappointed, the faithful prepared for their own trek north.

Sheehan went along to the Mile High City, too. Once there, he told a group of young New Mexican pilgrims that he'd seen only a few protesters, "but if I were one of them I'd be depressed when I saw the 200,000 Catholics here. I'd take my sign and go home."[24]

Several of those depressed picketers were determined clergy abuse activists who were not about to give up yet. Led by the author, four other members of the Alliance for Justice, including Susan Sandoval and Conrad Jiron, also went to demonstrate as the only group of clergy abuse protesters to be seen at the major events, including the final outdoor Mass at Cherry Creek Park.

Attended by some 500,000 enthusiastic pilgrims, hellish August heat turned it into a near-disaster by the end as many were overcome. Though there was some light heckling of the demonstrators by the crowd, the authorities kept a very tight rein. The event went peacefully but the marchers found themselves diverted to a penned area far out of view of the Mass arena. The toll made it their last, if most quixotic, group protest, however.

People on all sides had been hoping that John Paul would use this historic opportunity to say something inspiring about the clergy abuse crisis. But it was not ever to be, then or later. His homily at the final Mass merely condemned "the culture of death" and abortion. He had publicly mentioned the crisis in passing only to blame the failures of his priests on a "widespread false morality." Abuse was simply a North American problem.[25]

Previously, the pope's silence about the crisis had only been broken in a letter sent in June to the American bishops. In it, John Paul said he was "deeply pained" by the scandals, claimed that canonical penalties were "fully justified" and that a committee was working on how they could be applied in the United States.

But the main point of the pontiff's message to his bishops was to emphatically decry *"treating moral evil as an occasion for sensationalism."* Speaking of the "fundamental right of individuals not to be easily exposed to the ridicule of public opinion," John Paul clearly didn't like how his priests were being treated in the press. The letter ended with a warning that "America needs prayer – *lest it lose its soul*" (emphasis shown in original).[26]

Another decade would pass with more outbreaks across America and in Canada, Ireland, Australia, Austria, and elsewhere before the universal nature of the crisis would be undeniable to all save the Vatican. Finally, in 2002, Cardinal Bernard Law of Boston's concealment of the numerous molestations of John Geoghan and others were revealed, followed by *Crimen sollicitationis* the next year.

For his part, Law was rewarded with a major post in the Vatican, serenely immune from annoying American lawsuits and court summonses.

Not that it mattered much by then. A year before, as will be shown, then-Cardinal Ratzinger, the pope's right hand man, had already reinstituted the cover-up even more tightly than before with his boss's blessing.

Of course, none of this was known at the time.

Just like his successor would, John Paul II firmly believed that all scandals involving clergy should be kept secret for the Church to handle as it saw fit. He once said, "Like every house that has special rooms that are not open to guests, the Church also needs rooms for talks that require privacy." However, he was not speaking about the sanctity of Confession.

The supreme pontiff actually uttered this while privately scolding the bishops of Austria. He was disgusted by their failure to limit public debate and suppress the people's open fury over revelations of Cardinal Hermann Groer's sexual abuse of young boys.[27]

CHAPTER XV:
THE MONEY GAME

A Church nearly bankrupt

Bishop Sheehan had an audience with John Paul II in Denver. It could not have gone better for him. As soon as the pope returned to Rome, it was announced that the "boy bishop" from Lubbock would become the eleventh archbishop of Santa Fe.[1] He would be the second bishop from Texas to be so elevated.

Barely had the excitement died down after World Youth Day when it began to build again for Sheehan's installation. On September 21, he was raised to archbishop in a grand ceremony carried on live TV. Representatives from all the state's minorities participated. The papal nuncio himself performed the honors. Among the ecclesiastical dignitaries on hand were a platoon of bishops plus cardinals Joseph Bernardin of Chicago and Roger Mahony of Los Angeles.[2] The former would soon be accused of abuse (later recanted by the dying man under pressure) and the latter years later of covering up the numberless sins of his own priests.

Sheehan talked hopefully about progress and restoring the Church. He spoke of his friend Sanchez' accomplishments and encouraged the people not to leave. But signs that the Catholic Church was in trouble were evident in the numbers. In spite of the heavy publicity, the archdiocese admitted that only 4,500 showed up for the occasion, far less than the anticipated 10,500 sellout.[3]

But if the faithful present or watching on TV thought that their new leader could quickly end the crisis, they would be disappointed. Though indeed the worst was past, the New Mexican scandals would grind on into the next millennium.

Throughout the fall of 1993, the earlier lawsuits began to be settled even as more accusations continued. Elaine Montoya, who had been abused by Perrault over 300 times, starting when she was only fourteen, was awarded $600,000. Almost half of that went to her lawyers. She was also given $50,000 to cover her extensive hospitalization costs to date.[4] Earlier that week, her brother Paul had his claim dismissed because of the statute of limitations.[5]

To avoid trial and speed the settlement process, lawyers resorted to a new technique called "stipulated judgments." Under these agreements, the defendant being sued would assign its rights to the insurance payoff to the plaintiff up to an arranged sum. Eager to get out of the public spotlight, the Servants of the Paraclete quickly agreed. But the insurers of the archdiocese, who were already trying to avoid paying anything, balked.

The method was first tried successfully for the four New Mexican victims of James Porter who got $125,000 each. Months later, around the time Porter was sentenced, Pasternack used it again for seventeen victims of Jason Sigler for $13 million.[6] As part of the deal, he even got Sigler to apologize personally to the men in his office. Though officially the former priest admitted no liability, he did agree to reveal all he knew in a deposition.[7]

By this time, the archdiocese was distinctly feeling the financial pain. It was rich in land, including the vacant but prime site where St. Pius X High School originally stood, assessed at $2 million. But the Church in one of the poorest states was likewise poor in cash.

On paper Santa Fe already carried over $10 million in debt.[8] A $2 million settlement fund was rapidly being drained. The parishes had generously donated $350,000 to a counseling fund for victims, which was also emptying fast, though it was later doubled and in time would reach $1 million.[9] But after $280,000 had been spent, sharp restrictions were put into place. There would be no more inpatient therapy. Only approved therapists would be paid — but not those treating any victim suing the Church.[10]

Sheehan stoutly resisted any suggestion that the priests' own pension fund be tapped. He said that it wasn't that big anyway. There were only 34 retired priests who received just $1,000 to $3,000 a month.[11] He claimed that he himself only earned $550 a month plus expenses.[12]

Nor was the Vatican, which had an official deficit of $86 million in 1992 and more pressing global responsibilities, in any position to help.[13] Meanwhile, Sheehan said that victims were suing for as much as $51 million.[14] Desperate measures were called for.

Secret letters detailing allegations went out to ten dioceses that had sent perpetrators to the state asking for their help.[15] It is not known if any actually did. The insurance companies, however, who had been fighting the archdiocese in court, eventually agreed to pay up in most cases.

Soon after the Porter settlement, the archbishop announced that certain properties would be sold, but not at fire sale prices. Less than two weeks before Christmas, he sent a letter to the parishes again asking them for money. The alternative, he said ominously, could well be bankruptcy.

If so, Santa Fe would have been the first Catholic diocese in the nation to go down financially. Somehow, it avoided that fate. That dubious distinction went instead to Portland, Oregon in 2004, followed shortly by Tucson, then Spokane, Davenport, San Diego, and most recently, Fairbanks.[16]

San Diego had abruptly filed for bankruptcy protection shortly before trial was to begin on 42 lawsuits after four years of failed negotiations. It ultimately settled for $198.1 million, one of the largest of all time, and then sought to have its bankruptcy case dismissed.[17] Even the judge speculated that the filing had merely been a legal maneuver to avoid trial.

In any case, this time Sheehan's plea to the parishes produced the first open grumbling heard from his flock. Many parishioners could see no reason why they should pay for the sins of the estimated 40-50 abusive priests over 30 years, or their 200 victims.[18] One of the diocese's 91 parishes even voted against donating anything more at all, though it later did. Most, however, gave generously without complaint. The archbishop had asked for a million dollars and they gave him a half a million more. He even boasted that some accused clergy had donated, and one former priest had chipped in $2,500.[19]

In Albuquerque, the commercially valuable lot where Sanchez and Perrault once taught high school was eventually sold for redevelopment. A dozen other properties were put up for sale. Perhaps the most significant of these was the Dominican Retreat House.

This lovely 70-acre property had been run by a small group of nuns for 37 years. Open to all denominations, the sisters held workshops on everything from alcoholism to enneagrams. Moreover, it had acquired a reputation among victims of being one of the few places where they could find sympathy when disclosing their abuse to anyone associated with the Church. Some thought that was precisely why it was put on the block.

The nuns were offered space at the archdiocesan headquarters, but instead they temporarily moved over to the nearby Pius XII Villa. The Paracletes, who desperately needed some favorable publicity and had ended their halfway house experiment, gave it to the Dominicans rent-free for a year.[20] They have since moved to a different location.

There was now a Paraclete connection with the sisters' previous home. Their former retreat had been acquired by an order of monks popularly called the Norbertines, as a monastery and retreat house of their own. This order also ran several parishes and provided chaplains to a Catholic hospital and the local Air Force base. Two members were to give spiritual direction to guests of the Servants of the Paraclete in their retreat and renewal pro-grams.[21]

Significantly, there was never any talk whatsoever about the Paracletes themselves going bankrupt. One insurance company attorney complained that the Servants had a reputation of "extraordinary ruthlessness against in-surance companies."[22] The figures they and their insurers have paid out have never been divulged either, though doubtless many millions. It doesn't seem to have hurt them, however. Though the Paracletes have half-heartedly tried to turn some unused facilities to other purposes, they've never even had to hold a bake sale to raise funds.

Yet, even in "treatment," however, guests could help pay for their own keep. In the affidavit where he complained of the lack of therapy while at the Villa, David Holley revealed that he had instead been put to work saying Masses for money.

Holley testified he had been given the necessary permissions, or facul-ties, to say Masses, both by his own bishop and the archbishop of Santa Fe. There were too few priests to perform the sacred liturgy for all the needs of the people of Worcester, so their prayer intentions and the accompanying donations of $3-5 would be forwarded to Holley, who was supposed to say Masses privately for them.[23]

Trafficking in Masses is one of the oldest, most often used and dubious means for priests to make quick cash. At best, it flirts with the sin of simony but at worst, it is outright fraud. There's no indication of where Holley's ac-tivities fit on the scale, or how many other guests were similarly employed.

Despite the Church's solemn assurance that the efficacy of such rites are unaffected by the moral character of the performer, one can only wonder if the people got what they paid for. One thing is certain, however: it would take a lot of Mass donations to fully support a guest. From what is known of Fitzgerald's thinking, however, he might well have approved of the men be-ing employed in so spiritually profitable a manner.

Questions remain, such as, how much sacramental trafficking was going on? Was it a major source of income, or just something to keep the guests busy and out of trouble? And how much did supply priests bring in?

After the firestorm

January 1994 brought news of Sanchez' return to tell his side to the law-yers, but he said nothing to the people. In February, the agreement with the insurance companies was reached. It was a hopeful omen that a corner had been turned in the crisis. Another sign was a bit of a shock that came before the papers were even signed: the chancellor was reassigned, starting on Valentines Day.

Just the month before it had become embarrassingly apparent that Sheehan was not happy with his chief of staff. One day, Wolf informed the news media that he was no longer permitted to comment on cases. Several days later, he said he had misunderstood his instructions, but that he first had to clear all statements with his boss.[24] Apparently, his frank admission that Sanchez had to have known about his old pal Griego's abuse was just too honest to be tolerated.

Ron Wolf went back to parish work. His curt dismissal had been a public slap in the face of a man who had given so much to try to save the Church he loved. But he did appear to be genuinely content to be out of the hot seat.

There he stayed until he suddenly passed away on August 2, 1995. Both his wake and funeral were attended by overflowing crowds. The archbishop and thirteen priests concelebrated the service, and a survivor read the eulogy. Sheehan, the man who had fired him, said that Wolf had lupus and kidney disease, and had actually "begged" for the transfer. He admitted, though, that Ron Wolf "was strong medicine for a very sick patient."[25] Even Wolf's legal opponents praised him. Pasternack said simply but accurately, "He was a righteous man."[26]

The good feeling was evident all around. Afterwards outside the church, Kirsch, still wearing his Roman collar, was seen by the author chatting pleasantly with Archbishop Sheehan. It was like old times.

In fact, Sheehan had re-installed the man Wolf replaced, Richard Olona. Known to have been another close friend of Sanchez, the move was regarded dubiously by survivors and their supporters. A nun who had worked in family services, Sister Nancy Kazik, came in to serve as case manager and vice chancellor. Though she was the first female vice chancellor in the nation, her investigative powers in that position were restricted by canon law because she was not a priest.

She concentrated on reining in the scandals instead. Kazik limited counseling to victims, and abruptly cut off payments to Kirsch's victim, Susan Sandoval, who had not been awarded a settlement. Two professional full-time investigators hired by the archdiocese quit in disgust, publicly complaining that Kazik had changed the ground rules so that their inquiries would be far less effective.[27]

The buzz among survivors was that the real reason the investigators quit was because they had compiled a long list of names of both victims and perpetrators, many more than were generally known, but had been forbidden to present them to the Review Board.

Whatever the truth of that rumor, the archdiocese had indeed used its investigators against victims. Members of the Alliance for Justice had complained of being harassed, followed, spied upon, and even having had their phones tapped. Though Wolf had angrily denied authorizing the latter charge when privately confronted by the author, he had blustered angrily on occasion at reporters about having damaging personal information about another member of the Alliance.[28]

Confirmation that the Church investigated New Mexican victims came years later, surprisingly, from the East Coast. It was due to the release of testimony by then-bishop (and now retired cardinal) Edward Egan of Bridgeport, Connecticut, about one of his errant priests.

In 2002, it was revealed that one guest of the Paracletes, Laurence Brett, had been sent to them in 1964 after admitting biting a teenager during oral sex. Assigned to the archdiocese rather than return to Connecticut, he sought oral and anal sex from a boy in his room in a New Mexico rectory. He later went to Baltimore, and ultimately fled the country.

When the New Mexican victim told priests in 1992 about what had happened, the Archdiocese of Santa Fe hired an investigator to check into his background, Egan's testimony revealed. There was no sign that they had looked into that of the priest.[29] Sheehan later claimed that this was "not done to discredit victims. This was rather an effort to look at what priest had done and to talk to those who had made allegations about it."[30] However, the author knows of no victim in the state who ever talked to archdiocesan investigators about their case.

Yet, whatever else the investigators had been up to, their snooping had apparently borne some fruit. The Review Board was claimed to have advised removing a dozen or so priests from publicly ministry. But names such as that of popular pastor Ignacio Tafoya were only released when the accused occupied a highly visible position.[31] Likewise, another pastor, John C. Rodriguez, only stepped down after being sued.[32] If either had already retired, his sins would probably remain hidden like the rest.

In this manner, the primary means hyped to enforce accountability within the archdiocese was employed instead to reinforce secrecy. Eventually, however, the Review Board ran out of work. This "Inquisition Lite" was quietly dissolved as no longer needed, with the private thanks of the archbishop to its members for their good service to the Church.

Other tactics

Secrecy continued as before. Wolf had strongly recommended that Lipinski should voluntarily seek liacization. A year after becoming archbishop, Sheehan mentioned in the paper that the popular priest would face an ecclesiastical trial. Naturally, details have never been released but the archbishop later said Lipinski had indeed finally been defrocked.[33] And that was that.

In 1995, the archdiocese's lobbyists tried to get a bill through the state legislature that would have eliminated the Church's liability. Suits would only be allowed by the victim, not his or her family, and only against the individual perpetrator rather than the institution. The extended time granted by an earlier liberalization of the statute of limitations was to be sharply curtailed to events happening on or after July 1, 1993. Lawyers and victims sharply opposed the legislation, and the cut-off date and free pass for the Church were removed.

Olona weakly justified the ploy as an attempt to "clarify" the earlier law.[34] However, the proposed revision itself was a virtual admission that the Catholic Church had done no effective internal reform and expected more such trouble in the future.

Meanwhile, old lawsuits were settled secretly in batches. The process became so routinely confidential that most often lawyers only gave out the numbers of cases settled like sports scores. Little mention was made of the defendant or accuser, settlement amount, or liability. No reasons for such payouts, no matter how large, were even suggested any more.

Victims were paid off one by one, legally bound to maintain silence not only about the settlement, but also their abuse as well. And so, they, too, became more-or-less willing accomplices once more in keeping secret the sins of the Church.

But they weren't alone: Lipinski's criminal case was one of the few that went to trial. No civil suit ever did. Lawyers, judges, and the media all seemed more than happy to cooperate on preserving the cover-up, too. To the Church, it was well worth the immense fortune the archdiocese paid out of the people's donations in the course of suppressing the scandals.

Meanwhile, the Servants fought successfully against the insurance companies to keep the cases in state court and out of the federal system. In a state where the Church was so influential, this could not have hurt their cause. The courts also ruled that anonymity would no longer be allowed to plaintiffs.[35] Thus new victims coming forward were once more put in the spotlight's glare even as the Church slipped quietly back into the shadows.

This was substantially helped by pretrial gag orders inflicted in March, 1993 by four judges during Pasternack's open spat with Wolf and the archdiocese's lawyers in the buildup to Sanchez' fall. There had been plenty of leaks to the press. Then, and for most cases following, the courts slapped on gag orders – supposedly to protect victims and defendants.

It worked out substantially better for the latter than the former. Years later, Pasternack pleaded futilely to the judges to release the secrecy orders. He asked not only for those involving the Archdiocese of Santa Fe, but also for the dioceses of El Paso, Winnipeg, Worcester, and Fall River so that other victims could use the information.

Bruce Pasternack also implored the judges for sake of the future and for history. "The actual facts of what happened here have never been made known to the public," he said. "The time has come for them to be known lest the errors of the past be repeated."[36] But it was to little avail.

Years of legal wrangling all the way to the state Supreme Court had been required to get any of the former archbishop's deposition released. But when highly edited portions of Robert Sanchez' testimony were finally made available on September 17, 1996, the resulting media sensation nearly equaled that which surrounded his resignation. Old wounds reopened causing a wave of revulsion from victims and despair among the parishioners. Within a month, angry priests were writing to the papers to complain about all the negativity.

Another deposition of Sanchez did get out eventually with information on three clerics, including Griego and Lipinski. But not much more has ever been seen, including any of Sigler's promised revelations. It was once even rumored that Arthur Perrault himself was somehow deposed, but no testimony from his or hundreds of other cases has ever been released.

In response to the earlier revelations, Sanchez' replacement tried to smooth everything over, claiming all the "bad priests" were gone. He even offered a half-hearted public apology for his friend. Michael Sheehan said, "I hope that people won't only remember these tragic things but also will remember the good that he has done and the great amount of respect that people still have for him."

No abusive priests would be left in ministry, the archbishop claimed. The church had done "plenty" to avoid future misconduct, including written policies, sexual abuse prevention workshops, and careful screening of prospective priests. Every seminarian was to be subjected to an extensive background check, an AIDS test, and a review by a board, as well as a "battery of tests to make sure he is psychologically healthy."

Sheehan boasted of the financial contributions of the parishes and the rising number of seminarians.[36] He did not mention that the archdiocese had lost a quarter of its priests in the past several years and some parishes now had none at all. But he admitted that he had asked the Servites and Salesians – despite both orders having severe abuse issues of their own – to take over a few parishes.[37] Perhaps he did not know, or bother to ask.

However, he did say priests coming from outside the archdiocese were also to be checked out with their religious superiors. This last step was nothing new, however, but merely the traditional formality of granting permission or "faculties" required of newly arrived clergy to preach or administer the sacraments. This had proven so ineffective as to be practically worthless.

In 2002, a decade after it began in New Mexico, Sheehan remarked on how well the archdiocese had come through its "dark night of the soul." "The temple had to be cleansed," he admitted. He said that 23 seminarians had made it through AIDS tests and background checks, church ranks had swelled, and the archdiocese was free from debts.

But it wasn't cheap. 187 suits had been filed. Though earlier reports had claimed $50 million had been paid out, the head of the archdiocesan finance committee said it was closer to $25. Of that, the Church paid about one-third, with $2 million from savings and collections, $1 million from the sale of the Dominican Retreat House and $4.5 million from other land. The half-dozen insurance carriers picked up the rest after much litigation.[39]

Since the strategy had worked, the archbishop had every reason to be optimistic. "I believe that this process of regaining trust is going forward," Sheehan proclaimed even before Sanchez' depressing deposition had been released. "The healing process is taking place." And indeed, the archdiocese had launched a major public relations campaign to rebuild that trust and recoup their losses, called "Renew."[40]

Finally, a day after the Dallas Charter was passed, the Archbishop spoke proudly of New Mexico's own policies serving as a model for the nation. The

Church had turned around, and was flourishing again with a fresh crop of priests and 20,000 new families registered.[41]

Perhaps he would not have been quite so optimistic had he foreseen either Keating or Burke's remarks about the National Review Board, or how coolly the celebrated Dallas Charter would be greeted by Rome. Any rejoicing that problem was finally solved remained premature.

Sheehan still spoke optimistically in 2008, while celebrating his twenty-fifth anniversary in the priesthood. The archbishop claimed that he had ordained 60 priests and 100 deacons. Yet he also admitted that it was not enough – the archdiocese was importing priests from Mexico, Nigeria, and even Vietnam. Clearly, despite his best efforts, the Archdiocese of Santa Fe still had not yet fully recovered.[42]

What may be the last word on the cost came just as this book was being prepared for publication. When old allegations were made public about a priest in the neighboring Diocese of Gallup, Archbishop Sheehan was asked about conditions in Santa Fe. He indicated that the total payouts, including lawyers' fees, settlements, and the rest had come to over $30 million, and some 20 priests had been removed.[43]

The scandals cost a great deal, and not just monetarily. Thus far in New Mexico, they had already challenged the faith and patience of those in the pews. Though the few remaining cases might also test their credulity, the full extent of the horror that went on has not yet been revealed, and probably never will be.

CHAPTER XVI:
DARK SHADOWS

Later scandals

Cases kept coming into the new century but the flood dwindled into a trickle. Many of these, however, were stranger than the earlier ones.

This should not come as a surprise. With topics as painful and sensitive as sexual abuse, experience proves that disclosure tends to build upon disclosure. The most obvious and socially acceptable aspects are usually revealed first. The reactions of the hearers are carefully judged before anything more will be acknowledged.

Thus, a child might first tell his mother that Father spanked him and only if she responds with concern and not blame will any more be admitted. Last of all to be revealed, if ever, are the most horrible, painful, frightening, or bizarre parts of the story.

So it was with the clergy abuse crisis in New Mexico.

One woman accused a Franciscan, Lorenzo Ruiz, of recruiting her into a "girls club" of some 15-20 preteen girls. He used this to screen them. Ruiz would take them on outings and slowly conditioned them with gifts of money and presents, including lingerie, to accept his hugs, kisses, and ultimately sex. He also softened them up with alcohol and illegal drugs.[1]

Another woman claimed that nuns and a priest at an orphanage abused her. While temporarily at St. Anthony's Boy's School in the 1960s, members of the Poor Sisters of St. Francis Seraph of Perpetual Adoration would subject her to "cleansing rituals." The nuns would take her to a room where a priest, the late Clarence Schoeppner, would bathe her. Then, the monsignor and the nuns would perform nonconsensual sex on her.[2] This was the only suit filed against nuns in New Mexico, but these sorts of stories would be much more common elsewhere, especially in Ireland.

Other women accused Paul Baca, the pastor at Queen of Heaven, of molestation. One went public with claims that she was abused first in the early 1970s when she was 15. She later had a sexual relationship with him when she went back to him for counseling for depression and he took advantage of her. It stopped in the early 1990s once her awareness had been raised by the scandals. She even videotaped a conversation where he pleaded with her to try to make it right. But the counseling and the psychological manipulation continued for most of the decade.[3]

By this time in 1998, Pasternack had not filed any new lawsuits against the Church for five years. He said he had rejected many cases during his self-imposed moratorium, but took her case after she attempted suicide. He met with even more success than usual. These women received settlements before any claims could go to trial, even another accuser of Baca who had never even sued.[4]

However, this was to be Bruce Pasternack's last hurrah. The attorney unexpectedly died of an infection shortly before Christmas in 2001 at the age of 51. Revered as a courageous avenging angel by the more than 60 clergy abuse plaintiffs whose cases he took but equally scorned by many in the pews as an unethical opportunist, he had a major impact on the course of the scandals in New Mexico. Without Pasternack's relentless badgering of the largest and most powerful institution in the state, far fewer victims would have had the courage to come forward.

As for Paul Baca, his congregation gave him a standing ovation at his final Mass as pastor, where he had unexpectedly announced his retirement at the age of 75. But he was said to be going to teach Bible classes and minister to the sick, and there were no permanent restrictions placed on him as a priest.[5]

One of the last cases to come out thus far was also one of the oddest. Robert Malloy, 41, another popular pastor at Queen of Heaven, police chaplain, director of the Boy Scouts, and one of the two priests picked to sit on the Review Board, was indicted for hiring or attempting to hire teen-age boys for sexual purposes over four years.

This well-respected priest was accused in 1998 of 42 charges, including sexual offenses against boys and evidence tampering. After a long, peculiar investigation in which even his own attorney was briefly forbidden to see the evidence, Malloy was finally given nearly five years probation after pleading no contest to five counts of attempted criminal solicitation to commit tampering with evidence. He was suspended from working in a parish, forbidden to have unsupervised contact with minors, and required to attend therapy.

What he was really up to was not clear. The evidence was sealed for a long time, and when revealed, showed a strange and detailed scheme. Malloy apparently sent sexually explicit anonymous notes to somewhere between 5 and 14 teenaged boys requesting semen samples to be delivered to him through dead-drops right out of a spy novel in return for cash. He later asked them to destroy the notes, which led to the final charges.

Some teens complied – police even found a videotape Malloy had made of himself examining the sperm through a microscope in his own kitchen, making comments like a doctor. This puzzling and disturbing behavior, prosecutors thought, would undoubtedly have led to direct contact and attempted oral sex had he not been arrested.[6]

Among the last cases to be publicly mentioned to date was that of Ronald Bruckner. Short and pugnacious, he had been a colleague of Sanchez and Perrault at St. Pius High. Old rumors and accusations involving boys, sleepovers, and wrestling matches in their underwear finally caught up with him in 2005. The evidence was deemed insufficient until a man read about him on the Internet and wrote a letter to a victim's group alleging that he had been molested, which put public pressure on Archbishop Sheehan.[7]

Bruckner had been living in a house near his parish church that was like a teenagers' fantasy with a huge TV, pool table, and games. He has apparently since quietly retired.

But as the scandals opened with a criminal case, so too they have apparently ended with one. George Silva, 74, a priest in the northern town of Raton, pled guilty to charges in the fall of 2006. He was sentenced to five years in prison and an equal time on probation for having taken a fourteen-year-old boy to France and Portugal the year before where he abused him.

When the crime was reported to the archdiocese, law enforcement was notified, and Sheehan personally announced the news to the priests' congregations at Mass. Silva spent some time in a Church-backed treatment center in Ohio (possibly one run by the Servants) and decided to leave the priesthood.[8]

Perhaps by then something had been finally been learned by the Catholic Church. However, by pleading guilty, a criminal trial was cleverly avoided once again.

The Servants slip away

By late 1994, the Paracletes had soured on the bad publicity. Their programs for other problems than sex abuse suffered as priests who did not want to be labeled as such resisted being sent to Jemez Springs. Less than 30 priests staffed their facilities there anyway while their other programs around the world were still growing. So in the fall of that year they announced they were phasing out treatment at their foundation house.[9]

Several anonymous sources claiming to be insiders, however, alleged that despite this highly publicized act, they reopened the program two weeks later under a different name.[10] It is not known if this is true or where they shifted their guests. Complaining of the bad publicity, the Servants continued to insist they were part of the solution and not the problem.

The Paracletes, however, seemed to want to return to their original function at their birthplace, with a slight difference. They said they would now use the facility as a retreat house open to the public. But the stigma did not easily disappear and the effort was abandoned in 2002. In any case, it apparently only included the Foundation House, but not the other facilities in Jemez Canyon. Those still provide a refuge. At least one of the houses seemed still used as a retirement home for a half-dozen elderly clerics.

There were scandals at least one other Paraclete institution. Our Lady of Victory Trust in Stroud, Gloucestershire, England, treated over 1,800 priests. Though it treated substance abuse, emotional and other problems, it was also the only known residential pedophile treatment center for priests in the United Kingdom. It was brought to public attention when a priest guest, Sean Seddon, 38, was sent there after a 6-year affair with a teacher and threw himself under a train when he learned his lover had lost their baby.[11]

The Stroud center closed after questions were raised about sexual relationships between staff members and guests. They had led to a Vatican-ordered investigation by Chicago's Cardinal George, who is now under criticism himself for his handling of abusive priests. Servant General Hoare explained it as merely a "visitation."[12]

In any case, the results of the Stroud report are apparently still under wraps. Publicly, the closure was blamed on the fact that priests with other problems such as alcoholism objected to being sent there because of its known association with pedophiles.

Other centers also closed. The Albuquerque Villa was one of the first to go but the pastoral/residential center in Cherry Valley, California, and even offices in Rome have been shut. From a former novice and brief references in Paraclete documents, however, it seems that other sites may be in Cleveland, Ohio and Sturgis, South Dakota; while Vermont may have or had a novitiate in Bethel, plus ski chapels or other facilities in Barre and Randolph.[13] In France, the Servants helped the bishops set up a treatment center of their very own. Other foreign ministries have also been mentioned.

Apparently, the Paracletes maintain facilities in Nevis, Minnesota and at several locations in Missouri. In the town of Dittmer, where many of their records supposedly ended up, they run the Vianney Renewal Center. This is a supervised residential treatment center for about 30 men, most of whom are permanent. Perhaps their most notorious offender is Eleuterio "Al" Ramos of the diocese of Orange, California. With 25 victims, he had also been to St. Luke's and the House of Affirmation.[14]

Not far from the facility is an even more rigorous center, RECON, that sounds much like a monastery of strict observance. Little is known about that. The Servants are now headquartered in St. Louis, where they also run two programs. One is for chemical dependency and another for depression and emotional problems.[15]

Predatory patterns

The fifty or so known priests and monks whose cases made it to the news were certainly not all of the offenders in New Mexico. Three of them, including Perrault, had vanished. At least thirteen – about a quarter – had been guests of the Paracletes or another treatment center at one time or another. But there were likely more.

So, Pasternack's description of New Mexico as a "dumping ground" was not that far off. "Although New Mexico has only one-half of 1 percent of America's population," he noted, "it had 20 percent of America's priest pedophiles."

The bishops did indeed use Jemez Springs almost as a "job fair."[16] Just as the Servants of the Paraclete accepted priests from all over, they sent their guests back out everywhere as well. Over two dozen were later named as abusers and many had re-offended – far more than "about 10" that Servant General Lechner claimed.[17]

Many were Sons of Perdition as depraved as James Porter – like Ted Llanos of Los Angeles with 35 victims, who killed himself before imprisonment; Laurence Brett of Hartford who molested over two dozen in four states including New Mexico and later fled overseas; and Andrew Christian Andersen of Orange County, California, with 27 victims. He was arrested in Albuquerque after molesting a teenager in his car.

A closer look at the New Mexican situation confirms a complex picture among the offenders. Few abuses at all were reported in the capitol, Santa Fe, though there were at the seminary and the local high school and college.

A Christian Brother was active at the latter two locations. That order had achieved considerable infamy for abusive rings in orphanages in Canada and elsewhere.[18] Of other religious orders, only the Franciscans, who had played such an important role earlier in New Mexico, had several accused members. There was a lone Benedictine as well. Since in earlier times the regulars had the most abusers, it is likely that any offenses were discreetly handled in-house.

Perhaps significantly, most of the molestations had occurred in the very parishes in Albuquerque that were designated as recipients for graduates of the Paraclete program in 1967. But local priests, not former guests of the Servants, committed most of these crimes. Did the archdiocese corrupt the order and not the other way around?

Of these sites, Queen of Heaven was the worst with no less than seven predatory pastors and assistant pastors assigned there, one after another. These ranged from Paul Rodriguez, a psychologist, to Ron Bruckner and Robert Malloy. Perrault's last parish, St. Bernadette, and the author's home parish of Our Lady of Fatima were also hot spots. Abeywickrema, who molested three sisters at the former, served at all three. But then again, Ron Wolf's first assignment had been at Fatima, too.

Certain other churches seemed also to have a dark cloud over them, such as Our Lady of Sorrows in Las Vegas, New Mexico. However, the Paracletes' guests' assignments had not been restricted to the locations agreed on earlier. Porter, Sigler, and Holley all acted out elsewhere. Apparently, guests could be sent out as temporary "supply priests" on a weekend basis anywhere a parish priest would be needed due to vacations or other reasons.

It might be argued that in any diocese with around 250 priests and only 90 or so parishes, it would be inevitable that eventually some abusive priests would be stationed to the same places. It also means, however, that it would be easier for men of similar interests to get together. And pedophile priests in positions of power as deans or on staffing or pension committees could greatly influence where their fellow predators would be stationed and help cover for them.

For instance, there was Sabine Griego, whom Archbishop Sanchez sent to investigate Barney Bissonette. He assured his boss that the chaplain of the boy's school would get treatment. A year later, Bissonette was sent to St. Bernadette.[19] Though Sanchez probably did not know that Griego was himself molesting altar boys at the time, did his friend influence that decision?

Archbishop Sanchez' buddies Griego and Perrault were also linked. Both men were named the abusers of an anonymous man in a lawsuit along with John A. Gallegos, a priest who died of AIDS. The victim, who was also killed by HIV, claimed that all three priests had abused him in 1965 when he was in eighth grade, in church and on trips.[20] If so, multiple abusers are the very definition of a criminal pedophile network. Such claims have appeared in various other dioceses, also.

And what of Robert Malloy, with his strange fascination with teenage sperm? He served on the Review Board as well as a police chaplain. Did he ever use his influence to protect accused priests? Due to the secrecy of the Board's deliberations, it will probably never be known.

Very curious coincidences surround Monsignor Clarence Galli, who was on several occasions in the wrong place at the wrong time. He was pastor at St. Edwin when Porter acted out there. He was also in Las Vegas, New Mexico when Jason Sigler was busy there, too, claiming he was giving Sigler psychological therapy (and may have even given the authorities false evidence).[21] Finally, Galli later served as Vincent Lipinksi's never-interrogated superior at Our Lady of Fatima. What was that all about?

Other connections appear in the case of Sigler. Robert Kirsch first met him while at Via Coeli and invited him into his parish. Plus, there were those guests who had actually joined the Servants of the Paraclete. Not all their names are known. Did they corrupt the order, too?

Serpents in the garden

The parish priest in Jemez Springs, F. John Murphy, had bitterly complained to the American hierarchy about the problems some of the Servants had with alcohol and sexual issues of their own. There was also Gordon MacRae, who served as the Paracletes' admissions director, though not an actual member. Another one who had abused five boys in Pennsylvania worked on their computers at Via Coeli. One former guest ran their retreat house in Santa Fe and yet another, Jim Sampson, even became novice master in charge of training new recruits.

But one recruit with a criminal past had even greater importance.

The man who recommended that Porter and others be reassigned was John B. Feit. How he ever got into such a position is a genuine mystery. He apparently had no special training and a bad reputation with some in the order for being an unpleasant, unlikable character, even described as a "little Goebbels."[22]

Feit joined the Servants a few years after his arrival in Jemez Springs in the early 1960s. He was sent there after being removed from parish work by his order, the Missionary Oblates of Mary Immaculate. Feit had been convicted in connection with the attempted rape of a 20-year-old college student in South Texas, whom he had attacked inside a church as she knelt at the communion rail. He had been tried the year before on an even more serious charge that had resulted in mistrial.

Most ominous was Feit's connection to the murder of Irene Garza several weeks later. The 25-year-old beauty queen was sexually assaulted, beaten, suffocated, and her semi-clad body dumped in a canal in McAllen. The crime shocked southern Texas, especially after the priest was identified as a prime suspect.

The last person known to have seen her alive, Feit admitted he had heard her Confession that night in his rectory nearby. Her car was still parked at the church. Feit took four "inconclusive" lie detector tests, but he was never arrested.[23] Yet, an old slide viewer was found near her body that receipts showed belonged to the priest.

Later, in a monastery in Missouri, a monk was assigned to counsel him because he was told Feit was a murderer. In 2002 and no longer a monk, Dale Tachney confessed to being part of the cover-up for forty years. He told authorities that Feit had admitted the crime, but had claimed that Church and legal authorities had protected him from going to prison. Another priest, Joseph O'Brien, who had once been Feit's friend and supporter, also then broke his silence, saying he believed Feit did it also.[24]

The case was reopened. But Feit had left the Paracletes in 1972, married, and ultimately retired, living in Phoenix. Though the only suspect in the case, the authorities have been notably half-hearted in their efforts to prosecute, much to the frustration of the victim's family.

Peter Lechner, the Servant General, claimed that former administrators had only told him that they were aware of an "apparent incident involving a woman." But the staff somehow could not locate Feit's personnel records to see specifically what had been known.

Whatever technical qualifications Feit might possess to make such recommendations or how he came by that assignment have never been revealed. The head of the order said he was stunned to learn that a man with a criminal background made such important decisions. And this was well before Feit's ties with the Garza killing were made public.[25]

Lechner had once delicately explained in the Paracletes' newsletter that in some cases where priests who continue to re-offend, "the offender gained the confidence of someone who was in a position to affect reassignment."[26] He wouldn't have had to look very far to find the responsible party: Feit was a prominent member of the community. He served on various committees, worked on their *Manual of Procedures*, and even kept minutes of meetings.

Feit's explanation for helping Porter was quite simple. He said, "I tell you the man had me fooled. He was deceptively charming."[27] Such a basis for judgment was common. One Servant General, William Foley, when asked how he knew a priest required no more treatment, said with equal complacency, "We just get an intuition that they're going to work out."[28]

In both custodial treatment programs and religious orders, posts like admissions director, novice master, or assignment manager are all highly critical positions. Yet. men who had been sent to Via Coeli for their own serious, possibly criminal, problems, held them at times. Whether acting in concert or not, unethically or not, anyone with such a troubled history might be expected to be more than a little sympathetic with a kindred soul facing similar difficulties.

Tamed wolves do not make good sheepdogs. Yet unanswerable questions linger still: Did such former guests form an active ring of enablers? How intentional was their protection and reassignment of dangerous sex offenders? Did these guests and members deliberately corrupt the order and the archdiocese, or did they merely find a congenial environment easy to manipulate according to their desires?

In any event, the Servants' emphasis on unconditional forgiveness for priests along with an appalling lack of professionalism certainly helped promote a culture of permissive enabling. Add to that accusations of drinking, drug use, and homosexual solicitation by Paraclete staffers, and it goes far to explaining just how and why the Sons of Perdition and their friends were shielded and some later set loose upon the world.

"I can tell you what the atmosphere was," said Sylvia Demarest, an attorney for some of Kos' victims. "They flew in fresh fish and special food items and they went on hikes in the mountains and they were released over the weekend into local parishes where they continued to abuse children."[29]

As usual, Pasternack summed it up succinctly, if perhaps simplistically: "The center existed so that criminal priests did not have to pay criminal penalties."[30] Thus, Fitzgerald's noble dream gradually twisted into nightmare.

By the time of his passing, it was as if the inmates themselves had fully taken over the asylum. Perhaps in some ways they had.

Death draws nigh

Like the aroma of decay inevitably draws flies, the ills infecting the order seemed to attract violent death ever closer. The first known mortality was probably an accident though it could have been suicide. Robert Pospisil, a 64-year-old Jesuit who had run a retreat center in Oregon disappeared on a hike in the Jemez Mountains in late November 1993. Dressed in a light sweater, he was lost in a snowstorm. His body was finally found the next spring at the base of a cliff. The Servants said he had been there for personal problems, but not therapy for sexual issues.[31] But a treatment center seems an odd choice for a man who ran his own retreat, unless perhaps alcoholism or another delicate problem was involved.

The next, almost a year later, was the death by hanging of Philip Wolfe in his apartment in Albuquerque. Only 40, the man was a defrocked Franciscan priest. He had been a teacher and boys choir leader involved in the huge, multi-generational abuse scandal at the infamous St. Anthony's Seminary in Santa Barbara, California, which is still being fought over.

Wolfe served a year in jail for his part. His probation had only been finished barely a month when he hanged himself from his closet door. It was not known, but suspected, that he had been one of nine among the eleven abusive seminary staff members the Franciscans have admitted they sent to treatment. But the Servants declined to say whether Wolfe had ever been a guest of theirs.[32]

The third fatality was most definitely murder, and a brutal one at that. An elderly priest had his head bashed in by an ex-convict with a rock. And the site where it happened was as spectacular as the crime.

At the beginning of May 1998, Armando Martinez, a retired priest, 62, picked up a recently released prisoner, 38-year-old Dennis Carabajal, hitch-hiking north of Albuquerque. They were seen traveling together. Up past Jemez Springs, the road to Los Alamos opens onto a magnificent but lonely vista – the aptly named Valle Grande. It is formed from the bowl of the immense sleeping volcano, now a vast, peaceful sea of grass where distant grazing cattle and elk look as small as ants. The road skirts it below its rim of rounded hills draped with pine and aspen.

There, just past a popular overlook, horrified tourists witnessed the fatal beating. The priest even pleaded futilely for assistance from some Good Samaritans who were waved off by the killer who claimed his "friend" was drunk.[33]

Martinez' nude body was found nearby the next day, in a lonely spot now marked by a small memorial cross. Three days after that, Carabajal meekly surrendered to authorities. He was charged with murder, stealing the car and the priest's credit cards, and trying to cover up the crime.

Carabajal claimed that the priest had been drinking, and when Martinez attempted to fondle him, the ex-con responded in rage. The accusation outraged the family of the murder victim. It turned out, however, that Martinez had been relieved of his duties in 1993 after being accused of sexual misconduct with a minor. He retired the next year.[34]

Since the Valle Grande lies well above Jemez Springs, the pair almost certainly passed through town to reach it. Had Martinez originally been on his way to visit the Paracletes? Prosecutors tried to pry his records from them but failed. Neither side finally got to see them.[35] Carabajal pled guilty, apologized to the family, and won an agreement for a 50-year sentence.[36]

Finally, bloody murder savagely seized one of the Servants. Mike Mack, an almost 60-year-old Paraclete priest and former Dominican, was viciously hacked to death in one of the order's own houses. On December 8, 2000, the Feast of the Immaculate Conception, his pajama-clad body was found in the farthest hermitage. Lourdes House is up the road, remote from all the rest. It is rumored at various times to have been used for novices, the worst offenders, or important ecclesiastical visitors. It had been broken into and ransacked. Mack's wallet and keys were missing.[37]

A new resident in town, an apparently mentally disturbed cook, was the killer. Stephen DeGraff, however, loudly proclaimed his innocence, and like Carabajal, maintained that the priest had tried to rape him.[38] Nobody bought the story. The case was very quickly shut up, and little more information ever came out.

The Devil rides out

Sexual abuse in the archdiocese happened in many different locations, in numerous schools, rectories, and chapels, and even the chancery and the archbishop's own residence. Often it defiled the sacred precincts of churches themselves, in sacristies and confessionals. Violent rape, the spilling of semen and blood, spiritually polluted and desecrated all these sanctuaries, yet not a single one has ever been ritually purified by exorcism – neither publicly nor likely in private either.

This, too, is nothing new. No matter how horrific the obscenities recorded by the Spanish Inquisition as having occurred within holy places,
historian Lea could find no indication that any had ever been properly reconciled according to canon law. There too, fear of scandal had overridden
every other concern. Theologians even conveniently concluded that such
spiritual pollution only occurred when the act was public and not hidden.[39]

But there may have been still darker activities going on in the Archdiocese of Santa Fe. By the very nature of their job, priests are immersed in a
world of ritual. Belief in the effective power of ceremonial prayer defines
their entire existence. So, it is likely that there would be a tendency to ritual-
ize aspects of their sex lives, too.

The use of seemingly religious practices in molestation would have the
benefit of confusing, terrifying, and persuading the victim of his or her own
blame. He or she would much more easily believe that what just happened
was somehow part of the faith, especially if very young. Often the cruelest
molestation was presented as penance for sins or, most perversely, even as
sacramental in nature.

As noted previously, the Inquisition had pushed many unacceptable
clerical behaviors underground along with priestly sex. Together in the fetid
darkness of the clerical underground, heresy, sex, magic, and lingering pagan practices subversively fermented over time into various bizarre forms,
including varieties of Satanism.

During the Middle Ages, only the clerical class had the education and
free time – not to mention most of the tools readily available – to call up demons. With a growing surplus of poorly educated and underemployed
priests, many may well have been tempted to try to improve their lot with
secretly casting spells or raising the occasional devil for themselves or others,
especially just before the Reformation. But great caution was always needed
as the Inquisition constantly guarded against just such mischief.

The dark and dubious history of Satanism in the Catholic Church is
much too lengthy and contentious to be properly dealt with here. But
enough was going on that the figure of the diabolic priest entered European
folklore through such tales as that of Doctor Faustus, the theologian who
sold his soul to the Devil. Based on an actual alchemist who died around
1540, the tale inspired great plays by Christopher Marlowe and Goethe – the
latter who, by the way, portrayed Mephistopheles himself as a pederast.

There were actual satanic cases involving clerics, too. The most notorious trial was that of Urbain Grandier. A seductive chaplain of nuns like Ricasoli, who was active at the same time, Grandier was burned in 1634 for supposedly magically seducing an entire convent in France. Aldous Huxley wrote a classic study of the case, *The Devils of Loudon,* and the unsettling movie he co-wrote inspired an entire genre of sleazy films about naughty nuns. There was even a royal investigation of satanic priests and poisonous prostitutes in the court of Louis XIV of France. Like certain later inquiries of such things, it too was suppressed for reasons of state.

A few modern cases have overtly diabolical connections as well. Perhaps the most disquieting was the ritualistic murder of an elderly nun, Margaret Ann Pahl, by stabbing and strangulation in a Toledo hospital chapel on Holy Saturday in 1980. Over twenty years later it resulted in the conviction of the chaplain, priest Gerald Robinson. The case brought up other allegations of satanic priest abuse in Ohio as well, some quite weird involving priests dressed as nuns, but nothing that could be proven.[40]

One prime reason for priestly deviltry is quite simple. Even if they are excommunicated, expelled, and defrocked, the sacred powers given priests at ordination simply cannot be taken away. But the ability to bless and sanctify can be perverted to curse and blaspheme. Priests could just as easily bring Christ to Earth for abuse instead of adoration, if they so dared. Since only priests were capable of saying a Mass, some occultists felt that only such persons, defrocked or not, could "properly" perform a Black Mass, the satanic mockery of the Catholic rite.

In New Mexico and other places, though diabolic practices have never been spoken of in public at all, certain sinister rumors circulated among victims and survivors.

They indicate that a few priests, with possibly several nuns and laity, organized group satanic rites in central New Mexico during the 1960s and later. Their alleged activities, spoken of in hushed and halting tones, evoke the full gamut of dreadfulness. Ritualized sodomy, Black Masses, cult ceremonies in churches and cemeteries and even worse practices were whispered about. Names of several prominent clergymen were brought up in these contexts as either passive enablers or active participants.[41]

Of course, none of these appalling assertions could ever be proven. Nary a word of them has ever been spoken in court or to reporters either. Attorneys for victims strongly discouraged their clients from mentioning any such allegations at all if possible. They were rightly fearful that such extreme but unsupportable claims would likely have rendered their cases ridiculous and get them thrown out of court.

Circumstances suggest there may have been something to the stories, however. Alarmingly, many of these incidents supposedly took place at the very same churches where the most offenders, both guests and local priests, had been stationed. Perhaps the locales had some special significance or attraction, such as "Devil's Rooms" as have been reported in Ireland and elsewhere – out of the way closets, basements, attics, bell towers, or otherwise unfrequented areas within the sacred precincts where dark rituals could be regularly held.[42] Could the old English saying, that "the Devil has a chapel wherever God has a church," have been meant literally?[43]

A.W. Richard Sipe, a former priest and monk who has made a career of studying celibacy, interviewed thousands of clerics. He has noted the existence of sex rings, and that "other priests have encouraged *group sex* and organized sex clubs for adolescents. There have been scattered reports of *ritual* sexual abuse in which a priest participated. Priests who abuse adolescents frequently ply them with alcohol and drugs."[44]

Though deeply disturbing, there is also evidence indicating that Rome is deeply albeit secretly worried about satanic priests as well.

CHAPTER XVII:
SIN, SECRECY, AND THE VATICAN

What is truth?

In crises like the clergy abuse scandals, the paper trail is most important. While physical evidence, such as DNA, may make or break an individual criminal case, documentation is usually the only means of proving that more than one person in an institution was involved. In other words, that there was a conspiracy or a cover-up.

In situations where events under dispute are for the most part decades old and many of the principals are dead, oftentimes paperwork is all the evidence there is. Many a case has turned on the question of whether any documentation of abuse or its concealment can be found.

Catholic doctrine actually gives individual clergy members the "right" to equivocate or even outright lie while under oath. Known as "mental reservation" it must be rationalized as somehow necessary for the greater good of the Church.[1] To someone adequately trained in Jesuitical casuistry and Probabilism, this would be child's play.

Also, technical theological terms, especially in Latin, may be used as a code to baffle outsiders. "*In res turpis*" is a general term for sexual abuse, for example. Misdirection, euphemisms, and ambiguity have also been resorted to on occasion.

Names have been known to be misspelled in replies to requests for information from the Paracletes. Sometimes clerics are misidentified with others bearing similar names.[2] These may be honest mistakes, but who knows?

Even the Church's public guides, such as the *Official Catholic Directory*, are not entirely straightforward. Published every year, it gives data on all 50,000 or so clergy in the United States. However, it necessarily relies on information furnished by the nearly 200 dioceses across the land. Thus, clerical perpetrators are often said to be "on leave," "inactive," or "on assignment outside the diocese," even simply left out, if they are in treatment somewhere, for instance.

However, any ongoing enterprise, especially one as large and enduring as the Catholic Church, must maintain an institutional memory based on thorough record keeping. This is vital if it hopes to maintain any consistency in policies or even minimal track of members. Moreover, the organization needs clearly established procedures and internal regulations that specify both offenses and their penalties.

In other words, the Church needs a functioning "government by desks" — a bureaucracy, abounding with archives and guidelines. Blessed, if that's the word, as it is with the longest surviving such clerical establishment on Earth, the Church has had plenty of time and talent necessary to develop a full range of policies covering every situation it has ever confronted.

The Roman Catholic Church's rules are called "Canon Law." Originally, a hodge-podge of collected and often conflicting decrees of councils and popes, it included even some that had been falsified, as has been seen. Canon law grew organically through the centuries out of the intense interplay between legal theories based on Roman imperial law, theology, papal politics, and historical events. Some specific incident somewhere or other in history has most likely influenced every single provision.

In time, canon law became loaded with special privileges for the elite, that is, the clergy, and weighted against the lower class, the laity. As professional elite leaders, clergy have been granted everything from exemption from military service and taxes to a guaranteed right to a living. Clergy were even given the right to be tried by the Church rather than the State, which of course, understands them better.

At one time, all it took was for an accused man to read Latin from the parish Bible to prove he was an educated cleric. Then he would be turned over to the Church for judgment and discipline, which was usually less harsh. This is what the term "benefit of clergy" actually means. It buttressed the expectation that the Catholic Church took care of its own, good or bad.

Codified in the early years of the twentieth century, the most recent compilation of ecclesiastical legislation dates from 1983. Amid intricate details of church structure and governance, the *Code of Canon Law* tells exactly how and where documentary evidence of clerical malfeasance must be kept.

The diocesan personnel files are an obvious place for evidence of clergy crime but they are usually incomplete and out of date. Even if an attorney or other outsider could gain access, rarely have any smoking guns seemed to turn up. The reasons are manifold.

For one thing, in many dioceses, access is not as rigorously controlled as it might be, or the filing system may be neglected or confused. Sensitive correspondence will often rely on discrete language, veiled references, and euphemisms, anyway. It is even conceivable that fearful prelates might hold midnight shredding parties to dispose of potential embarrassment, particularly of their own involvement or inaction.

Any notice of interest can put perpetrators or their enabling friends on alert. When subpoenaed by attorneys, it has happened on occasion that vital documents that should have been in the files such as ordination records may be gone. Stretches of years might be missing, or the chronological order reversed or jumbled, indicating that the file had been thoroughly weeded at some time.[3]

Unfortunately, although suspicious, the absence of a paper trail proves nothing. Yet, as it is said in another context, "absence of evidence is not evidence of absence." In any case, documents seriously detrimental to anyone's career would not usually be placed in an open file.

But the hierarchy still desperately needs information on which apples are rotting the barrel. So where then are the records of clerical misconduct kept?

In at least one case, a bishop was discovered to be holding "confidential files" in his office that he alone was supposed to have access to. However, this was not the most secure location either, as correspondence disappeared from there as well. It is likely from just such instances that canon law evolved its rules for the keeping of records.

Canon law mandates archives of several kinds and levels of security. First, there are the parish archives, which contain the registers of baptisms, confirmations, marriages, and deaths, "together with episcopal letters and other documents which it may be necessary or useful to preserve."[4] These are to be maintained by the pastor and are open to inspection by the bishop or his representative. Copies of inventories and other items are to be kept at the next level, in the diocesan archives.

The relationship between the personnel files and the diocesan or curial archives is rather obscure, but they do seem to be different entities. The diocesan archives are under the care of the chancellor, vice-chancellor, and staff notaries, all of whom serve at the pleasure of the bishop. They must be "of unblemished reputation and above suspicion. In cases which could involve the reputation of a priest, the notary must be a priest."[5]

This guarantees that all the most sensitive documents are generated and controlled only by trusted male clerics. Any nun, or layman for that matter, who becomes chancellor or vice-chancellor, however progressive such a promotion might appear, is still kept carefully out of the loop. Leadership in the Catholic Church strictly remains a members-only boys' club.

The chancellor and notaries write the documents, sign them, noting date, time and place, and "while observing all that must be observed, showing acts from the archives to those who lawfully request them."[6] This is peculiar phrasing, to say the least. Just what is "all that must be observed" – does this mean the form of the document or the code of silence, perhaps?

Canon law goes on to demand that all documents be kept with "the greatest of care." In each diocesan curia, the archive is to be kept in a "safe place" under lock and key, along with a catalog of documents kept there and a short synopsis of each. Only the bishop and chancellor are to have the key and no one may enter without either the bishop's or the both the chancellor and vicar's permission.

Persons concerned (i.e., accused priests, not their accusers) have the right to receive copies of documents "which are of their own nature public and which concern their own personal status." So, even they cannot see private evaluations and exchanges between prelates.

In any case, it is not permitted to remove any document except for a short time.[7] In addition, there is also supposed to be an historical archive of some kind.[8]

Secret archives

And that's just the ordinary archives. This level of security is not deemed sufficient for truly sensitive matters. Canon law states:

> There is also to be a secret archive, or at least in the ordinary archive there is to be a safe or cabinet, which is securely closed and bolted and which cannot be removed. In this archive, documents, which are to be kept under secrecy, are to be most carefully guarded. Each year, documents of criminal cases concerning moral matters are to be destroyed whenever the guilty parties have died, or ten years have elapsed since a condemnatory sentence concluded the affair. A short summary of the facts is to be kept, together with the text of the definitive judgment.[9]

Other materials to be kept in the secret archives include information on dispensations involving marriages, impediments to becoming a priest, and for leaving the clerical state. Decrees of dismissal from the priesthood or the invalidity of holy orders, and all records of internal investigations and trials are to be stored there.[10]

Only the bishop is to have the key to the secret archive, though the diocesan administrator may open it personally when the see is vacant "in a case of real necessity."[11]

Thus, sitting silently in the heart of every single diocese is a potential time bomb; an appendix where every sordid crime committed by apprehended clergy is forever preserved. Even when the perpetrators are dead and buried, canon law says that there still should be some record of what they were caught doing. As long as access is limited only solely to priests, however, the world will never know the full extent.

In any event, just as each diocese has its own secret archives, so too does the Vatican. The Secret Archives of the Holy See (their actual name) are as vast as they are ancient. Headed by a cardinal like the Vatican Library, another rumored trove of secrets, they are partially open today to a few approved scholars. These are let in only with specific purposes and with permission of the reigning pope.

> *It is one of the most mysterious institutions in the papal city, for in its more than thirty miles of shelving are reputed to be the accumulated records of scandals, secrets, and revelations of the most shocking and explosive kind, blithely boxed and filed away with the insouciance born of centuries of silence and discretion.*[12]

The Secret Archives are so vast, disorganized, and secret that no one even knows their full extent — one expert claims that there are "only" 24 miles or so of shelves, though the Vatican itself admitted that there are "85 linear kilometers (52 miles) of shelves." Pope Leo XIII opened them to selected scholars in 1881.[13]

The collection contains 135 *fondi*, or individual archives. These include not only records of papal decrees, chancery business, and similar paperwork, but much other material as well, including the records of prominent papal families, suppressed religious orders and monasteries, and various church embassies. Most of this has never even been examined, much less properly indexed and cataloged.

There have been several attempts to create indices by past archivists, but they were incomplete to begin with. Plus, the archives have been moved and looted several times during their long history. Most of the medieval records that survived the papal exile to Avignon and resulting struggle were lost during the Sack of Rome in the sixteenth century. Napoleon seized the archives and brought three thousand cases of records to Paris in the eighteenth century to be part of his planned world library. There, however, to the horror of archivists, many volumes were recycled into butcher paper after his fall; and much fell into the hands of the Italian government later on.[14]

Moreover, the paperwork generated by the various curial organizations, while technically belonging to the Secret Archives, remains under the control and often in the possession of the department that produced it. Access to the Secret Archives is strictly controlled, and the period when records cannot be examined is long, even by institutional standards. Pope Paul VI advanced the cut-off date up to 1878. Meanwhile, Vatican officials are carefully and discreetly examining the period of the Second World War and the Holocaust in hopes of refuting the charges of Pope Pius XII's negligence during that time.[15]

So could there be truly hidden Secret Archives, just like Dan Brown put forth in his novel (and now film) *Angels and Demons*? One woman who worked there wrote:

> *The Italian anticlerical party was disappointed in its hope of finding the Secret Archives a repository for records of usurpations, crimes, and sexual perversions. But the question still remains as to whether the Secret Archives exercises internal censorship over its materials. What action is taken by a scriptor, custodian, or prefect when, in the course of his work, he comes across material that is morally or theologically controversial? Has a closed (chiuso) fondo [individual archive] gradually accumulated, the much-talked-of fondo about which nothing is actually known, a closed fondo which is categorically denied by the Archives authorities? This is a question which puzzled me during the long time I spent working in the Secret Archives, and to which I still have not found any answer. My own personal impression is that no such material is destroyed. The men of the Archives have too much sense of the past, too much reverence for scholarship, too much obligation to learning, for that. But such documents may be omitted from the inventories, bound in volumes containing documents of a very different kind, and relegated to some fondo that is closed because of chronological limitation or very seldom consulted.*
>
> *This happened with the personal letters of Pope Borgia to the little clan of his devoted women, and with the original summary of the process [or trial] of Giordano Bruno, and may have happened many other times that we do not know about. Such documents may eventually reappear in the future.*[16]

The Secret Archives are probably not the final repository of most reports of all kinds of dirty deeds done by clergy. Still, the Roman curia is infamously protective of their contents, especially those of the Apostolic Penitentiary. In the late 1980s, a long-approved priest, Filippo Tamburini, wrote two books, said to be "spicy stories from the penitentiary." They were "fairly innocuous" about erring clergy who lived centuries ago. Yet he was fired, demoted from his rank of monsignor, and banned. The archives are said to be very carefully screening applications since then to keep out "scandalmongers."

The Roman Inquisition's records, which were also quietly opened up to approved scholars on a very limited basis in the late 1990s are also extremely restricted. On their grand opening, the congregation's secretary, Archbishop Tarcisio Bertone, "stated that 'naturally,' neither materials subsequent to 1903 nor anything having to do with such 'delicate matters' as solicitation of sexual favors in the confessional would be made available for consultation."[17]

Truly, Rome clings to its secrets most jealously. That it is the Penitentiary's documents the Vatican seems most worried about may in itself be most significant.

CHAPTER XVIII:
BEYOND THE PURPLE CURTAIN

When in Rome

The first public act of every new cardinal, as one of the pope's advisors or head of a Vatican agency, is to swear to preserve the secrets of the Roman Church. During his follow-up meeting with the pontiff in the second or Secret Consistory, one of the closing ceremonies of his elevation was historically called the rite of the "Opening and Closing of the Mouth." In it, each new member of the college, as a "prince of the Church," received personal permission from the pope to offer him wise counsel, and then also "to keep the secrets of their office," that is, their mouths shut.[1]

This makes trying to find out which officials in the Vatican, if any, which are dealing with abuse questions extremely difficult. To outsiders, such institutions present a blank outer wall and an impenetrable inner maze of arcane titles and unwritten rules, truly Byzantine in its complexity. Glimpses and speculation are sometimes the only means of constructing a picture of who or what is involved.

Of course, in the organization of the Holy See, the key institution would seem to be Holy Office, now called the Sacred Congregation for the Doctrine of the Faith. There the records of the old Roman Inquisition are kept safely locked up. But the Prefect may not be the only one concerned with actively maintaining the rigid rule of secrecy.

The CDF is a "dicastery," as Vatican departments are sometimes called, that before its historic role was discovered, seemed to be more concerned with keeping theologians under control than sexual perpetrators. Access to its records was virtually impossible. But as noted, Ratzinger in his effort to modernize the office opened them to a few select scholars also.

Other likely Congregations that could be involved would seem to be ones for the Clergy or the Institutes of Consecrated Life and Societies for the Apostolic Life (professed religious) or even Divine Worship and the Discipline of the Sacraments. These are concerned with "the life, discipline, rights, and duties of the clergy" and members of religious orders while the latter deals with "abuses to the sacred liturgy."[2]

Possibly they might have some interest, but probably have as little to do with handling these cases as any one of the Vatican's three ecclesiastical tribunals: the Apostolic Penitentiary, the Apostolic Signatura, or the Roman Rota.

The Rota deals with big-name divorces, while the Signatura serves as the "Supreme Court" of the Vatican. That leaves the Apostolic Penitentiary, which, despite its name, is not a prison for erring evangelists, but the oldest court of the Holy See, in charge of granting absolutions, dispensations and other favors. It also determines indulgences. And its head has a very particular role to play after the pope dies.

The cardinal-prefect in charge, known as the Major (or formerly, Grand) Penitentiary of the Holy Roman Church, "is the only Curia official who remains in power, with the full authority of his office, during the Sede Vacante," that is, the period between popes.

> *This is so that he may continue to confer necessary pardon and dispensations during the duration of the vacancy... [He] is also the only cardinal that who may maintain a steady stream of outside contact during the sealed conclave as the nature of his office requires his continued attention in severe matters of internal forum. "In the event he dies during Conclave, the conclavists must immediately elect a successor for the duration of the Conclave. The mystery of the mercy of God, which is exercised through the Penitentiary, thus does not suffer interruption."[3]*

This may sound touchingly pious but the provision is really quite unusual. It's generally thought that nobody, but nobody, could communicate with the cardinals in Conclave – that being the entire point of the exercise. Indeed, the revised rules for John Paul II's succession were full of precautions so that those locked up have no means of communication with the outside world (such as cell phones), or that the Conclave is bugged.

Yet, this Cardinal Penitentiary, currently Cardinal James Francis Stafford, formerly of Baltimore, alone of all his peers is specified in the rules to do his job when the pope dies, even during Conclave. Not only that, but he even has his own personal revolving drum dumbwaiter, smaller than the one used to give food and medicine to the sequestered cardinals, but just for him – and him alone – to pass secret documents through while isolated.[4]

Some researchers claim that other cardinals continue with their appointed duties, and have limited contact with their staff.[5] But certainly not to the degree he does. Nor are any other cardinals considered so important to the continuing life of the Church that their immediate replacement, if necessary, is more important than the pope's.

Furthermore, the argument that the Penitentiary is needed at all times to issue forgiveness falls flat. Mercifully, *any* priest, even defrocked ones, can fully forgive *any* sin or censure of persons who are dying, even those usually reserved to the supreme pontiff alone to forgive. Everything else, one might think, could wait for the new pope.

Is the Major Penitentiary, then, the cardinal in charge of maintaining the cover-up? It's quite possible, as he is the official most concerned with the "internal forum." This has to do with sacred matters of conscience, that is, Confession and absolution, the realm of the deepest and darkest secrets of the soul.

Possible confirmation of all this comes from a journalistic peek through the crack between the basilica's doors. The following is excerpted from such a scene involving Pope Paul VI's daily paperwork in July 1978:

> *Much of the work near the bottom of the tray requires no more than careful reading and initialing. The Apostolic Penitentiary handles complex problems of conscience... It also advises the penalties a pope may impose for such a dire crime as* a priest saying a black mass. Every year there are a number of such cases; *they frighten Paul more than anything else. He regards them as proof the devil is alive and well and hiding inside the Church. Cardinal Giuseppe Paupini* [the Major Penitentiary]... *is the Vatican's resident expert on sorcery of all kinds. His work is adjudged so important and urgent that* he will be the only cardinal allowed during the next Conclave to remain in contact with his office.[6]

Since John Paul II retained such arrangements, it seems no coincidence that the pope's point man on clerical black magic is the chief pardoner of the Church. As the case of the banned writer Tamburini demonstrated, the Apostolic Penitentiary is extremely zealous in its protection of the secrecy of Confession. It would be a natural choice to handle these most sensitive issues. As the papacy's oldest court of law, it has possibly had jurisdiction for a very long time, too.

So perhaps the Cardinal Penitentiary merits such consideration because the papacy takes the threat of diabolic clergy most seriously indeed, believing that both constant vigilance and total secrecy are necessary.

Other possibilities might not be much better. Maybe the Papal Penitentiary stills sells dispensations on the sly and any interruption would be bad for the trade. Or since the office deals with Confession, he might have to stay constantly available should vital information come forward during the dangerous and delicate transitions between papal regimes. As mentioned earlier, the so-called "seal of Confession" prohibits revelations of most sins except heresy. It's likely that other, even more secret loopholes also exist. Could the Major Penitentiary, then, be the Vatican's Director of Central Intelligence?

It can be quite tempting to imagine the worst. For if the modern clergy sexual abuse crisis has revealed anything about the Roman Catholic Church, it is that the hierarchy can and will go to great lengths to hide its dirty laundry. The Vatican has had millennia of experience, and it just may still be covering up even more monstrous secrets than anything imagined so far.

But the sinister question of satanic influence in Rome is age old, perplexing, and ultimately unanswerable. How it is regarded also depends entirely on how the papacy itself is viewed. Too much extreme propaganda from both sides since the Reformation has thoroughly befouled the entire issue. Just about anything from the late insider and former Jesuit Malachi Martin's dark speculations to Dan Brown's baroque thrillers are equally as believable as they are also laughably absurd.

Beyond scandal

At one time, the Church freely admitted its internal problems with unvarnished honesty that would literally be unthinkable today. Not just priests having sex, either. Every variety of moral failure of clergymen and consecrated women were discussed with remarkable frankness, despite any fear of scandal. Pictures of Hell were often depicted as brimming with as many roasting popes, bishops, monks, priests, and nuns as every variety of kings and lords and lay sinners.

Of course, society has greatly changed since then. Modern people prefer to see themselves as more refined and sophisticated than their ancestors. Crude exploitation is as unfashionable as superstition – yet both are still eternal facets of the human experience. Pretending to be above such things opens the door to them.

Once it had separated the clergy as a class apart from the laity, the Church that was expected to provide for them was supposed to limit their excesses, too. It was allowed to judge its failed ministers and keep them away from the vulnerable, usually hidden away in monasteries.

In modern times, abbeys were replaced by "treatment centers" developed just for clerics. Only media celebrities are treated in a similar manner, it seems. Certainly no other profession, no matter how prestigious – not even medicine, the law, or politics, has anything quite like them to rehabilitate their own fallen colleagues. This is a direct legacy of the fervent clericalism of the medieval Church.

There is one key difference nowadays, however. For many generations, the Catholic Church was the sole provider of spiritual solace in Western civilization. Since the fourth century, criticizing the Church had been like talking about the weather. Catholicism was as universal as the sky, completely overarching the people. Their lives entirely depended upon the grace it gave or withheld like the rain. Because there were no competing alternatives, its faults could be freely discussed. Reforming preachers and saints vigorously blasted conditions that they abhorred with some confidence because the health of the Church vitally concerned everyone.

The theologian Peter Comestor, who died in 1178, was esteemed in his day as one of the most cultured men in France – his last name means "devourer" as he was such a bookworm. His orthodoxy was never questioned though he boldly taught in his public lectures that, "the devil had never inflicted so severe a blow on the Church as in procuring the adoption of celibacy."[7] Such liberty could not last. Already in his day, the wide deployment of the thought police had made pointing out blemishes on the Bride of Christ considerably more dangerous.

So, two and a half centuries later, Thomas Connecte, another popular preacher who spoke similarly, ended up quite differently. He was a Carmelite who moralized so eloquently against vice and luxury that huge piles of cards, dice, chessboards, even ladies' headdresses, would be piled up and torched during his sermons.

His real source of popularity, however, came from his bitter attacks on clerical immorality, particularly priests living with concubines. Having concluded that the only solution was to restore clerical marriage, Connecte went to preach it in Rome in 1432. For his trouble, he was promptly seized, hauled before the pope, examined by cardinals, condemned, and duly burnt.[8]

A century later, the Reformation, with the successful secession of entire nations from obedience to Rome, made any mention of such failings even more dangerous in Catholic lands, if that was possible. To publicly denigrate systemic malfunctions of any kind was to invite being targeted as a foe of the pope, a heretic, and hated enemy of God's holy Church.

For the Catholic rebuttal, the Counter-Reformation, had little positive about it. By the time the Council of Trent finally convened over a generation after Luther's defiance, Rome was no longer in any mood to modify a single

point of theology nor to allow any concessions whatsoever that might mol-
lify the Protestant rebels. A few abuses such as outright indulgence fraud
and the papal sin tax were abolished, but no major changes were even admitted as necessary.

In pointed defiance of the Reformers, the Roman Catholic Church went
old school instead. Trent brought about that inward turning of the Church
that Vatican II attempted to reverse. Primarily a visceral reaction that created
a "fortress Church," the Council glorified and exalted ancient traditions. In
effect, the existing ecclesiastical order from pope on down was canonized
just as it stood. The structure was hailed as divinely decreed, revealed, and
necessary for salvation – and therefore utterly immune to criticism.

The failure of the Second Vatican Council to shake off this closed, trium-
phant attitude means that Catholicism remains a faith besieged to this day.

Reformers gleefully mocked the inability of Roman clergy to live up to
their lofty ideals, especially celibacy. Along the way, radicals dismissed one
by one almost all the sacred powers peculiar to the priesthood. Rome's fateful reaction was to desperately shore the system up by grounding it in absolute chastity as the necessary basis for the entire sacerdotal edifice.

What distinguishes Catholic priests from Protestant preachers are the
holy abilities to bless and forgive. But celibacy is what really sets them apart
socially. Chastity became more than a requirement for the job but the priesthood's special halo. Celibacy was thus elevated into an ennobling sacrifice
defining their entire existence as a class. In return, the clergy merited their
privileges of status, economic support, and freedom from secular duties.

Such a superhuman offering must come from some mysterious divine
grace transmitted during ordination to enable these men to be sexless and
forgetful of everything heard in Confession. Or so the simple thought. Their
pastors cannily did not dissuade them of this happy illusion.

Thus, laymen freely entrusted their wives and children to the men in
black. And if that person got abused, the failure was ascribed only to the sinner – or more often the victim. In any case, it surely had nothing to do with
the magnificent temple they were told that Christ himself had built.

Silence of the cloisters

Long after the Inquisition surrendered its terrible powers and retired to
the background, this triumphal clericalism persisted. It formed the foundation of Fitzgerald's dream. Only in the late 1960s during the flowering of
Vatican II could Catholics contemplate any alternative to such a divinely ex-

alted virginal male clergy. But, as has been shown, the mere admission that celibacy was unnecessary helped spark the catastrophic clerical flight of the late twentieth century. In reaction, the papacy anxiously re-hardened its position as fast as it could.

In 1992, Pope John Paul II invoked Vatican II to encourage vocations and shore up priestly discipline in no uncertain terms: "The Synod does not wish to leave any doubts in the mind of anyone regarding the Church's firm will to maintain the law that demands perpetual and freely chosen celibacy for present and future candidates for priestly ordination in the Latin Rite."[9] The principle of absolute priestly chastity, while it cannot be official Roman Catholic dogma, endures as a key corporate directive.

Yet, while celibacy is but one factor, the drastic decline in the priesthood continues despite the Catholic population boom resulting from the banning of contraception. "The stark facts are that, while the diocesan priesthood population will have declined by 40 percent between 1966 and 2005, the lay population is increasing by 65 percent."[10]

The fall in the number of monks and nuns is even more remarkable. The Vatican itself revealed they diminished by a full ten percent in just one year. Worse, the numbers of consecrated women, whose ill-paid efforts actually keep the institution running from day to day, declined by no less than 25% – a full quarter – while John Paul II was in office.[11]

Clearly, if one out of every four sisters voted with her boots to get out during one reign, even the second longest, that's not just a decline – it's a full-fledged stampede. In losing 10% of its religious per year, then within a mere eight years half will be gone. Within a little over two decades, there will be only 10% left. If the current rate of decline continues among priests – which admittedly is not likely – there will be less than 10,000 Catholic clergy worldwide in less than three hundred years.

Yet, even now, thousands of married former priests wait hopefully for a call to take up their vocations again. Many devout Catholic women would likewise jump at the chance to be ordained. But by excommunicating any female who attempts it, the Church has clearly demonstrated that this option will never be adopted in the near future either.

It seems the time has truly passed when celibacy could be rejected as a failed experiment or even made optional. If the Roman Church were at this late stage to repudiate such an important position now, what would become of all its other edicts and divine authority?

But with such an already urgent and steadily growing need for priests, is it even possible that the high standards the Church should insist upon could be maintained? Or will the shortfall lead to more men like Kos or Perrault, who should never have been ordained? Will the entire world thus come to resemble colonial New Mexico in its desperation for priests?

Gay seminaries and lavender rectories

Celibacy is not the only challenge facing the priesthood. Oddly enough for such supposedly asexual beings, sexual identity itself is a problem. Like the shamans of many cultures, including the Pueblo Indians, Catholic priests traditionally present themselves as sexually ambiguous, androgynous figures. Though presumably perpetual virgins, everyone calls them "father" – but clerical business wear consists of feminine dress-like cassocks overlaid by gorgeous gowns, beautiful vestments of embroidered and brocaded silks and satins. If even St. Jerome, a Father of the Church, might well be a transvestite, it would be remarkable if there weren't others among the clergy.

Some experts believe that almost half the clergy is homosexual and most of those are sexually active.[12] The actual figure is quite controversial not only because of the secrecy surrounding all sexual activity in the clergy in general, but that particularly surrounding homosexuality. Yet there is no doubt that the percentage of gay men in the priesthood is widely perceived to be higher than in the general population and steadily increasing.

Seminarians, surrounded only by males, were particularly vulnerable to such temptations, and not just from their teachers. With no feminine companions save close relations permitted in their lives, they had also long been warned about the dangers of "particular friendships" with their male comrades, but not told much else. Fitzgerald himself had noticed the steadily increasing percentage of gays among his guests and worried about ever more gay-friendly seminaries. He clearly thought a homosexually permissive atmosphere could destroy the entire priesthood.

It's almost a joke that gay men would be attracted to the Catholic priesthood. And not just for the purely masculine environment either. Arts and service have long attracted many sincere, sensitive homosexual men and women, and their selfless contributions throughout the entire life of the Church have been as measureless as they are unrecognized.

The contribution of gays to the crisis is also quite contentious. Advocates point out that logically, homosexuality does not imply pedophilia of itself any more than heterosexuality does. However, the proportion of homosexual perpetration is overwhelmingly high: three out of every four victims of priest abuse were boys during the 1960s. And it only increased over time: from 64% male in the 1950s, to 76% in the 1960s, up to 86% in the 1970s, about where it stayed during the 80s.[13]

Though far from definitive, the *John Jay Report* thus confirmed the impression the late victims advocate Tom Economus had about this. After talking with hundreds of clergy abuse victims of all denominations, he felt that by far the most targeted group were 12-year-old Catholic boys. Statistically, his intuition was precisely correct.

How much is due to true homosexual preferences or the easy availability of altar boys is also highly debatable. Since the percentage of boys actually increased in the 1970s despite the fact that girls were also allowed to serve for the first time in many places after Vatican II, this may be indeed indicative of a growing homosexual population among the priesthood.

What there is little question about is that the culture of silence surrounding the forbidden lifestyle has been greatly conducive to hiding all manner of secrets, including child abuse. "There is no other single element so destructive to sexual responsibility among clergy as the system of secrecy, which both shields behavior and reinforces denial."[14]

The greatest appeal of the priesthood, however, might be the attraction of a prestigious, comfortable way of life where the absence of female company is completely accepted, and even praised. The celibate clergy thus provides a refuge not only for committed homosexuals, but also for those confused, conflicted, or ashamed about their sexual identity for any number of reasons. Asexuality, abuse, guilt, and transgender issues are all among those that could play a part.

As Dr. Jay Feierman, a Paraclete psychologist, pointed out, "The typical homosexual has no interest in pubescent boys. Ones who are involved with boys are rarely involved with men. Celibacy tends to attract people who have no socially acceptable outlet for their proclivities."[15]

A Roman collar, as Porter wistfully noted, provides a great place to hide. It therefore attracts a great number of disturbed individuals of all kinds. Many are drawn simply because they feel they cannot fit into the secular world. Such disastrously misplaced souls are probably the source of much unhappiness and insanity marring the history of the Church.

Yet Pope Benedict has made it abundantly clear that even chaste, mature, well-intentioned, sexually inactive homosexuals are not welcome in his clergy. Strict standards and psychological testing to root out deviants has been promised to keep them out of the seminaries.[16] Against the passive resistance of already well-situated gays and their allies, some in very high places, there may be little he can do, however. In fact, effective testing might only serve to identify future victims or partners to administrators so inclined.

In any case, official condemnation of gays in the clergy is still the only actual incentive for them to leave. The priestly lifestyle itself remains a agreeable men's club. Heterosexual men who fall in love nowadays, however, have plenty of reasons to leave the clubhouse behind. So it is likely that the priesthood will only become ever more gay – and ever more secretive and hypocritical along with it – even as it continues to shrink in size.

Insufficient grace

Perhaps what is most disturbing about all this is the failure of moral theology it reveals. Catholic priests are elite members of the Church. Despite any lapses in screening or training, these men are as carefully prepared and closely watched throughout their years of instruction as professional athletes. Moreover, all the resources of a worldwide enterprise back them up, including two thousand years of moral teaching and experience in spiritual direction.

And as has been seen, even when priests stumble and fall, they are often given second and third chances. Lavish mercy is often offered in situations where non-clerics would be facing certain disaster. Priestly sinners are showered with every incentive to reform, have every spiritual aid and tool in the Catholic arsenal at their disposal, and are supported in such efforts not just by their superiors and spiritual directors, but also by the earnest prayers of the faithful. Yet, for some that is just not enough.

Perhaps it is unfair to judge the Servants of the Paraclete and other stewards just by their fiascos. After all, their successes are generally unknown to all but them while their grossest failures were caught and displayed for all to see. Who can say how many drunken priests quietly dried up, how many sex-crazed clerics secretly reformed over the years? Only God knows.

Yet Christ said, "By their fruits shall you know them."[17] The grim but undeniable fact is that the numbers of clerics who fell or were saved form only a tiny portion of the consequences of the clergy sex crisis. They are overshadowed by the damages not just to the primary direct victims of their lust but also the secondary victims, the families involved, too. For sexual abuse can create a domino effect that can wreck lives for generations.

Fitzgerald believed that even if a sinful priest were never caught, his loss of grace and lack of faith would still cause his congregation to drop away. There is an incalculable bad effect on the Church as a whole and upon the larger society as well.

Perhaps the most dismal but significant results are from the toxic effects of the system developed to keep all that wicked fruit hidden. On that basis will stand the judgment of history on the Roman Catholic Church in these matters. At this point, perhaps the faithful should just pray that the judgment of God might be more merciful than that of the future.

Beyond that, should it not be disturbing to believers that so many of their revered holy men have failed so badly and so often? What does this say about the faith of the fathers if it is sometimes so utterly and tragically inadequate to save even its most privileged and pampered standard bearers?

CONCLUSION:
THE RETURN OF THE INQUISITION

Meanwhile in Rome

Research has revealed that the Holy Office of the Inquisition had jurisdiction over clergy sexual abuse for at least half a millennium. The Second Vatican Council seriously compromised that secret system. For decades afterwards, bishops transferred abusive priests and sent them to treatment in hopes of being cured.

Yet, despite several major eruptions, the crisis has gradually diminished everywhere since the early days of this century. Most cases still winding their way through the legal system deal with events decades old. The story of how this change came about, and what it implies for the future, is possibly the most interesting part of the history.

It involves one of the men who broke the power of the Inquisition. This one, however, later rebuilt it. Not only was his turnabout from liberal to conservative most remarkable, it was to have the most profound effects on the Roman Catholic Church. The full extent cannot yet be seen at the time of this writing. For that man became the current pontiff, Pope Benedict XVI.

Originally a liberal, Joseph Ratzinger changed greatly in the two decades since the Council. His thoughts and attitudes had grown far more pessimistic. He began doubting the directions the reforms were leading even before the council's conclusion. But it was the shock of student rebellions in 1968 that decisively spurred his defection to the conservative camp.[1]

By the time the Polish pope was elected a decade later, now-Cardinal Ratzinger's transformation was complete. Within a few years, John Paul II made him prefect of the Congregation for the Doctrine of the Faith. The protestor against the intolerance of the Inquisition had somehow become the grand inquisitor himself.

If Ratzinger ever sensed this irony, he has kept it safely hidden. As has been well documented, the new prefect soon launched a number of serious public campaigns against certain movements that had arisen in the wake of Vatican II. Liberation theology, women's hopes for ordination, gays' demands for inclusion, the ecumenical dreams of Anglicans, even the legislative ambitions of national bishops conferences, one by one, all came in for condemnation.

Cutting-edge theologians, from liberationist Leonardo Boff to old friends and allies including Küng and Rahner, were silenced, denied employment, or forced out of the priesthood for their theories.[2] Even if Ratzinger has never publicly acknowledged any change in his own views, his turnabout was complete and dramatic. His deliberate long-term efforts to redefine the Council's teachings to enhance papal power seem almost as if they were some sort of a self-imposed penance to pay for his former liberality.

As prefect, he was criticized in much the same terms as he had used decades before against Ottaviani. Arbitrariness, lack of defense afforded to the accused, the only options being submission or exile – all the old familiar complaints returned. When finally stripped of his qualifications as an approved theologian after long resisting summonses, Küng said, "Whatever the name, it is still the old Inquisition. There is no due process in Rome."[3]

Although the cardinal strongly objected to John Paul II's millennial apology for the excesses of the Inquisition, Ratzinger went along with the refurbishing of the Holy Office. He implemented some of the Council's recommended changes by modernizing procedures, hiring consultants, and ending some secrecy. Seminars were held where approved scholars minimized the Inquisition's terrors. The department's own secret archives were opened to select researchers who soon found confirmation of its early ongoing involvement in clergy abuse cases.[4]

But the most powerful head of the doctrinal police force in modern times was out to repair all of Vatican II's "mistakes." For instance, he carefully designed a statement, *Dominus Iesus*, "Lord Jesus," repealing the freedom of conscience Pope John XXIII had upheld for all humanity in *Pacem in terris*. Once again, only within the Roman Catholic community under the leadership of the pope, could true communion with Christ be found. Boff passionately criticized the document as a "very clear presentation of totalitarian rule" and "the grave of the ecumenical movement."[5]

Even before that, however, Ratzinger targeted the national bishops conferences as threats to papal authority. Despite the authorization of the council, he claimed they had no power. Thus, there may be another reason for the failure of *The Manual*. It is quite possible that it failed due to Ratzinger's efforts behind the scenes to thwart the bishops, for the Vatican's approval was required.[6] Most likely, interests among the American bishops as well as the Vatican both had reasons to want to see it buried, and so it was.

This likelihood is increased by the fact that when the American bishops finally got around to seriously tackling clergy abuse again in 1992, they found their efforts blocked by Rome. It took another decade and much negative publicity to erect a zero tolerance policy, which then met substantial obstacles behind the Vatican's closed doors.[7] Apparently the danger of independent action by synods of bishops was seen as even greater than the activities of pedophile priests.

Secrecy triumphant

Ratzinger had already dealt with the latter problem himself anyway. He had drafted new secret instructions and a cover letter on clergy sex abuse. Signed by John Paul II on April 30, 2001, the decree, an apostolic letter named *Sacramentorum sanctitatis tutela,* "Safeguarding the Sanctity of the Sacraments," clandestinely replaced *Crimen sollicitationis* as if the latter had remained in force all along.[8]

If anything, the new policy seems even more repressive than the old one. Whereas the earlier document gave detailed instructions on how to conduct trials just like the Inquisition, the new one simply authorizes the Congregation for the Doctrine of the Faith to do its thing. The cover letter Ratzinger furnished made sure the highest levels of secrecy still covered all.[9]

The new policy still deals with sexual solicitation in Confession and associated offenses such as priests granting absolution to their partners or having sex with minors of either gender.

On the other hand, there are certain other offenses, some formerly reserved to the pope to forgive, that now rest exclusively in the tender care of the CDF. These include violations of the seal of Confession, various Eucharistic sacrileges including keeping blessed hosts for blasphemous purposes such as Black Masses, and even the awful crime of celebrating Holy Communion with others than Roman Catholics.

So, the faithful are shielded once again from priestly sex, sorcery, as well as dangerously promiscuous ecumenism. There's a sacred statute of limitations, too: a decade for the crimes above, as opposed to three for most lesser ones. This is actually an upgrade for child abuse, as in the 1983 *Code of Canon Law,* it had a limit of only five years, like murder, kidnapping, rape, living with a woman, and procuring an abortion, considered the worst typical crimes of priests by Rome.[10]

Significantly, the "worst crime" of clerical homosexuality is no longer even mentioned at all in the new policy. Could this be because the high percentage of sexually active gays in the clergy?

The new policy also seems even more ruthless than before. Whereas previously it took three denunciations by different victims within a month of occurrence to initiate a case, nowadays any suspicion, rumor, or complaint will do to start an investigation. It would seem that a bishop or superior is free to start proceedings against an underling for any reason, which will doubtless further curb clerical independence of any sort. Once wheels are in motion, however, transfers are still forbidden.

In some ways, this makes sense as the inquisitors of the CDF doubtless have the "experience" necessary. They are to be informed after the initial investigation, and may take the case to judge if they feel like it. Even the leaked policy itself is still wrapped in the profoundest pontifical secrecy. Automatic excommunication remains the unholy fate for any who would dare breach the silence.[11] The only outward sign that such trials are even taking place would be the cessation of new cases – which seems to be happening. Despite huge settlements, church apologists happily reported that for the second year in a row, sex abuse claims went down in 2006.[12]

Thus, two years before it was even discovered to have ever existed, then-Cardinal Joseph Ratzinger had carefully replaced the inquisitorial lid he had accidentally helped dislodge and break. This is one reason Rome takes such a long, sanguine, and altogether self-satisfied view.

Whether or not he ever admits it even to himself, the crisis had been, in some ways, partly his fault. What more, then, will he accomplish as pope?

How much could Benedict change the Church if he wanted? Theoretically, a great deal. The Roman Catholic Church remains an absolute monarchy. For good or ill, it is totally governed by the opinions of one man. But though all-powerful on paper, in practice the pope is on a fairly short leash. His freedom of action is sharply restrained by the curia, hemmed in on all sides by the oldest continual bureaucracy on the planet, and above all, confined by the crushing dead weights of ancient dogma and sacred tradition.

Trapped beneath the suffocating baggage of all his predecessors' claims, the pope cannot speak beyond those limits any more than his underlings can tell him anything contrary. All are constrained by doctrine and history to play roles increasingly unreal in the third millennium after Christ. Real reform remains out of reach. And so it is that the magnificent façade of the Roman Church ever more resembles that of a monolithic tomb.

Church v. State in the Third Millennium

The scandals still smolder. High-profile incarcerated offenders are now occasionally involuntarily laicized in public as if in a modern *auto da fé*. Pope Benedict travels the globe proclaiming that pedophile priests will not be tolerated. He announces no reform programs or anything suggestive of real change, but his flock seems strangely content anyhow.

So, the Church has once again instinctively retreated from reform on all fronts. As if by reflex, Rome has merely reinstated the cover-up more firmly than ever before. That, obviously, doesn't seem like what Jesus would do.

Meanwhile, Church spokespeople are quick to point out that most cases in the news now relate to events decades old, as if there has been great moral progress made, though the main solution now seems to be expulsion.

Could there really be no new sex abusers in the clergy? Or are the traditional methods of coping by secrecy and intimidation, now coupled with payoffs, once again successfully concealing recent crimes? If given a chance, clerical child molesters these days might gladly opt for secret discipline, even harsh, over public disgrace.

There is little evidence that reporting laws are being observed any better than before when the Church is not compelled by publicity or that transferring problem priests has ceased. In any case, it is said that the CDF's global backlog for involuntary liacization is now so great, it takes a bishop eighteen months to even get a reply.[13]

More money yet fewer cases while more priests are quietly thrown out or otherwise internally dealt with is exactly what might be expected if the secret system were fully operational again. But whether such medieval policies can succeed in modern democratic societies remains an open question.

The Catholic Church stands eternally apart from the State. The kingdom it focuses upon is not of this world, after all. Having begun as a faith persecuted by the Roman Empire, it was forced to develop its own basic institutions, which served it well when that empire collapsed. In the wake of the barbarian invasions, the Christian Church then had to bear the entire weight of preserving what was left of civilization. It has ample reason not to rely too much on kings and parliaments.

Unlike Islam, where the division between Church and State is unknown, this distinction forms a fundamental chasm in the West. For the Church to determine its own structure and rules seems quite natural to us. The question is, and has always been, how much governing power it should possess over itself and society in general.

Were the scandals due to modern society or the failure of the secret system? The Church claims the former; as has been shown, the temporary curbing of the Inquisition seems to be a more direct influence. But is allowing that power to be restored a wise solution?

The problem is not so much that the Catholic Church metes out its own justice, but that it consistently appears to be so overwhelmingly bad at it. People did not lose faith in the ability of their Church to effectively govern its members for no reason. They lost faith simply because the hierarchy failed them. Their leaders betrayed the flock in favor of their fellow shepherds.

As has been shown, consistent patterns of covering up for abusive priests are evident throughout the scandals. As Richard Sipe, a noted expert on clergy abuse has emphatically maintained, the reason bishops and cardinals can't fix it is because some prelates are abusers themselves.

Sipe, a former Benedictine priest and now a practicing psychologist, has spent his life studying celibacy. Interviews with thousands of priests have convinced him that true celibacy is a rare but valuable attainment, a Holy Grail rightfully prized for its contributions to human society as selfless charity. How difficult is true chastity to achieve? As hard as one might think. For buried among all his anecdotes and carefully shaded definitions lurks one, simple, inescapable statistic: 80% of all priests masturbate.[14]

The figure is only remarkable because priests are not supposed to have *any* sexual activity whatsoever; not even that which was once but is no longer considered a grave sin is allowed. Regardless, the fact means that only one in five priests is ever truly chaste or pure.

The choice, then, it would seem, would be between a tiny priesthood composed of living saints or a larger but far more human clerical class. It is Pope Benedict's unfortunate dilemma that neither option really seems viable.

A medieval strategy

A monarchical system only performs well when the leader is strong, upright, and principled and insists on the same from his underlings. That, unfortunately, has not always been the case with the Church in its long history. After two thousand years, an immense burden of bureaucratic corruption and expedient compromises has built up like ineradicable grime.

The record of the Catholic Church's handling of the sexual activities of its clergy has been frankly abysmal. And it's not just the pope stonewalling and bishops covering up for their priests, either. Those answerable for cleaning up the mess afterwards have been shown to be equally irresponsible, shortsighted, and as overtly enabling.

The Servants of the Paraclete may be especially guilty in this respect. But virtually all churchmen concerned seem to have performed very poorly – even by their own alleged standards. They have not prevented scandal at all by the cover-up but merely guaranteed that the scandal would be far greater and more devastating when finally revealed.

The hierarchy has consistently ignored demands from survivors and reforming lay organizations like Voices of the Faithful or Call to Action. The Roman Church seems blindly determined to continue to handle affairs just as it sees fit. Possibly, it can do nothing else.

If anything, history sadly suggests that the system just might in fact be unfixable. Almost five hundred years ago in a similar crisis, the Catholic Church found itself unable to make the changes necessary and lost the allegiance of half of Europe. Every attempt since then has been strangled by the fear of losing further influence. Holy Mother Church's last recourse has always been to wrap itself in hoary tradition and mystery and stubbornly insist that its antique privileges are divinely granted rights.

How much of that can be allowed? "Privileges" or private laws must stop where they harm the health and well being of the whole society. At that point, secret actions must be opposed. In a certain sense, it is immaterial whether the Church is intent on punishing wicked priests or merely shifting them about. Because there is no public accountability in a secret system, secrecy should not be allowed. Justice, to be done, needs to be seen being done.

A truly horrific price has been paid due to the scandals, and the immeasurable monetary fortune given by the faithful that the Church has squandered is the least of it. The coin of untold misery has most dearly bought a far more prudent understanding of human frailty and the flagrant misuses of the authority of God.

The gravest sin of all would be to waste that by allowing the Roman Catholic Church to again privately tidy up its messes for the Vatican's sole benefit. Time alone, however, will tell if the hierarchy can continue to get away with such a haughty and deeply cynical strategy.

Victims and survivors should not be required to solely shoulder the duty of demanding a true and faithful rendering of their abusers. Nor should this burden be limited to Catholic laity or even all Christians. These issues affect everyone in our pluralistic society, Catholic and non-Catholic, Christians, heathen, and atheists alike. Independent civil watchdogs are needed to guard every flock of all faiths, not merely against their erring shepherds, but also their deep purses.

A monument in the canyon

Meanwhile, the Servants of the Paraclete and their sister order, the Handmaidens of the Precious Blood, still maintain their homes in Jemez Springs. But an even deeper silence reigns at the monastery now. Though well kept, most facilities look little used these days. Many buildings stand silent and forlorn, like a college campus abandoned between semesters.

In fact, the Servants' once infamous "ecclesiastic prison" and former "byword for healing" is no longer even the "Fr. Fitzgerald Retreat Center." Those offices have been rented out for the last several years to the non-profit organization now in charge of running the new Valles Caldera National Preserve up the road.

The whitewashed church next door with its distinctive silver sculpture poking up like some futuristic antenna stands unchanged. But the sign reading "Mary, Mother of Priests" hanging out front announces a new role. It now serves as the town's parish church. During the glory days of the center, the sanctuary invited adoration of the holy Eucharist at all hours. Now it's locked and deserted save for a lone Mass on Sundays.

Several large dedication plaques, proudly sandblasted out of gleaming black marble, are still set in the front of the building. One, opposite the ruins, mounted upon a white stone pillar in front of the doors poignantly proclaims Fitzgerald's heartfelt gratefulness to his order's patrons:

**DEDICATED
TO HIS EXCELLENCY
ARCHBISHOP EDWIN V. BYRNE, D.D.
OUR BELOVED FATHER IN CHRIST
THAT OUR GRATITUDE TO GOD,
OUR LADY, AND OUR CO-FOUNDER
MAY RING OUT FOR MANY CENTURIES
OVER THIS CANYON
OF THE BLESSED SACRAMENT
SERVANTS OF THE PARACLETE
PALM SUNDAY, 1963**

To this devout sentiment, the spirits of the friars who raised and labored in the mission across the highway over three centuries earlier would surely whisper, "Amen!"

The plaque is dated mere months before the archbishop's passing and a little over a year after the issuing of *Crimen sollicitationis*. It marks what was probably the supreme high point of Father Gerald's accomplishments. His refuge, now firmly established, had just been blessed with a fine place of worship, his order approved, and plans were underway to truly purify the Church with the island penitentiary. His vision was coming true. There was every reason to believe that Heaven would answer this fervent prayer positively. Wayward priests would find a welcoming sanctuary and haven of last resort there for ages to come.

Yet, it was not to be. The ecumenical council also already in the works would soon convulse the entire Catholic world and totally wreck his dreams. In a few short years, the founder himself would be shoved aside by the need for change. Because of the urgent need for priests after Vatican II, his plans were doomed to be tossed into the trash before they could ever be realized. The tragic results would devour most of the good work the founder had already accomplished.

And so the exuberant confidence the tablet expresses seems as touchingly naïve now as the pious aspirations of those long-dead missionaries. Although, considering Fitzgerald's penchant for lost causes and his choice of a ruined mission to make his stand, who can say he did not foresee it?

To outsiders, now the plaque reads almost like an epitaph to the Servants' struggles. The Paracletes must have been as deeply disappointed in their quixotic quest there in Jemez Canyon just as the Franciscans had been. For although physically sound, unlike the neighboring ruins of San José Mission, their church of Mary is likewise a dead monument to human obstinacy.

All these priests had splendid intentions and faith enough to move mountains, yet their wisdom tragically faltered before the great task of converting souls. From 1947 until at least 1994, the Servants also tried mightily to open the hardened hearts of their charges there in the "Canyon of the Blessed Sacrament." They had almost as much time as had the friars long before them. But their mission was ultimately as bitterly futile as that of their predecessors had been, and for much the same reason.

For the Spirit, it is written, goes where it wills. Grace can neither be forced nor conjured into the souls of the unwilling or the unable, be they heathens or sinners. Even if those sinners had been consecrated as conduits of grace, whose crimes made a mockery of infinite forgiveness.

But is it really their tombstone? Have the Servants truly given up? Does the plaque mark the demise of the order's ambitions in general, or just in Jemez Springs? If the Servants of the Paraclete still quietly minister to the fallen servants of God, where is it done and how?

After all, the Paracletes have never said they were abandoning their purpose to provide a refuge for priests. Servant General Hoare only complained during the scandals that "the media in its reporting did not always avoid sensationalism and inaccuracy, and this coupled with a prevailing litigious spirit, ultimately led us to close the therapeutic program at our Mother House."[15] There was never talk of abandoning the effort, just shifting their programs to someplace less conspicuous beyond the canyon's walls.

They still apparently run several centers in Missouri and Minnesota, but what about outside the country? Even the Archdiocese of Santa Fe's official history celebrating its hundredth anniversary in 1975 boasted of their foreign mission. Along with the other orders, it spoke of the "Paraclete Fathers" in Jemez Springs devoted to "aged priests and others with various needs. From here other such houses have been founded in other parts of the world."[16]

By the time of the founder's death six years previously, seven houses had indeed already been established overseas, according to Father Gerald's reverent biography. They were in England, Scotland, and Italy, along with one in France "owned and financed" by the French bishops, plus two more in South America and one in Africa, too.[17] A former novice, however, identified those houses as being in Argentina, Bolivia, and Tanzania.[18]

No names or more precise locations are known for most of these, much less any hint of any other refuges since founded. However, with as many as 23 centers running at their height in the 1970s, supposedly only three were still operating by 2007, according to one outside expert.[19]

Only the facility in England, Our Lady of Victory Trust at Stroud, in Gloucestershire, ever became publicly known, and that was solely because of its own scandals. Due to them, it too was officially shuttered just like the Villa, Cherry Valley, and ultimately Via Coeli itself had been.

It's quite possible none of those closings makes any difference whatsoever in the larger scheme of things. Other places, maybe even other orders, might have stepped in to fill the gap.

But Fitzgerald had a global ministry transcending political borders in mind from the start. Already in a joint begging letter with his co-founder in August 1956, he bragged, "Priests come to Via Coeli from all parts of the United States, from Canada, Europe and South America."[20]

Undoubtedly, some among the foreign hierarchy were acquainted with his program and utilized it, too, not just American bishops. The fourth Servant General, Liam Hoare, also boasted that the program was known around the world by the time the founder died.

However, no foreign sexual abusers have ever been exposed as one-time visitors to Jemez Springs or any other Paraclete facility in the US as far as is known. Not even in the case of Abeywickrema, the single priest from overseas accused in the New Mexican scandals, was there ever any hint of a stay at Via Coeli. Perhaps he hadn't been a guest, but what of those foreigners who were? Whatever became of them?

Obviously, there is still much more to this story.

Where did all the fallen priests go? It is the weightiest question left hanging. What finally happened to them all? Were they expelled like Adam into the secular wilderness as accursed sinners to find their own way? Or have they been passed on to other monasteries in even more obscure locations – perhaps to other facilities run by the Servants in far-off lands?

Has "Paraclete Island" or a similar priest prison finally become a reality after all? Or have predators posing as men of God been welcomed yet again into distant parishes with trusting parents and unsuspecting children?

Perhaps as it once was, it is again. In this world, quite possibly only Pope Benedict alone knows for sure.

TIMELINE

Here are a few of the highlights in the history of sex and the clergy of the Roman Catholic Church. This is not meant to be a comprehensive survey by any means.

In the beginning

- c. 305 – The Council of Elvira in Spain first prescribed absolute chastity for priests.
- 312 – Constantine wins the Battle of the Milvian Bridge and legalizes Christianity.
- 325 – The first ecumenical Council of Nicea establishes the Creed and organizes the basic form of the Church.
- 604 – Pope Gregory the Great dies, after establishing a policy of "zero tolerance" that was never followed.
- c. 855(?) – "Pope Joan" is supposedly revealed as a woman while giving birth during a papal procession, and is slain on the spot with her lover.
- c. 900 – The *False Decretals* alter Gregory's policy to favor repentance.
- 955 – Possibly the worst pope ever, John XII, ascends the throne, arranged by his powerful mother, papal mistress Marozia.
- 1051 – Pope Leo IX orders all priests' women in Rome enslaved, and that other bishops do the same.
- 1072 – Monastic reformer and cardinal, St. Peter Damian dies. He wrote *The Book of Gomorrah*, a fiery denunciation of clerical immorality.
- 1080 – First mention of tax on clerical mistresses, "cullagium," at the Synod of Lillebonne.
- 1085 – Reforming pope Gregory VII dies. He enforced clerical chastity and tried to free the Church from the influence of secular lords.
- 1123 – First Lateran Council declares all ties to the Church are superior to other human bonds.
- 1139 – Second Lateran Council forbad priestly marriages.
- 1215 – Fourth Lateran Council admits celibacy is a local rule of Western Church. It also orders yearly confession and Communion for Catholics, and launches the **Albigensian Crusade** against the Cathar strongholds of southern France.

- **April 20, 1233** – **Medieval Inquisition** founded by Pope Gregory IX to fight heresy in the wake of the crusade.
- **c. 1255** – *Taxes of the Penitentiary*, the infamous papal sin tax, codified.
- **1302** – Pope Boniface VIII issued *Unam sanctum*, which defines disobedience to the pope as heresy.
- **1439** – The Council of Florence, in order to bring about reunification with the Eastern Churches, notes that celibacy is not required for them.

The Inquisition reborn

- **1478** – Ferdinand and Isabella found the Spanish Inquisition. Run and jealously guarded by the crown, its prime focus is mainly on protecting the state from divisions caused by converted Jews and Moslems, as well as heresy and clergy misconduct.
- **1484** – *Malleus Maleficarum*, or aptly named *The Hammer of the Witches*, by the Dominicans Heinrich Kramer and James Sprenger is published, and is an early bestseller across Europe thanks to the newly-invented printing press. Its instructions on detecting and destroying witches empowered the witchcraft craze, which may have killed millions in the ensuing centuries.
- **1521** – Martin Luther evades capture by the Inquisition after standing up to the emperor at the Diet of Worms. He goes into hiding, continues to write, and inspires what becomes the Protestant Reformation.
- **1542** – Pope Paul III revives the Roman Inquisition in the wake of the Protestant heresy. From the beginning, the Roman version is mainly concerned with intellectual dangers to the Church at large, such as Lutheranism and modern science as well as clerical discipline. It publishes the *Index of Forbidden Books*, and remains to this day (although under a different name) as it began: the most powerful department of the Vatican.
- **1559** – Pope Pius IV authorizes the Spanish Inquisition to actively seek out and punish priests who seduce women through misuse of the sacrament of confession, known as "**solicitation in the confessional.**"
- **April 15, 1561** – The pope, pleased by its success, extends its sexual jurisdiction over all Spanish dominions. The recently revived papal Roman Inquisition is given similar broad powers.

- **The crime of solicitation** is first published as one that must be denounced to the Inquisition under penalty of excommunication. It would be quickly and quietly removed from the list, even while later popes steadily extended the powers and jurisdiction of the Inquisition over clergy sex cases.
- **Around 1565,** St. Charles Borromeo installs an early **confessional booth** in Milan, as a screen between two chairs. The idea is to prevent sexual contact between priests and penitents. Within half a century, the Vatican would order them installed in every church in the world.
- **1622** – Pope Gregory XV decrees that priests are still obliged to individually inform penitents of their duty to inform on sexually predatory clergy, but the whole process becomes cloaked in secrecy. In areas where no Inquisition is active, bishops are empowered to set up their own secret tribunals and inflict the most extreme punishments.
- **1641** – Canon **Pandolfo Ricasoli**, abbess Faustina Mainardi, and another accomplice are condemned to "perpetual and irremissible confinement" for running a sex cult and prostitution ring in a Florentine convent and school for poor girls.
- **1643** – Confessor Urbain Grandier is burnt for allegedly magically seducing an entire convent of nuns in Loudon, France.
- **1646** – The pope abolishes the **Piarists**, a highly successful order teaching poor boys across Italy, for child sexual abuse. Founded by the patron saint of Catholic education, St. José Calasanz, the order had been taken over by a pedophile ring. The order will be quietly revived later, but these scandals are successfully concealed until the opening of the Inquisition's own archives at the dawn of the twenty-first century.

Modern times

- **July 15, 1834** – Though its dismantlement was first decreed in 1820, the Spanish Inquisition is finally abolished. Archives show its continual intervention in clergy sex cases until the very end.
- **1836** – "Maria Monk," an alleged escapee from a Canadian convent, is the first to break silence about sexual and other abuse in nunneries. She is nearly universally reviled and disbelieved.
- **1867** – American historian Henry Charles Lea publishes a three-volume study on celibacy in the Catholic Church, which reveals the long and

often futile struggle to impose chastity on clerics. He also publishes other equally massive studies on both the medieval and Spanish Inquisitions as well as the sacrament of Confession.

- **1880** – Personal friend of Lincoln and former American priest, Charles Chiniquy, bitterly complains of the current ongoing dangers and results of solicitation in *The Priest, The Woman, and the Confessional*.
- **1908** – The now-Universal Roman Inquisition is renamed the "Supreme Sacred Congregation of the Holy Office" and given authority across the globe.
- **1922** – Any knowledge at the Holy Office's entire role in sex crimes is now deemed too scandalous. New secret rules were written.
- **1924** – *Là Bas*, or *Down There*, the first modern novel on clerical Satanism, is published.
- **1947** – The **Servants of the Paraclete**, a religious order dedicated to helping fallen priests, is established with headquarters in Jemez Springs, New Mexico by Fr. Gerald Fitzgerald.
- **1954** – An American ex-Franciscan, Emmett McGloughlin, in his autobiography first reveals the existence of the Jemez Springs establishment as one "ecclesiastic prison" among others where priests are sent without trial for sexual offenses, alcoholism, and insubordination.
- **1962** – Reporting laws that mandate disclosure of sex abuse appear for the first time. McGloughlin publishes another book with a few more details on Jemez Springs. Prophetically, he writes, "The sexual affairs of priests in the U.S. are more closely guarded secrets than the classified details of our national defense."
- **March 16** – Cardinal Alberto Ottaviani, the head of the Holy Office, presents Pope John XXIII with *Crimen sollicitationis*, in English, *Instruction on the Manner of Proceeding in Cases of Solicitation*. This is a highly secret document containing instructions for bishops on how to proceed in trying cases of sexual abuse and homosexuality among clerics like the Inquisition.

Vatican II

- **October 11, 1962** – the Second Vatican Council formally begins.
- **October 13** – On the first working day, the head of the liberal faction, Cardinal Josef Frings of Belgium, opposes Ottaviani's proposed plan

of discussion. Ottaviani boycotts the Council for weeks out of pique, giving liberals the chance to determine their own agenda. Among them is **Joseph Ratzinger,** one of Frings' trusted theological advisors.

- **November 8, 1963** – Frings gives a rousing speech that Ratzinger wrote calling for reform of the Holy Office and its "medieval ways." It is enthusiastically applauded. Pope Paul VI calls Frings that evening to tell him that the reform will go through.
- **Heated discussions over celibacy** and the clergy also consume the Council. Finally, in the *Decree on the Life and Ministry of Priests*, carefully coded language reveals that 1) **priests will no longer be punished** for sexual transgressions but treated with "with fraternal charity and magnanimity" and 2) **celibacy is not necessary** for the priesthood but would still be demanded of Latin-rite priests. This sets the stage for the great clergy exodus.
- **December 7, 1965** – Vatican II ends. On the very last day of the Council, the reform of the Holy Office is announced. It will henceforth be called the "Congregation for the Doctrine of the Faith" (CDF). Some secrecy will be ended, priests would be given certain rights of appeal and representation, and the *Index of Forbidden Books* will be discontinued. Ominously, the CDF is given the power of questioning faith and morals anywhere in the entire Church. Only the Pope retains more power.

In the wake of the Council

- **August 23, 1965** – Archbishop Davis removes Fitzgerald from control of Via Coeli.
- **March 23, 1966** – Cardinal Ildebrando Antoniutti authorizes rehabilitation programs at Via Coeli over Fitzgerald's objections.
- **1966** – Southdown, a treatment center in Toronto, is founded.
- **June 14, 1967** – Finally bowing to pressure, Pope Paul VI issues an encyclical that removes certain restrictions of the Holy Office on clergy wishing to leave, and the flight of disgruntled religious begins.
- **1968** – Returning to academic life, Ratzinger is traumatized by anticlerical student protesters. His doubts about the direction of the Council grow, and he becomes a reactionary.
- **July 4, 1969** – Gerald Fitzgerald, founder of the Servants of the Paraclete, is laid to rest in Jemez Springs with full military honors.

- **1976** – With few other options available, the Paracletes' Jemez monastery becomes a major center for treating priests with sexual problems, over the objections of founder Fitzgerald, who wanted to imprison them on an island for life. Instead, the order opens up more treatment centers, even halfway houses, and loans priests in treatment out to local communities without warning anyone.
- **April 4** – The Vatican declares this as a "Day of Consolation" to quell rumors of Pope Paul VI's alleged homosexual involvement with a young priest.
- **1981** – Pope John Paul II names Ratzinger as Prefect of the CDF. The former protestor becomes the "Vatican's enforcer." He begins a highly publicized series of campaigns against liberal causes that have sprung up since the Council – and attacks many of his former allies, too, such as Hans Küng and Karl Rahner. National bishops councils established by the Council are also opposed as threats to papal power.
- **St Luke Institute** for troubled priests opens in Suitland, Maryland.
- **1983** – **Canon Law revised**, complete with a statute of limitations for clergy sex crimes.

The Age of Scandals

- **1984** – The first significant modern scandal begins with the exposure of **Gilbert Gauthe**, a serial child molester in Louisiana. His attorney, Ray Mouton, calls for help. Priests Tom Doyle, then working in the nunciature in Washington, and Michael Peterson, a psychiatrist who had recently founded St. Luke Institute for troubled priests, become involved. Together, they write a proposal for American bishops, most simply known as *The Manual*. It calls for a "crisis control team" to fly around the country putting out hotspots, with little concern for victims.
- **1985** – *The Manual* is presented to the bishops at their June meeting. It would even be shown to Pope John Paul II. Nothing happens.
- **Late 1980s** – The Paracletes are advised to stop shredding documents by the bishops, and directed the New Mexico archdiocese to do the same.
- **March 25, 1992** – Pope John Paul II issues an apostolic exhortation making celibacy as close to dogma as possible.

- **July** – The scandals first receive extensive national media attention when the notorious **James Porter** cases surface. His tracks lead to Jemez Springs, which leads to scandals breaking out in New Mexico. By this time, some 1,200 other religious had also passed through their programs.
- **Ireland** – Bishop Eamonn Casey flees the country after his having an illegitimate son in the US is exposed.
- **American bishops** find themselves again frustrated by Rome, which blocks their proposals.
- **March 21, 1993** – Archbishop Robert Sanchez of New Mexico becomes the first high-ranking prelate to fall as his affairs are exposed on CBS' *60 Minutes*.
- **August 15** – At **World Youth Day** in Denver, Pope John Paul II infamously dismisses the crisis as a largely North American affair due to a corrupt secular society.
- **St. Anthony's Seminary** in Santa Barbara is rocked by revelations of almost a quarter century of abuse by a fourth of the Franciscan faculty; lasting so long it became multi-generational.
- **1994** –The **Servants of the Paraclete** scale back their treatment programs in New Mexico.
- **1995** – Cardinal Hans Groer of Austria resigns as archbishop due to allegations of sexual misconduct. He will also have to leave a later position as prior of a monastery due to fresh allegations.
- **AIDS** presumably claims Bishop Emerson Moore, the first African-American bishop in the New York archdiocese, who died in a hospice.
- **Ireland** – The scandals begin with over 25 other priests and religious were being investigated. At least one, Danny Curran, had been treated at the Servants' house in Stroud, England.
- **1996** – Four priests in a Washington, DC sex ring, including two that had been sentenced to 16 years in prison, all go free due to leniency from a judge largely due to their advanced age.
- **Canada** – Bishop Hubert O'Connor of Prince George is convicted of sex crimes committed as a young priest at a residential school. Near genocidal abuses on a massive scale against native peoples would be revealed in the years to come.

- **Scotland** – Bishop Roderick Wright of Argyll resigns after running off with a divorced mother of three, whom he later marries.
- **Washington, DC** – Ted Llanos of Long Beach kills himself in the midst of lawsuits and criminal proceedings, accused of sex with 24 teen boys.
- **1997** – Rudy Kos is sentenced to prison, later defrocked, and the largest award to date of $120 million, later reduced to $23 million, is given to 10 altar boys and the family of one who killed himself.
- **Ireland** – Brendan Smyth died shortly after beginning to serve his sentence for 74 instances of sexual abuse. His case brought down the Irish Government for delaying his extradition from Northern Ireland.
- **Rome** – The Inquisition's own secret archives are opened to select scholars by Prefect Ratzinger, allowing for the rediscovery of the Inquisition's role in the cover-up.
- **Australia** – A government investigation of the **Sisters of Mercy** reveals atrocities against hundreds of orphans for over 90 years. They were also investigated in Ireland, the US, and elsewhere for similar abuses.
- **1998** – Bishop J. Keith Symons of Palm Beach resigns after admitting the molestation of 5 boys.
- **Canada** – In St Johns, Newfoundland, trials began for 7 accused members of the **Christian Brothers**, accused of physical and sexual abuse of boys at the infamous Mt. Cashel Orphanage. The order would also be sued in Australia for their treatment of British orphans.
- **1999** – Three Jesuits at the elite Stonyhurst College in England were charged with sex crimes against students, bringing the number of accused staff to 8.
- **California** – Bishop Patrick Ziemann of Santa Rosa resigns after being accused of sexually abusing a Costa Rican priest, Jorge Salas, who claimed the bishop hired 5 men to defame him. Bishop Daniel Ryan of Springfield, Ohio, also resigns under a cloud of homosexual allegations.
- **Washington, DC** –Ted Llanos of Los Angeles kills himself before he can begin serving his sentence for molesting 35 altar boys.
- **Ireland** – The government officially apologized to the victims of 59 church-run reform schools financed by state for their failure to save them.

- **Canada** – The Church refused to offer compensation or even apologize for the treatment of the **Duplessis Orphans**, poor children housed and abused in orphanages and psychiatric facilities as mentally ill to earn their keepers, the Sisters of Providence higher rates. They would also be sued in Vermont.
- **2000** – The Boston scandals, after simmering for years, finally take off when defrocked priest John Geoghan, suspected of abusing over 100 boys, faces trials and numerous lawsuits.
- **Portland, Oregon** – In one of the largest cases, 22 men settled their suit over a quarter-century of sexual abuse by Maurice Grammond, 80, for an undisclosed amount.
- **December 8** — The hacked body of Mike Mack, 60, a Paraclete priest, is discovered in one of the order's residences.

The crisis wanes

- **April 6, 2001** – The European Parliament votes for a symbolic condemnation of the Vatican for rapes suffered by nuns in Africa.
- **April 30** – The CDF secretly issues *Sacramentorum sanctitatis tutela*, or *Safeguarding the Sanctity of the Sacraments* under Pope John Paul II's name. This replaces *Crimen sollicitationis* with a policy even more secret and ruthless than before. All priestly sex crimes are to be placed under the CDF, which usually will authorize the bishops to conduct trials themselves. However, clerical homosexuality is not even mentioned.
- **May 18** – Cardinal Ratzinger quietly adds the cover letter for the new policy, making cases "subject to the pontifical secret." In other words, absolute secrecy is imposed on all who know about them under pain of automatic excommunication that only the pope can forgive.
- **Boston** – The scandals return with John Geoghan (again), and later Paul Shanley and other cases. At the end of the next year, Cardinal Bernard Law resigns, having been exposed as a prime enabler of the cover-up.
- **2002** – American bishops issue the so-called "Dallas Charter" calling for audits and zero tolerance.
- **Ireland** – The Church offers a settlement of $110 million to cover over 3,000 victims. Over 20 clergy had been convicted.

- **Louisville, Kentucky** – Bishop J. Kendrick Williams resigns after allegations of abusing altar boys surface.
- **Milwaukee** – Archbishop Rembert Weakland resigns after hush money paid to a former lover is revealed.
- **2003** – *Crimen sollicitationis* is discovered among diocesan legal papers in Boston. A comprehensive settlement of $85 million is offered for 500 victims.
- **National Review Board** chairman, Frank Keating, resigns after comparing the bishops to the Mafia.
- **Cincinnati** – The Archdiocese is symbolically found guilty of covering up abuse after Archbishop Pilarzyck admits 5 occasions.
- **2004** – Pope John Paul II apologizes for the excesses of the Inquisition and asks for forgiveness.
- **Springfield**, Massachusetts' Bishop Thomas Dupré resigns the same day he's accused of abusing two youths 20 years previously.
- **Portland**, Oregon becomes the first diocese to go bankrupt due to the abuse crisis.
- **Rome** – Cardinal Bernard Law of Boston is rewarded for his role in the scandals there with the important post as head of one of the most important churches in Rome, St. Mary Major.
- **National Review Board** issues a report claiming 10,000 child sexual abuse victims of over 4,000 Catholic priests just in the US over the last 50 years, undoubtedly severely underestimated.
- **April 19, 2005** – Joseph Ratzinger becomes Pope Benedict XVI.
- **June** – The US Conference of Catholic Bishops finally gets a toothless version of the *Charter for the Protection of Children and Young People* approved.
- **2006** – The Vatican finally announced that Marcial Macial Degollado, the founder of the **Legionaries of Christ**, was giving up his public ministry. Nine men first accused the head of the powerful order in 1997 of molesting them over three decades.
- **2007** – David Yallop, in his critical biography of John Paul II, reports that so many referrals for action against priests are sent to the CDF that it takes 18 months just to get a reply.
- **2008** – The Vatican reports that for the third year in a row, the number of new cases has gone steadily down, despite record high financial settlements.

BIBLIOGRAPHY

The Internet's immense and ever-growing resources have made much of this research far easier than it could have been done only a few years ago using only print sources. Many of the Church documents cited are online in English at the website of the Holy See, *www.vatican.va*, some long-out-of print books are available in PDF format from the Internet Archive, *www.archive.org*, and other materials can be located through other online archives and also tools like Google's new Book Search.

The 1917 *Catholic Encyclopedia* at *www.newadvent.org/cathen/index.html* was most informative about the pre-Vatican II structure and definitions.

An important trove of documents important to the clergy abuse crisis are at the Bishop Accountability website, at *www.bishop-accountability.org*.

The website of the Servants of the Paraclete, *www.theservants.org*, provided rare insights into their perspective. Many of their internal documents that were released after the trials were obtained online at Kay Ebeling's City of Angels blog, *www.cityofangels4.com*.

News clippings, particularly in regard to the crisis in New Mexico, came mainly from the author's own archives. They are chiefly from the two main dailies, the *Albuquerque Journal*, and the now-defunct *Albuquerque Tribune*, but also from the *Santa Fe New Mexican*, *National Catholic Reporter*, and others. Due to the hundreds of print articles and TV segments reviewed, many re-petitive, most are cited only by source and date.

Anthologies, Dictionaries, Encyclopedias

Apperson, G. L., *The Wordsworth Dictionary of Proverbs*, (Wordsworth Editions, Ltd., Ware, Herfordshire, 1993).

Bretzke, James T., *Consecrated Phrases: A Latin Theological Dictionary*, (The Liturgical Press, Collegeville, Minnesota, 2003).

Broderick Robert C., *The Catholic Encyclopedia*, (Thomas Nelson Inc., Publishers, Nashville, Tennessee, 1976).

Bunson, Matthew. *The Pope Encyclopedia*, (Crown Trade Paperbacks, New York, 1995).

Hardon, John A., *The Pocket Catholic Dictionary*, (Doubleday, New York, 1980).

Hillgarth, J. N., *The Conversion of Western Europe, 350-750*, (Prentice-Hall, Inc., Englewood Cliffs, New Jersey, 1969).

Kuhner, Hans, *Encyclopedia of the Papacy*, trans. by Kenneth J. Northcott, (Philosophical Library, New York, 1958).

Robbins, Rossell Hope, *The Encyclopedia of Witchcraft and Demonology*, (Crown Press, New York, 1959).

Robinson, J. H., *Readings in European History*, (Ginn, Boston, 1905).

Ross, James Bruce and McLaughlin, Mary Martin, ed., *The Portable Me-

dieval Reader, (Viking Press, New York, 1949).

Stelten, Leo F., *Dictionary of Ecclesiastical Latin*, (Hendrickson Publishers, Inc, Peabody, Massachusetts, 1995).

Books

Allen, John L., Jr., *Pope Benedict XVI: A Biography of Joseph Ratzinger*, originally published as *Cardinal Ratzinger: The Vatican's Enforcer of the Faith* (Continuum, New York, 2000).

Ambrosini, Maria Luisa with Willis, Mary, *The Secret Archives of the Vatican*, (Barnes & Noble, New York, 1969).

Barber, Malcolm, *The Trial of the Templars*, (Cambridge University, New York, 1978).

Barraclough, Geoffrey, *The Medieval Papacy*, (Harcourt, Brace, & World, Inc., Norwich, England, 1968).

Benko, Stephen, *Pagan Rome and the Early Christians*, (Indiana University Press, Bloomington, 1986).

Berry, Jason, *Lead Us Not Into Temptation: Catholic Priests and the Sexual Abuse of Children*, (Doubleday, New York, 1992).

Burkett, Elinor, and Bruni, Frank, *A Gospel of Shame: Children, Sexual Abuse, and the Catholic Church*, (Harper Collins, New York, 2004).

Burman, Edward, *The Inquisition: Hammer of Heresy*, (Dorset Press, New York, 1984).

Cather, Willa, *Death Comes for the Archbishop*, (Alfred A. Knopf, New York, 1927).

Chamberlin, E. R., *The Bad Popes*, (The New American Library, New York, 1969).

Chiniquy, Charles, *Fifty Years in the Church of Rome*, (S.R. Briggs, Toronto, 1886).

—. *The Priest, The Woman, and the Confessional*, (Adam Craig, Chicago, 1880).

Doyle, Thomas, P., Sipe, A.W. Richard, and Wall, Patrick J., *Sex, Priests, and Secret Codes: The Catholic Church's 2000-year Paper Trail of Sexual Abuse*, (Volt Press, Los Angeles, 2007).

Ellis, Bruce, *Bishop Lamy's Santa Fe Cathedral*, (University of New Mexico Press, Albuquerque, 1985).

Eusebius, *The History of the Church from Christ to Constantine*, trans. by G. A. Williamson, (Dorset Press, New York, 1965).

Fitzgerald, Gerald, *Letters from Father Page, CSC*, (Longmans, Green and Co., New York, 1940).

Hardon, John A., *A Prophet for the Priesthood*, (Eternal Life, Bardstown, Kentucky, 1998).

Harris, Michael, *Unholy Orders: Tragedy at Mount Cashel*, (Viking, New York, 1990).

Held, Robert, *Inquisition/Inquisición*, (Qua D'Arno, Florence, Italy, 1985).

Hoffman, Paul, *Anatomy of the Vatican: An Irreverent Look at the Holy See*, (Robert Hale, London, 1985).

Howlett, William J., *Life of the Right Reverend Joseph P. Machebeuf, D.D.*, (Franklin Press Company, Pueblo, Colorado, 1908).

Investigative Staff of *The Boston Globe*, *Betrayal: The Crisis in the Catholic Church*, (Little, Brown and Company, Boston, 2002).

Katz, Jack, *Mysteries and Miracles of New Mexico*, (Rhombus Publishing Co., Corrales, New Mexico, 1988).

Kennedy, William H., *Lucifer's Lodge: Satanic Ritual Abuse in the Catholic Church*, (Reviviscimus, South Egremont, Massachusetts, 2004).

Kessell, John, L., *Kiva, Cross, and Crown: The Pecos Indians and New Mexico 1540-1840*, (University of New Mexico Press, Albuquerque, 1987).

Kramer, Heinrich and Sprenger, James, *Malleus Maleficarum*, trans. by Montague Summers from the Latin text originally published 1484, (Dover, New York, 1971).

Lea, Henry Charles, *A Formulary of the Papal Penitentiary in the Thirteenth Century*, (Lea Brothers & Co., Philadelphia, 1892).

—. *A History of Auricular Confession and Indulgences in the Latin Church*, 3 vol., (Lea Brothers & Co., Philadelphia, 1896).

—. *A History of the Inquisition in Spain*, 4 vol., (Macmillan Co., New York, 1906-7).

—. *A History of Sacerdotal Celibacy in the Christian Church*, 3 vol., (Lea Brothers & Co., Philadelphia, 1867), reprinted in one, (University Books, New York, 1966).

—. *The Inquisition of the Middle Ages*, abridged by Margaret Nicholson, (Macmillan Company, New York, 1961, originally published in 3 vol. By Lea Brothers & Co., Philadelphia, 1887-9).

—. *The Inquisition in the Spanish Dependencies*, (Macmillan Co., New York, 1908).

Liebreich, Karen, *Fallen Order: Intrigue, Heresy, and Scandal in the Rome of Galileo and Caravaggio*, (Grove Press, New York, 2004).

Lux, Annie, *Historic New Mexico Churches*, photos by Daniel Nadelbach (Gibbs Smith, Layton, Utah, 2007).

Martin, Malachi, *The Decline and Fall of the Roman Church*, (G.P. Putnam's Sons, New York, 1981).

—. *The Keys of this Blood: The Struggle for World Dominion Between Pope John Paul II, Mikhail Gorbachev, and the Capitalist West*, (Simon & Schuster, New York, 1990).

McGloughlin, Emmett, *Crime and Immorality in the Catholic Church*, (Lyle Stuart, Inc., New York, 1962).

—. *Letters to an Ex-priest*, (Lyle Stuart, Inc., New York, 1965).

—. *People's Padre*, (The Beacon Press, New York, 1954).

McGuire, Michael A., *The New Baltimore Catechism and Mass No. 2 Official Revised Edition*, (Benziger Brothers, Inc., New York, 1949).

McHugh, John A., *Catechism of the Council of Trent for Parish Priests*, Charles J. Callan, trans., (Joseph F. Wagner, Inc. New York, 1934).

Mills, George and Grove, Richard, *Lucifer and the Crucifer: The Enigma of the Penitentes*, (The Westerners, Inc, Denver, 1955).

Monk, Maria (psued.), *Awful Disclosures of Maria Monk, or, The Hidden Secrets of a Nun's Life in a Convent Exposed!*, (T.B. Peterson, Philadelphia, 1836).

Morrello, Giovanni, ed., *Vatican Treasures: 2000 Years of Art and Culture in the Vatican and Italy*, (Electa, Milan, 1993).

Morris, Charles R., *American Catholic: The Saints and Sinners Who Built America's Most Powerful Church*, (Random House, New York, 1997).

Noonan, James-Charles, Jr., *The Church Visible: The Ceremonial Life and Protocol of the Roman Catholic Church*, (Viking, New York, 1996).

Northland Editors, *Kachinas: A Hopi Artist's Documentary*, (Northland, Flagstaff, Arizona, 1973).

Partner, Peter, *The Murdered Magicians: The Templars and Their Myth*, (Thorsons Publishing Group, Rochester, Vermont, 1987).

Rahn, Otto, *Crusade Against the Grail: The Struggle Between the Cathars, the Templars, and the Church of Rome*, trans. by Christopher Jones (Inner Traditions, Rochester, Vermont, 2006, orig. pub. 1933).

Ranke-Heinemann, Uta, *Eunuchs for the Kingdom of Heaven*, (Penguin Books, New York, 1991).

Rappaport, Angelo S., *The Love Affairs of the Vatican or the Favourites of the Popes*, (Barnes & Noble Books, New York, 1995, orig. pub.1912).

Reese, Thomas J., *Inside the Vatican: The Politics and Organization of the Catholic Church*, (Harvard University Press, Cambridge, Masachusetts, 1996).

Roberts, David, *The Pueblo Revolt: The Secret Rebellion that Drove the Spaniards Out of the Southwest*, (Simon & Shuster, New York, 2004).

Salpointe, J. B., *Soldiers of the Cross*, (Documentary Publications, Salisbury, North Carolina, 1977).

Schiffer, Nancy L., *Contemporary Hopi Kachina Dolls*, (Schiffer Publishing, Atglen, Pennsylvania, 2003).

Schieler, Caspar E., *Theory and Practice of the Confessional: A Guide in the Administration of the Sacrament of Penance*, ed. By H. J. Heuser, (Benziger Brothers, New York, 1905).

Schlichte, George A., *Politics in the Purple Kingdom: The Derailment of Vatican II*, (Sheed & Ward, Kansas City, Missouri, 1993).

Sipe, A.W. Richard, *A Secret World: Sexuality and the Search for Celibacy*, (Brunner/Mazel, New York, 1990).

—. *Sex, Priests, and Power: Anatomy of a Crisis*, (Brunner/Mazel, New York, 1995).

Stanford, Peter, *The Legend of Pope Joan*, (Berkley Books, New York, 1999).

Steele, Thomas J., *Saints and Santos: The Religious Folk Art of Hispanic New Mexico*, (Ancient City Press, Santa Fe, 1982).

Stoyanov, Yuri, *The Hidden Tradition in Europe*, (Penguin Books, New York, 1994).

Thomas, Gordon and Morgan-Witts, Max, *Pontiff*, (Doubleday, New York, 1983).

Torjesen, Karen Jo, *When Women Were Priests*, (Harper San Francisco, 1993).

Weigle, Marta, *The Penitentes of the Southwest*, (Ancient City Press, Santa Fe, 1970).

Wilson, Ian, *Jesus: the Evidence*, (Harper and Row, San Francisco, 1984).

Yallop, David, *The Power and* the Glory: Inside the Dark Heart of John Paul II's Vatican, (Carroll & Graf Publishers, New York, 2007).

Magazine and Online Articles

Anderson, C. Colt, "When magisterium becomes imperium: Peter Damian on the accountability of bishops for scandal," *Theological Studies*, December 1, 2004.

Burge, Don, "Crypto-Jews in New Mexico," *UNM Quantum*, Summer 1992.

Cafardi, Nicholas P., "Before Dallas," *The Catholic World*, June 17, 2007.

"A Cardinal Carabiniere," *Time Magazine*, Monday, August 13, 1979.

"The Cardinal's Setback," *Time Magazine*, Friday, November 23, 1962.

Doyle, Thomas, *The Archives and the Secret Archives Required by Canon Law*, at *the author's website*

Filtreau, Jerry, "U.S. experts at Vatican II recall history-making years", Catholic News Service, at *www.catholicnews.com/data/stories/cns/0505792.htm*.

Hechler, David, "Sins of the Father," *McCall's*, September 1993.

Ingels, Gregory, "The Loss of the Clerical State," undated, found at *www.opusbonosacerdotii.org*.

Laughlin, Corrina, *The Second Vatican Council*, reminiscences of Abp. Connally at *www.stjames-cathedral.org/Prayer/vatican2-3.htm*.

"Ratzinger explains opening of Inquisition files," *Catholic World News*, January 23, 1998.

Smith, Mike, "Al Capone's Hideout," *New Mexico Magazine*, July 2007.

Sullins, D. Paul, "Empty Pews and Empty Altars," *America*, May 13, 2002.

"U.S. Catholic abuse crisis starts to fade," Associated Press, July 11, 2007.

Church Documents and Decrees

Biblical quotes are from the authorized Douay-Rheims translation of the Latin Vulgate.

Aquinas, Thomas, *Summa Theologica,* Supplement.

Augustine, *Confessions.*

Burke, Anne, et al., *A Report on the Crisis in the Catholic Church in the United States,* also known as the *John Jay Report,* (USCCB, Washington, DC, 2004).

Chavez, Angelico, *The Lord and New Mexico,* (Archdiocese of Santa Fe, 1975).

The Code of Canon Law, (William B. Eerdsmanns Publishing Company, Grand Rapids, Michigan, 1983).

Councils: Elvira, Nicea, Lateran II, III, IV, Constance, Florence, Vatican II

Damian, Peter, Letters; *Monumenta Germaniae Historica,* Vol. 1.

Lateran Pacts between Italy and the Holy See, signed February 11, 1929.

Ottaviani, A. Cardinal, *Crimen sollicitationis,* known as "Instruction on the Manner of Proceeding in Cases of Solicitation," (The Vatican Press, Rome, 1962), March 16, 1962.

Pope Boniface VIII, Encyclical *Unam sanctam,* "One Holy," November 18, 1302.

Pope Gregory XV, Constitution *Omnipotentis Dei,* "Omnipotent God," March 16, 1623.

Pope John Paul II, Apostolic exhortation *Pastores dabo vobis,* "I Will Give You Shepherds," March 25, 1992.

—. Apostolic letter *Ordinatio sacerdotalis,* "On Reserving Priestly Ordination to Men Alone," May 22, 1994.

—. Apostolic letter *Sacramentorum sanctitatis tutela,* "Safeguarding the Sanctity of the Sacraments", April 30, 2001.

—. "Letter of His Holiness John Paul II to the Bishops of the United States of America," June 11, 1993.

Pope John XXIII, Encyclical *Pacem in terris,* "Peace on Earth," April 11, 1963.

Pope Paul VI, Apostolic letter *Integrae servandae,* "Preserving Intact," December 7, 1965.

—. Encyclical *Sacerdotalis caelibatus,* "On the Celibacy of the Priest," June 24, 1967.

Ratzinger, Joseph Cardinal, Declaration *Dominus Iesus,* "Lord Jesus," issued by the Congregation for the Doctrine of the Faith, August 6, 2000.

—. "Letter ... On More Grave Delicts Reserved to the Same Congregation for the Doctrine of the Faith," May 18, 2001.

NOTES

Preface: By Way of an Apology

1. Matt. 18:1-7. See also the parallel sayings in Mark 9:33-7, 42, and Luke 9:46-8, 17:1-2.
2. John 8:32.
3. Matt. 10:26-7, parallels Mark 4:22 and Luke 12:2-3.

Chapter I: A Church Exposed

1. "Pope calls for continuous prayer to rid priesthood of paedophilia," *The Times Online*, Jan. 7, 2008.
2. Attorney Bruce Pasternack quoted in "Priest Treatment Unfolds in Costly, Secretive World," by Ellen Barry, *Boston Globe*, April 3, 2002.
3. Ian Wilson, *Jesus: the Evidence*, (Harper and Row, San Francisco, 1984), frontispiece.
4. "Keating's Parting Shots For Church," CBS News, June 17, 2003.
5. Joe Feuerherd, "Review board head charges bishops 'manipulated' sex abuse panel and withheld information," *National Catholic Reporter*, May 11, 2004.
6. Gregory Ingels, "The Loss of the Clerical State," undated, found at *www.opusbonosacerdotii.org*.
7. Henry Charles Lea, *A History of Auricular Confession and Indulgences in the Latin Church*, (Lea Brothers & Co., Philadelphia, 1896) Vol. II, p. 22.
8. Henry Charles Lea, *A History of Sacerdotal Celibacy in the Christian Church*, (originally in 3 vol., Lea Brothers & Co., Philadelphia, 1867), these cita-

tions are from a one-volume 1966 University Books reprint, p. 572.
9. Anne Burke, et al., *A Report on the Crisis in the Catholic Church in the United States*, also known as the *John Jay Report*, (USCCB, Washington, DC, 2004), pp. 22-23, claims 4,392 priests between 1950 and 2002 sexually abused 10,667 minors. Due to incomplete data, those figures are undoubtedly much too low.
10. John A. McHugh, *Catechism of the Council of Trent for Parish Priests*, trans. by Charles J. Callan, (Joseph F. Wagner, Inc. New York, 1934), p. 318.

Chapter II: From Chastity to Celibacy

1. Lea, *Celibacy*, pp. 363-4.
2. Gospel of Philip, II, 3, 63:32-64:6.
3. Eusebius, *The History of the Church from Christ to Constantine*, trans. by G. A. Williamson, (Dorset Press, New York, 1965), Book 2, Sect. 22, pp. 99-103.
4. Eusebius, *History*, Book 3, Sect. 11, pp. 123-4.
5. Pope John Paul II, Apostolic letter *Ordinatio sacerdotalis*, "On Reserving Priestly Ordination to Men Alone," May 22, 1994, Sect. 3, para. 4.
6. Matt. 8:14.
7. 1 Timothy 3:3-5.
8. Karen Jo Torjesen, *When Women Were Priests*, (Harper San Francisco, 1993), pp. 9-10.
9. Uta Ranke-Heinemann, *Eunuchs for the Kingdom of Heaven*, (Penguin Books, New York, 1991), p. 25.
10. Ranke-Heinemann, *Eunuchs*, pp. 228-9.

11. A.W. Richard Sipe, *Sex, Priests, and Power: Anatomy of a Crisis*, (Brunner/Mazel, New York, 1995), p. 74.

12. Ranke-Heinemann, pp. 90-2.

13. Op. cit., p. 99.

14. Eusebius, *History*, Book 6, sect. 8, pp. 247-8.

15. Elvira, Can. 27, also, Lea, *Celibacy*, p. 30.

16. Elvira, Can. 33, 18, 71, 30, and 24.

17. Lea, *Celibacy*, pp. 107-8.

18. David Yallop, *The Power and the Glory: Inside the Dark Heart of John Paul II's Vatican*, (Carroll & Graf Publishers, New York, 2007), p. 322.

19. Lea, *Celibacy*, p. 83.

20 Op. cit., p. 108.

21. Peter Stanford, *The Legend of Pope Joan*, (Berkley Books, New York, 1999), pp. 11-2.

22. Stanford, *Legend*, p. 16.

23. Op. cit., p. 19.

24. Op. cit., p. 162.

25. Op. cit., pp. 138-41.

26. Lea, *Celibacy*, pp. 114-5.

27. Angelo S. Rappaport, *The Love Affairs of the Vatican or the Favourites of the Popes*, (Barnes & Noble Books, New York, 1995, orig. pub.1912), pp. 79-81.

28. Hans Kuhner, *Encyclopedia of the Papacy*, trans. by Kenneth J. Northcott, (Philosophical Library, New York, 1958), p. 67.

29. Rappaport, *Love Affairs*, pp. 81-2.

30. Lea, *Celibacy*, p. 145.

31. Giovanni Morrello, ed., *Vatican Treasures: 2000 Years of Art and Culture in the Vatican and Italy*, (Electa, Milan, 1993) p. 302.

32. A.W. Richard Sipe, *A Secret World: Sexuality and the Search for Celibacy*, (Brunner/Mazel, New York, 1990), pp. 38-9.

33. Lea, *Celibacy*, pp. 121-2.

34. Op. cit., p. 117.

Chapter III: Sex and the Single Priest

1. Lea, *Celibacy*, p. 150.

2. Op. cit., p. 157-8

3. Op. cit., p. 152.

4. Peter Damian, Letters, 31.7-8; *Monumenta Germaniae Historica*, vol. 1, 287.

5. Lea, *Celibacy*, p. 172.

6. C. Colt Anderson, "When magisterium becomes imperium: Peter Damian on the accountability of bishops for scandal," *Theological Studies*, Dec. 1, 2004.

7. Ibid.

8. Ibid.

9. Ibid.

10. Lea, *Celibacy*, p. 184

11. Rappaport, pp. 122-146.

12. Lea, *Celibacy*, pp. 211-2

13. Op. cit., p. 233.

14. Op. cit., pp. 258-9.

15. Op. cit., pp. 153-4.

16. Op. cit., pp. 198-9.

17. Op. cit., p. 166.

17. Op. cit., pp. 264-5.

18. Odericus Vitalis, "An Attempt to Enforce Clerical Celibacy" from *Ecclesiastical History*, trans. by T. Forester (London, Bohm, 1853-1856) in *The Portable Medieval Reader*, ed. by James Bruce Ross, and Mary Martin McLaughlin, (Viking Press, New York, 1949), pp. 75-8.

19. Lea, *Celibacy*, p. 264.

20. Op. cit., p. 268.

21. Op. cit., p. 276.

22. Lateran IV, Canon 14.

23. Lea, *Celibacy*, pp. 290-1.

24. Lea, *Confession*, p. 253.

25. Lea, *Celibacy*, pp. 271-2.

26. Op. cit., pp 281-2.

27. Op. cit., pp. 363-4.

28. Henry Charles Lea, *A Formulary of the Papal Penitentiary in the Thirteenth Century*, (Lea Brothers & Co., Philadelphia, 1892), p. xvii.

29. Geoffrey Barraclough, *The Medieval Papacy*, (Harcourt, Brace, & World, Inc., Norwich, England, 1968), p. 121.

30. Sipe, *Secret World*, pp. 46-8.

31. Lea, *Celibacy*, pp. 455-6.

32. Torjesen, *Women*, pp. 234-7.

33. Lea, *Celibacy*, pp. 465-7.

Chapter IV: Solicitation and the Confessional

1. Lateran IV, Can. 21.

2. Jerome on Isaiah 3:9, quoted in Thomas Aquinas, *Summa Theologica*, Supplement, Ques. 6, Art. 6, Obj. 1.

3. Lea, *Confession*, Vol. I, p. 16.

4. Op. cit., Vol. I, pp. 22-5.

5. Op. cit., Vol. I, pp. 30-1.

6. Deacons: Lea, *Confession*, Vol. I, pp. 56-8; laymen and nuns: pp. 218-26.

7. Caspar E. Schieler, *Theory and Practice of the Confessional: A Guide in the Administration of the Sacrament of Penance*, ed. by H. J. Heuser, (Benziger Brothers, New York, 1905), pp. 29-39.

8. Lea, *Confession*, Vol. II, pp. 103, 108.

9. Schieler, *Theory*, pp. 37-9.

10. Lea, *Confession*, Vol. 2, p. 174.

11. Schieler, p. 54.

12. Schieler, p. 316, *ff.*

13. *The Code of Canon Law*, (William B. Eerdsmanns Publishing Company, Grand Rapids, Mich., 1983), Can. 976.

14. Lea, *Confession*, Vol. I, p. 432.

15. Lea, *Celibacy*, pp. 496-7.

16. Lateran IV, Can. 21.

17. Lea, *Celibacy*, pp. 496-8.

18. Lea, *Spain*, Vol. IV, p. 96.

19. Lea, *Celibacy*, p. 499.

20. Lea, *Confession*, Vol. I, p. 394.

21. Op. cit., Vol. I, p. 395.

22. Sandro Magister, "Emerging Trends: The Return to the Confessional," *L'espresso*, Sept. 6, 2007.

23. Schieler, p. 354.

24. Lea, *Celibacy*, pp. 512-3.

25. Charles Chiniquy, *The Priest, The Woman, and the Confessional*, (Adam Craig, Chicago, 1880), p. 66. Emphasis in original.

26. Lea, *Celibacy*, pp. 510-1.

27. Op. cit., p. 500.

Chapter V: The Edict of Faith

1. Robert Held, *Inquisition/Inquisición*, (Qua D'Arno, Florence, Italy, 1985), p. 16, emphasis in original.

2. Lea, *Inquisition*, pp. 661-2.

3. Edward Burman, *The Inquisition: Hammer of Heresy*, (Dorset Press, New York, 1984), pp. 16-7.

4. Burman, *Hammer*, pp. 20-1.

5. Lateran IV, Can. 3.

6. Henry Charles Lea, *The Inquisition of the Middle Ages*, abridged by Margaret Nicholson, (Macmillan Company,

New York, 1961, originally published in 3 vol. by Lea Brothers & Co., Philadelphia, 1887-9), pp. 190-4.

7. Lea, *Inquisition*, p. 197.

8. Henry Charles Lea, *A History of the Inquisition in Spain*, (Macmillan Company, New York, 1906), Vol. II, pp. 90-8.

9. Lea, *Inquisition*, p. 207; *Confession*, Vol. I. p. 423.

10. Burman, pp. 63-5.

11. Lea, *Inquisition*, p. 200.

12. Lea, *Spain*, Vol. III, pp. 164-72.

13. Lea, *Confession*, Vol. III, p. 178, also *Taxes*, p. 60.

14. Held, *Inquisition*, p. 82.

15. Lea, *Spain*, Vol. III, pp. 180-2.

16. Lea, *Inquisition*, pp. 389-90.

17. Peter Partner, *The Murdered Magicians: The Templars and Their Myth*, (Thorsons Publishing Group, Rochester, Vermont, 1987), pp. 51-2.

18. Malcolm Barber, *The Trial of the Templars*, (Cambridge University Press, New York, 1978) p. 179.

19. Barber, *Trial*, pp. 99-101.

20. Lea, *Inquisition*, p.770 *ff*.

21. Heinrich Kramer, and James Sprenger, *Malleus Maleficarum*, trans. by Montague Summers from the Latin text originally published 1484, (Dover, New York, 1971), Part I, Quest. 1, p. 1.

22. Rossell Hope Robbins, *The Encyclopedia of Witchcraft and Demonology*, (Crown Press, New York, 1959), "Spain, Witchcraft in," pp. 474-7.

Chapter VI: Harsh Measures

1. Lea, *Spain*, Vol. IV, pp. 97-8.

2. Lea, *Confession*, Vol. I, p. 385.

3. Lea, *Celibacy*, pp. 500-1.

4. Lea, *Spain*, Vol. IV, p. 105.

5. Karen Liebreich, *Fallen Order: Intrigue, Heresy, and Scandal in the Rome of Galileo and Caravaggio*, (Grove Press, New York, 2004), p. 144.

6. Lea, *Celibacy*, pp. 504-5.

7. Lea, *Spain*, Vol. IV, p. 101.

8. Op. cit., Vol. IV, p. 128.

9. Op. cit., Vol. IV, pp. 120-1.

10. Lea, *Celibacy*, p. 517.

11. Lea, *Spain*, Vol. IV, pp. 126-7.

12. Lea, *Celibacy*, p. 503.

13. Op. cit., pp. 503-4.

14. Op. cit., p. 505.

15. Op. cit., pp. 506-7.

16. Op. cit., pp. 510-1.

17. Op. cit., pp. 513-4.

18. Op. cit., p. 514.

19. Lea, *Spain*, Vol. IV, pp. 116-7.

20. Lea, *Celibacy*, p. 509.

21. Op. cit., pp. 509-10.

22. Op. cit., p. 518.

23. Op. cit., p. 520.

24. Op. cit., pp. 518-9.

25. Op. cit., p. 517.

26. Summary of the major theme of Liebreich, *Fallen Order*.

27. Maria Luisa Ambrosini with Mary Willis, *The Secret Archives of the Vatican*, (Barnes & Noble, New York, 1969), pp. 219-21.

28. Lea, *Spain*, Vol. IV, pp. 43-4.

29. George Frederick Young, *The Medicis*, Vol. 2, (E.P. Dutton, New York, 1911), pp. 412-3.

30. Liebreich, pp. 135-6.

31. Ambrosini, *Archives*, p. 212.

32. Lea, *Celibacy*, pp. 525-6; *Spain*, Vol. IV, pp. 135-6.

33. Lea, *Celibacy*, pp. 502-3.

34. Op. cit., pp. 520-1.

35. Op. cit., pp. 569-70.

36. Op. cit., pp. 526-7.

Chapter VII: Crime and Punishment

1. Sipe, *Priests*, p. 11.

2. Lea, *Celibacy*, p. 560.

3. Quote from an article in *Time Magazine* in "Irish Protection" under "Religious Socio-Politics Around the World," *The Realist*, Issue 12, Oct. 1959, p. 12.

4. *The Boston Globe* Investigative Staff, *Betrayal: The Crisis in the Catholic Church*, (Little, Brown and Company, Boston, 2002), pp. 44-5.

5. Maria Monk, (psued.), *Awful Disclosures of Maria Monk, or, The Hidden Secrets of a Nun's Life in a Convent Exposed!*, (T.B. Peterson, Philadelphia, 1836), p. 24.

6. "Nuns targeted in Africa and elsewhere," by John Allen and Pamela Schaeffer, *National Catholic Reporter*, March 16, 2001.

7. Lea, *Celibacy*, p. 567.

8. Op. cit., pp. 562-3.

9. Lateran Pacts, 1. Conciliation Treaty, Article 23. Signed Feb. 11, 1929.

10. Lateran Pacts, 3. Concordat, Articles 5 and 8 respectively. Signed Feb. 11, 1929.

11. Emmett McGloughlin, *People's Padre*, (Beacon Press, New York, 1954), p. 64.

12. Charles R. Morris: *American Catholic: The Saints and Sinners Who Built America's Most Powerful Church*, (Random House, New York, 1997.)

13. Paul Valley, s.P., "In the Belly of the Whale," *Priestly People*, Nov., 2000.

14. Thomas P. Doyle, A.W. Richard Sipe, and Patrick J. Wall, *Sex, Priests, and Secret Codes: The Catholic Church's 2000-year Paper Trail of Sexual Abuse*, (Volt Press, Los Angeles, 2007), p. 47.

15. Cardinal A. Ottaviani, *Crimen sollicitationis*, known as "Instruction on the Manner of Proceeding in Cases of Solicitation," March 16, 1962, (The Vatican Press, Rome, 1962).

Chapter VIII: Revolution at the Council

1. On Frings and the Council, John L. Allen, Jr., *Pope Benedict XVI: A Biography of Joseph Ratzinger*, originally published as *Cardinal Ratzinger: the Vatican's Enforcer of the Faith* (Continuum, New York, 2000), pp. 52-3. Also, Corrina Laughlin, *The Second Vatican Council*, reminiscences of Archbishop Connally at *www.stjamescathedral.org/Prayer/vatican2-3.htm*; "The Cardinal's Setback," *Time Magazine*, Friday, Nov. 23, 1962; Jerry Filtreau, "U.S. experts at Vatican II recall history-making years," *Catholic News Service*.

2. "A Cardinal Carabiniere," *Time Magazine*, Monday, Aug. 13, 1979.

3. Pope John XXIII, Encyclical *Pacem in terris*, "Peace on Earth," Sect. 9, para. 14, April 11, 1963.

4. Cardinal Joseph Ratzinger, Declaration *Dominus Iesus*, "Lord Jesus," issued by the CDF, Aug. 6, 2000.

5. Allen, *Benedict*, pp. 64-5.

6. Ibid.

7. Pope Paul VI, *Presbyterorum ordinis*, "Decree on the Life and Ministry of Priests," Dec. 7, 1965, Chap. 1, Sect. 7.8, para. 3.

8. Op. cit., chap. 2.16, para. 1, 3.

9. Pope Paul VI, *Sacerdotalis caelibatus*, "Encyclical on the Celibacy of the Priest," June 24, 1967, Sect. 17, 88.

10. Pope Paul VI, *Integrae servandae*, Apostolic letter, "Preserving Intact," Dec. 7, 1965, described in Allen, pp. 260-1.

11. Summary of the Gauthe case and the history of *The Manual* derived from Doyle, *Sex*, pp.87-92.

12. Doyle, et al., *The Manual*, included as Chap. 4 in Doyle, *Sex*. See Sect. III, pp. 165-74.

13. Doyle, *Sex*, pp. 91-8.

14. Nicholas P. Cafardi, "Before Dallas," *The Catholic World*, June 17, 2007.

15. Ann Rodgers, "Duquesne U. dean's book tells how church dealt with pedophile priests," *Pittsburgh Post-Gazette*, April 7, 2008.

16. Sipe, *Priests*, p. 4.

17. See the database at the Bishop Accountability website.

18. Doyle, *Sex*, pp. 92-3.

Chapter IX: A Refuge in the Outlands

Some of the information in this section first appeared in the author's article, "Mysteries Remain in New Mexico," *Albuquerque Tribune*, May 7, 2002.

1. Jack Katz, *Mysteries and Miracles of New Mexico*, (Rhombus Publishing Co., Corrales, New Mexico, 1988), p. 41.

2. Mike Smith, "Al Capone's Hideout," *New Mexico Magazine*, July 2007.

3. Information provided by a former Paraclete novice, "Fr. Pious," private communication to the author.

4. Liam J. Hoare, s.P., "The Beginning," in "Father Gerald Fitzgerald: Extraordinary Servant, Vessel of Priestly Love," undated, found at *www.theservants.org/gerald.html*.

5. John A. Hardon, *A Prophet for the Priesthood*, (Eternal Life, Bardstown, Kentucky, 1998), p. 144. Hoare, above, in "Calling of the Holy Spirit," gives his age as 47.

6. *Albuquerque Journal*, April 2, 1993.

7. "Fr. Pious," private communication to the author.

8. Affidavit of Joseph T. McNamara, s.P., para. 12, no date given, found at *www.cityofangels11.com*.

9. KRQE TV, Dec. 30, 2008.

10. J. B. Salpointe, *Soldiers of the Cross*, (Documentary Publications, Salisbury, North Carolina, 1977), pp. 126-7.

11. Salpointe, *Soldiers*, p. 28.

12. John L. Kessell, *Kiva, Cross, and Crown: The Pecos Indians and New Mexico 1540-1840*, (University of New Mexico Press, Albuquerque, 1987), p. 14.

13. Salpointe, p. 126.

14. Angelico Chavez, *The Lord and New Mexico*, (Archdiocese of Santa Fe, 1975).

15. Kessell, *Kivas*, p. 29.

16. Op. cit., p. 12.

17. Salpointe, p. 53.

18. Kessell, p. 90.

19. Op. cit., p. 93.

20. Henry Charles Lea, *The Inquisition in the Spanish Dependencies*, (Macmillan Company, New York, 1908), p. 256.

21. Kessell, p. 271.

22. David Roberts, *The Pueblo Revolt: The Secret Rebellion that Drove the Spaniards Out of the Southwest*, (Simon & Shuster, New York, 2004), p. 15.

23. Salpointe, p. 64.

24. Kessell, p. 287.

25. Op. cit., pp. 348-9.

26. Op. cit., App. III, pp. 496-503.

27. Northland Editors, *Kachinas: A Hopi Artist's Documentary*, (Northland, Flagstaff, Arizona, 1973), p. 50. Also, Nancy L. Schiffer, *Contemporary Hopi Kachina Dolls*, (Schiffer Publishing, Atglen, Pennsylvania, 2003), pp. 57-9.

28. Roberts, *Revolt*, p. 226.

29. Kessell, p. 319.

30. Robbins, *Witchcraft*, p. 477.

31. Annie Lux, *Historic New Mexico Churches*, photos by Daniel Nadelbach (Gibbs Smith, Layton, Utah, 2007), pp. 70-1.

32. Kessell, p. 139, 153.

33. Op. cit., pp. 47-8.

34. Don Burge, "Crypto-Jews in New Mexico," *UNM Quantum*, Summer 1992.

35. Arlynn Nellhaus, "Spanish Jews still practice religious secrecy," *Alb. Tribune*, Nov. 12, 1992.

36. Kessell, p. 150.

37. George Mills, and Richard Grove, *Lucifer and the Crucifer: The Enigma of the Penitentes*, (The Westerners, Inc, Denver, 1955), p. 21.

38. Marta Weigle, *The Penitentes of the Southwest*, (Ancient City Press, Santa Fe, 1970), pp. 17-8.

39. Bruce Ellis, *Bishop Lamy's Santa Fe Cathedral*, (University of New Mexico Press, Albuquerque, 1985), pp. 35-6.

40. Salpointe, p. 162.

41. William J.Howlett, *Life of the Right Reverend Joseph P. Machebeuf, D.D.*, (Franklin Press Company, Pueblo, Colorado, 1908), p.164.

42. Willa Cather, *Death Comes for the Archbishop*, (Alfred A. Knopf, New York, 1927), p. 7.

43. Affidavit of Joseph T. McNamara, s.P., para. 33.

Chapter X: Ministers to the Fallen

1. "Fr. Pious."

2. Gerald Fitzgerald, *Letters from Father Page, CSC*, (Longmans, Green and Co., New York, 1940), pp. 46-7.

3. Deposition of Joseph T. McNamara, s.P., June 21, 2007.

4. "Fr. Pious."

5. Hoare, under "Handmaids of the Precious Blood," in "Father Gerald." Also confirmed by "Fr. Pious."

6. Hardon, *Prophet*, p. 92.

7. Op. cit., p. 20.

8. Op. cit., p. 107.

9. Op. cit., p. 66.

10. Op. cit., p. 72.

11. Op. cit., p. 134.

12. Op. cit., pp. 10-1, 34, 56.

13. "Fr. Pious."

14. Op. cit., pp.37-8.

15. Letter from Fitzgerald to Rector William J. Kenneally, C.M., July 21, 1960.

16. "Fr. Pious."

17. Ibid.

18. Ibid.

19. *Alb. Journal*, Nov. 25, 1994; "Fr. Pious."

20. "Fr. Pious."

21. Letter from Fitzgerald to Archbishop Edwin Byrne, Sept. 18, 1957.

22. Letter from Fitzgerald to Bishop Joseph A. Durick, Sept. 10, 1964.

23. Doyle, *Sex*, p. 211, puts the proportion of gay priests at 40-50%. Sipe estimates 30% have a homosexual orientation with half of them active.

24. Affidavit of Father Joseph McNamara, s.P., November 17, 1993, para. 9-11.

25. Op cit., para. 13.

26. Letter from Fitzgerald to unnamed cardinal, undated.

27. McNamara Affidavit, para. 33.

28. Personal experience of the author, who served at several of these Masses.

29. "Fr. Pious."

30. Ron Russell, "Camp Ped," *Los Angeles New Times*, Aug. 15, 2002.

31. "Fr. Pious."

32. McNamara, Affidavit, para. 15-7; "Fr. Pious."

33. Op. cit., para. 24-6.

34. Hoare, under "Death of Father Gerald," in "Father Gerald."

35. Letter from Card. Ildebrando Antoniutti to Fr. David Temple, March 23, 1966, quoted in McNamara, Affidavit, para. 28.

Chapter XI: The Operation of Error

1. McNamara, Affidavit, para. 31, *Alb. Tribune*, March 12, 1993.

2. Doyle, *Sex*, p. 73.

3. McNamara, Affidavit, para. 33.

4. *Alb. Tribune*, April 16, 1993.

5. *Alb. Journal*, March 13, 1993.

6. *Alb. Tribune*, March 12, 1993.

7. *Alb. Tribune*, March 13, 1993.

8. *Alb. Journal*, March 15, 1993.

9. Doyle, *Sex*, p. 54.

10. "Fr. Pious." Pious said that an elderly guest who confessed to being on the list told him about it shortly before he died.

11. *Santa Fe Reporter*, Aug. 5-11, 1992.

12. Private communication with the author.

13. *Alb. Tribune*, March 13, 1993.

14. "Fr. Pious."

15. *Alb. Tribune*, Dec. 17, 1992.

16. *Alb. Journal*, March 12, 1993.

17. Personal experience of the author.

18. "Fr. Pious."

19. *Alb. Journal*, May 23, 1993.

20. *St. Louis Post-Dispatch*, Aug. 30, 1992.

21. *Palm Beach Post*, June 28, 1998.

22. Ron Russell, "Camp Ped."

23. *Alb. Tribune*, May 15, 1993.

24. *Alb. Tribune*, Jan. 8, 1993.

25. *Alb. Tribune*, Nov. 18, 1992.

26. Doyle, *Sex*, p. 125,

27. Op. cit., p. 74.

28. McGloughlin, *Padre*, pp. 63-4.

29. Hardon, pp. 147-8; Hoare, under "Spread of the Ministry" in "Father Gerald;" *www.theservants.org/ servants.htm*; and Peter Lechner, "Cri-

sis in the Church," *Priestly People*, April 2002, cites 2,000 while Doyle, *Sex*, p. 74, puts the figure at 2,100.

30. Jason Berry, *Lead Us Not Into Temptation: Catholic Priests and the Sexual Abuse of Children*, (Doubleday, New York, 1992), pp.372-3.

31. *Alb. Journal*, Aug. 23, 1992.

32. *Alb. Journal*, May 23, 1993.

33. *Alb. Tribune*, March 12, 1993.

34. Emmett McGloughlin, *Crime and Immorality in the Catholic Church*, (Lyle Stuart, New York, 1962), p. 143.

35. McGloughlin, *Crime*, pp. 97-100, 169.

36. Personal experience of the author.

Chapter XII: Thunder in the Desert

1. ABC News, *PrimeTime Live*, July 23, 1992.

2. *Alb. Journal*, Feb. 1, 1994.

3. *Alb. Tribune*, Nov. 16, 1992.

4. *Alb. Journal*, Oct. 4, 1992

5. *Alb. Journal*, May 29, 1993; *Alb. Tribune*, Jan. 21, 1994.

6. *Alb. Journal*, Sept. 21, 1996.

7. *Alb. Journal*, Jan. 6, 1993.

8. *Alb. Journal*, Oct. 10, 1992.

9. KRQE-TV, March 21, 1993.

10. *Alb. Tribune*, Oct. 29, 1992, *Journal*, Jan. 6, 1993.

11. *Alb. Journal*, Oct. 10, 1992.

12. *Alb. Journal*, Dec. 1, 1992.

13. Personal communication with the author.

14. *Alb. Journal*, Nov. 25, 1992.

15. *Alb. Journal*, Oct. 23, 1992.

16. *Alb. Tribune*, Dec. 1, 1992.

17. *Alb. Journal* and *Tribune*, Oct. 23, 1992.

18. *Alb. Journal*, March 18, 1993.

19. *Alb. Tribune*, Oct. 30, 1992.

20. *Alb. Journal*, Aug. 1, 1993.

21. *Alb. Journal*, Feb. 2, 1993.

22. *Alb. Tribune*, Dec. 17, 1992.

23. Elinor Burkett and Frank Bruni, *A Gospel of Shame: Children, Sexual Abuse, and the Catholic Church*, (Harper Collins, New York, 2004), p. 38.

24. *Alb. Journal*, Oct. 18, 1992.

25. *Alb. Journal*, Sept. 17, 1993.

26. KRQE-TV, March 21, 1993.

Chapter XIII: Doom Comes for the Archbishop

1. *Alb. Tribune*, Oct. 24, 1992.

2. *Alb. Journal*, March 4, 1993.

3. *Alb. Tribune*, March 9, 1993.

4. KOB-TV, March 11, 1993, *Alb. Journal*, March 12.

5. *Alb. Tribune*, March 12, 1993.

6. *Alb. Journal*, March 6, 1993; *Journal, Tribune*, March 13; *Journal*, March 17.

7. *Alb. Journal*, March 13, 1993.

8. KRQE-TV, March 21, 1993.

9. CBS News, *60 Minutes*, "The Archbishop," produced by Robert G. Anderson, March 21, 1993.

10. *Alb. Tribune*, Sept. 18, 1996; *Journal*, Sept. 19; Deposition of Robert F. Sanchez, Vol. 1-4, Jan. 12-5, 1994. Much of the following analysis was originally published as "The Secrets of Archbishop Sanchez" by the author in *Missing Link*, Vol. 4, No. 3, Fall 1996/Winter 1997.

11. *Alb. Journal*, Dec. 22, 1993.

12. *Alb. Journal*, Dec. 28, 1993.

13. *Alb. Journal*, May 24, 1994.
14. *Alb. Journal*, Dec. 28, 1993.
15. *Alb. Journal*, Feb. 27, 1995.
16. *Alb. Journal*, July 15, 1995.
17. KRQE-TV, March 21, 1993.
18. See note 10, above.
19. *Alb. Journal*, Sept. 19, 1996.
20. KOB-TV, Nov. 4, 1998.

Chapter XIV: After the Fall

1. *Alb. Tribune*, April 7, 1993.
2. *Alb. Tribune*, April 7, 1993.
3. *Dallas Morning News*, July 25, 1997.
4. *Alb. Journal*, Sept. 14, 1997.
5. *Alb. Journal*, April 30, 1993; June 16.
6. *Alb. Tribune*, May 17, 1994.
7. *Alb. Tribune*, Nov. 11, 1992.
8. *Alb. Tribune*, Nov. 13, 1992
9. Hechler, David, "Sins of the Father," *McCall's*, Sept. 1993.
10. *Alb. Journal*, April 13, 1993.
11. *Alb. Journal*, April 28, 1993.
12. *Alb. Journal*, Aug. 1, 1993.
13. *Alb. Journal*, March 1, 1995.
14. *Alb. Tribune*, April 1, 1993.
15. *Alb. Journal*, July 1, 1993.
16. *Alb. Journal*, July 2, 1993.
17. *Alb. Journal*, May 6, 1993.
18. *Alb. Journal*, May 7, 1993.
19. *Alb. Journal*, May 8, 1993.
20. Letter from Peter Lechner, s.P. to John McCormack, Bishop of Manchester, Nov. 30, 2001.
21. *Alb. Journal*, Aug. 1, 1993.
22. *Alb. Tribune*, Dec. 22, 1993.
23. *Alb. Journal*, Nov. 14, 1994.
24. *Alb. Tribune*, Aug. 14, 1993.
25. Yallop, *Power*, pp. 312-3.

26. Pope John Paul II, "Letter of His Holiness John Paul II to the Bishops of the United States of America," June 11, 1993. Portions italicized for emphasis in the original.
27. Yallop, *Power*, p. 314.

Chapter XV: The Money Game

1. *Alb. Journal*, Aug. 17, 1993.
2. *Alb. Journal*, Sept. 23, 1993.
3. Ibid.
4. *Alb. Journal*, Nov. 24, 1993.
5. *Alb. Journal*, Nov. 21, 1993.
6. *Alb. Journal*, Nov. 30, 1993.
7. *Alb. Journal*, Dec. 3, 1993.
8. *Alb. Journal*, Nov. 13, 1993.
9. *Alb. Journal*, Dec. 9, 1993.
10. *Alb. Journal*, Oct. 22, 1993.
11. Ibid.; *Alb. Journal*, Nov. 12, 1993.
12. *Alb. Journal*, Dec. 17, 1993.
13. *Alb. Journal*, Dec. 24, 1993.
14. *Alb. Journal*, Dec. 14, 1993.
15. *National Catholic Reporter*, Jan. 28, 1994.
16. *Catholic World News*, Feb. 28, 2007
17. *San Diego Union Tribune*, Oct. 7, 2007
18. *National Catholic Reporter*, Jan. 28, 1994.
19. *Alb. Journal*, March 4, 1994.
20. *Alb. Journal*, Feb. 10, 1996
21. *Alb. Journal*, Sept. 9, 1995.
22. *Alb. Journal*, Jan. 6, 1996.
23. Affidavit of David A. Holley, para. 11-2, May 14, 1993.
24. *Alb. Journal*, Feb. 1, 1994.
25. *Alb. Tribune*, Aug. 5, 1995.
26. *Alb. Journal*, Aug. 3, 1995.
27. *Alb. Tribune*, April 4, 1994.

28. Private telephone conversation with the author.

29. *Alb. Journal*, March 23, 2002.

30. Ibid.

31. *Alb. Journal*, Aug. 29, 1994.

32. *Alb. Journal*, March 24, 1995.

33. Associated Press, Sept. 17, 1994; June 15, 2002.

34. *Alb. Journal*, Feb. 28, 1995; March 14.

35. *Alb. Journal*, Jan. 26, 1995.

36. *Alb. Journal*, July 29, 1998.

37. *Alb. Journal*, Sept. 20, 1996.

38. *Alb. Journal*, July 1, 1996.

39. *USA Today*, March 26, 2002.

40. *Alb. Journal*, April 7, 1996.

41. Associated Press, June 15, 2002.

42. *Alb. Journal*, June 18, 2008.

43. KOAT-TV, May 12, 2009.

Chapter XVI: Dark Shadows

1. *Alb. Journal*, May 5, 1995.

2. *Alb. Journal*, Aug. 1, 1994.

3. *Alb. Journal*, Jan. 17, 2000.

4. *Alb. Journal*, June 8, 2000.

5. *Alb. Journal*, Jan. 17, 2000.

6. *Alb. Journal*, Dec. 29, 1998; Feb. 17, 1999.

7. *Alb. Journal*, March 22, 2005.

8. *Santa Fe New Mexican*, Sept. 29, 2006.

9. *Alb. Journal*, Nov. 25, 1994.

10. Anonymous source, Nov. 1995, as well as from a former nurse.

11. *The Guardian*, April 18, 2001, Nov. 10, 2004.

12. *The Wanderer*, Jan. 11, 1998.

13. "Fr. Pious."

14. *The Tribune-Star*, Feb. 16, 2007.

15. *St. Louis Post-Dispatch*, March 19, 2005.

16. Dan Moffet, "Ground Zero for Molestation in the Catholic Church," *Palm Beach Post*, June 28, 1998.

17. Peter Lechner, s.P., "A Church in Crisis," *Priestly People*, April 2002.

18. Michael Harris, *Unholy Orders: Tragedy at Mount Cashel*, (Viking, New York, 1990).

19. *Alb. Journal*, April 28, 1993.

20. *Alb. Journal*, April 28, 1994.

21. *Alb. Tribune*, Oct. 30, 1992, *Alb. Journal*, Nov. 11.

22. "Fr. Pious."

23. Ron Russell, "Camp Ped."

24. Gary Tuchman, "Retired Priest Questioned about 1960 Murder," CNN, May 30, 2007.

25. *Dallas Morning News*, July 16, 2002.

26. Peter Lechner, s.P., "A Church in Crisis," *Priestly People*, April 2002.

27. *Dallas Morning News*, July 16, 2002.

28. Burkett, *Gospel*, p. 197.

29. *Boston Globe, Betrayal*, p. 174.

30. *Palm Beach Post*, June 28, 1998.

31. *Alb. Journal*, March 14, 1995.

32. *Alb. Journal*, Nov. 10, 1994.

33. *Jemez Thunder*, May 15, 1997.

34. *Alb. Tribune*, May 10, 1997.

35. *Alb. Journal North*, Nov. 21, 1997.

36. *Alb. Journal*, March 3, 1998.

37. *Alb. Journal*, Dec. 10, 2001; Peter Lechner, s.P., "One Priest's Life and Death," *Priestly People*, Jan. 2002.

38. *Alb. Journal*, Jan. 5, 2002.

39. Lea, *Spain*, Vol. IV, p. 130.

40. *Toledo Blade*, April 21, 2005.

41. Some of these, along with personal experiences, served as the basis of the author's 2002 novel, *The Harrowing*.

42. William H. Kennedy, *Lucifer's Lodge: Satanic Ritual Abuse in the Catholic Church*, (Reviviscimus, South Egremont, Massachusetts, 2004), pp.12, 86.

43. Apperson, G. L., *The Wordsworth Dictionary of Proverbs*, (Wordsworth Editions, Ltd., Ware, Herfordshire, 1993), under Devil, 50, p. 146, lists its first appearance as in 1560.

44. Sipe, *Priests*, p. 31. Emphasis in original.

Chapter XVII: Sin, Secrecy, and the Vatican

1. John A. Hardon, *The Pocket Catholic Dictionary*, (Doubleday, New York, 1980).

2. Personal experience of the author.

3. Ibid.

4. *The Code of Canon Law*, (William B. Eerdsmanns Publishing Company, Grand Rapids, Michigan, 1983), Can. 535 §4.

5. 1983 *Code*, Can. 483 §2.

6. Op. cit., Can. 484 1°.

7. Op. cit., Can. 486-8.

8. Op. cit., Can. 491 §2.

9. Op. cit., Can. 489.

10. Thomas P. Doyle, *The Archives and the Secret Archives Required by Canon Law*, April 6, 2002.

11. *Code*, Can. 490.

12. Matthew Bunson, The Pope Encyclopedia, (Crown Trade Paperbacks, New York, 1995), p. 26.

13. "Secret Archives Accessible Online", ZENIT, Jan. 10, 2006.

14. Ambrosini, pp. 291-5.

15. Op. cit., pp. 308-9.

16. Op. cit., p. 303.

17. Anne Jacobson Schutte, "Palazzo del Sant'Uffizio: The Opening of the Roman Inquisition's Central Archive," American Historical Association *Perspectives*, May, 1999.

Chapter XVIII: Beyond the Purple Curtain

1. James-Charles Noonan, Jr., *The Church Visible: The Ceremonial Life and Protocol of the Roman Catholic Church*, (Viking, New York, 1996), p. 24.

2. Noonan, *Visible*, pp. 69, 73.

3. Noonan, p. 75.

4. Gordon Thomas, and Max Morgan-Witts, *Pontiff*, (Doubleday, New York, 1983), p. 75.

5. In a private communication, May Ying Welsh, a researcher in Rome, took the author to task about this. She claimed that many other cardinals retain their offices also. "These are the Cardinal Camerlengo, the Cardinal Vicar of the diocese of Rome, the Cardinal Arch-Priest of St. Peter's Basilica, the Sostituto (Chief of Staff) of the Secretariat of State, and the Secretaries of each of the dicasteries of the curia. The Supreme Tribunal of the Apostolic Signatura (the Church's Supreme Court) and the Tribunal of the Roman Rota also continue their operations. Instead of reporting to the Pope, they all report to the College of Cardinals." Others, she said, also have contact with the outside, though only in emergencies. She dismissed the idea that the rules cited makes the Apostolic Penitentiary even more significant than the Pope, though filling his

position takes precedence even over the election of a new pontiff.

Ms. Welsh also maintained that it is necessary for the Major Penitentiary to be in touch with the outside world in order to be able to forgive those on their deathbeds. See the text for the refutation of this argument.

6. Thomas, *Pontiff*, p. 55.

7. Lea, *Celibacy*, p. 275.

8. Lea, *Inquisition*, p. 665.

9. Pope John Paul II, Apostolic exhortation *Pastores dabo vobis*, "I Will Give You Shepherds," March 25, 1992, Sect. 29, para. 3.

10. D. Paul Sullins, "Empty Pews and Empty Altars," *America*, May 13, 2002, quoting *Full Pews and Empty Altars*, by Richard Schoenherr and Lawrence Young, 1993.

11. "Catholic nuns and monks decline," *BBC*, Feb. 5, 2008.

12. Doyle, *Sex*, p. 211.

13. Burke, *Crisis*, p. 26. Of the 10,667 victims tabulated, 81% overall were male, with 50.9% in the ages 11-14.

14. Sipe, *Priests*, p. 141.

15. Berry, *Temptation*, pp. 267-8.

16. "Pope Approves Barring Gay Seminarians," *Catholic World News*, Sept. 22, 2005.

17. Matt. 7:16.

**Conclusion: The Return
of the Inquisition**

1. Allen, pp. 82-83.

2. Ratzinger's record summarized from Allen's thoughtful analysis in *Benedict*, especially Chap. 6-7.

3. Paul Hoffman, *Anatomy of the Vatican: An Irreverent Look at the Holy See*, (Robert Hale, London, 1985), p. 91.

4. Allen, pp. 312-3. Also, "Ratzinger explains opening of Inquisition files," *Catholic World News*, Jan. 23, 1998; Liebriech, *Fallen Order*, p. xxxix.

5. Leonardo Boff, "On the Vatican Declaration 'Dominus Jesus'," Munsteraner Forum fur Theologie und Kirche, March 2000.

6. Allen, pp. 61-4.

7. Yallop, *Power*, pp. 320-323.

8. Doyle, *Sex*, p. 50.

9. Pope John Paul II, Apostolic letter *Sacramentorum sanctitatis tutela*, "Safeguarding the Sanctity of the Sacraments," April 30, 2001. Also, Cardinal Joseph Ratzinger, "Letter … On More Grave Delicts Reserved to the Same Congregation for the Doctrine of the Faith," May 18, 2001.

10. *Code*, Can. 1362.

11. Ratzinger, "Letter."

12. "U.S. Catholic abuse crisis starts to fade," Associated Press, July 11, 2007.

13. Yallop, *Power*, p.351.

14. Sipe, *Secret World*, p. 74.

15. Hoare, "Father Fitzgerald," under the heading, "To the Present," *www.theservants.org/servants.htm*.

16. Chavez, *Lord*, under the heading "Orders of Men."

17. Hardon, p. 148.

18. "Fr. Pious."

19. *Reno Gazette-Journal*, July 22, 2007.

20. Letters from Fitzgerald and Byrne, dated Aug. 1956, downloaded from *www.cityofangels4.com*.

INDEX

Other works by Jay Nelson:

The Harrowing

A Dark Psychological Horror Novel

Available through Booksurge and Amazon.

Once Upon an Inquisition

A Comic Medieval Screenplay

Please visit my website:

www.sarabite.info